Applying Cognitive Linguistics to Second Language Learning and Teaching

C000161075

Also by Jeannette Littlemore

ICT AND LANGUAGE LEARNING, INTEGRATING PEDAGOGY AND PRACTICE (*edited with Angela Chambers and Jean Conacher, 2004*)

FIGURATIVE THINKING AND FOREIGN LANGUAGE LEARNING (*with Graham Low, 2006*)

Applying Cognitive Linguistics to Second Language Learning and Teaching

Jeannette Littlemore
University of Birmingham, UK

First published in hardback 2009
This paperback edition published 2011 by
PALGRAVE MACMILLAN

Palgrave Macmillan in the UK is an imprint of Macmillan Publishers Limited,
registered in England, company number 785998, of Houndmills, Basingstoke,
Hampshire RG21 6XS.

Palgrave Macmillan in the US is a division of St Martin's Press LLC,
175 Fifth Avenue, New York, NY 10010.

Palgrave Macmillan is the global academic imprint of the above companies
and has companies and representatives throughout the world.

Palgrave® and Macmillan® are registered trademarks in the United States,
the United Kingdom, Europe and other countries.

ISBN 978–0–230–21948–9 hardback
ISBN 978–0–230–30235–8 paperback

This book is printed on paper suitable for recycling and made from fully
managed and sustained forest sources. Logging, pulping and manufacturing
processes are expected to conform to the environmental regulations of the
country of origin.

A catalogue record for this book is available from the British Library.

A catalog record for this book is available from the Library of Congress.

Printed and bound in Great Britain by
CPI Antony Rowe, Chippenham and Eastbourne

For Dan, Joe and Oscar, with love

Contents

List of Tables and Figures

Tables

Figures

Acknowledgements

First and foremost I would like to thank the anonymous reviewers whose comments pointed me in the right direction. I would also like to thank Dan Malt for his endless patience, intelligent insights, and thorough proofreading. My thanks go to Jill Lake, Melanie Blair and Priyanka Pathak at Palgrave Macmillan, whose constant support and encouragement have helped me finish this book. I have had a number of engaging and useful discussions with various friends and colleagues who have helped me put together my ideas for this book. These include: Masumi Azuma, John Barnden, Frank Boers, Nicholas Groom, Susan Hunston, Almut Koester, Seth Lindstromberg, Graham Low, Fiona MacArthur, Narges Mahpeykar, Rachael Manamley, Joanne Neff, Veronica Ormeno, John Taylor, Wolfgang Teubert, Andrea Tyler, and Mona Zeynab. I would particularly like to thank Martin Pütz for inviting me to the LAUD Symposium on Cognitive Linguistics and Second Language Learning, which took place in Landau, Germany, in March 2008. At this symposium, I heard many papers and spoke to numerous people who helped me shape my ideas about cognitive linguistics and its applications to second language learning and teaching. A number of people have acted as linguistic and cultural informants. I would particularly like to thank Yeongsil Ko, Hung So Lee, Yasuo Nakatani, Richard Spiby, Ayumi Takahashi, Grace Wang, Fei Fei Zhang, and the Kodankan Judo Institute, Niigata, Japan. Finally, I would like to thank my insightful MA students at the University of Birmingham, with whom I discussed many of my early ideas.

1
Introduction

1.1 What is 'cognitive linguistics'?

Cognitive linguistics is a relatively new discipline which is rapidly becoming mainstream and influential, particularly in the area of second language teaching. It embraces a number of closely related theories of language, all of which are based on the following key claims:

- there is no autonomous, special-purpose 'language acquisition device' that is responsible for language acquisition and language processing;
- language is 'usage-based' in that it is a product of physical interaction with the world;
- a single set of cognitive processes operates across all areas of language, and these processes are involved in other types of knowledge and learning besides language;
- words provide only a limited and imperfect means of expression;
- language is inherently meaningful although grammatical meanings are more abstract than lexical meanings.

Let us examine each of these claims more closely. By asserting that there is **no special-purpose language acquisition device**, cognitive linguists directly challenge generative approaches to language, and the concept of Universal Grammar. I refer here to Chomsky (1965) and others (e.g. Fodor, 1983) whose theories about language are based on the conviction that the human mind includes a faculty for language acquisition which is largely 'walled-off' from the rest of cognition. Unlike generative linguists, cognitive linguists argue that the cognitive processes governing language use and learning are essentially the same as those involved in all other types of knowledge processing, or as Croft and Cruse (2004: 2) put it:

> the organization and retrieval of linguistic knowledge is not significantly different from the organization and retrieval of other knowledge in the mind, and the cognitive abilities that we apply to speaking and understanding language are not significantly different from those applied to other cognitive tasks, such as visual perception, reasoning, or motor activity.

The language that we encounter every day serves as input from which we can draw inferences about form–meaning relationships, typical patterns and schemata. We constantly modify our mental lexicon in response to the language that we hear and use. There is therefore no distinction between language competence and language performance, as performance equates to usage. Language knowledge and learning are thus **usage-based**, in that our knowledge of language is 'derived from and informed by language use' (Evans and Green, 2006: 111). The fact that we use language in interactive settings, and that we use contextual cues to work out what our speaker is trying to say, is an important part of this process.

The set of **key cognitive processes** that are thought to be involved in language learning and use include comparison, categorization, pattern-finding, and blending. They operate across all areas of language and are the same as those involved in other areas of cognition. In other words, the processes that we use to make sense of our surroundings are the same as those that we employ when dealing with and learning languages.

The fact that words provide only a **limited and imperfect means of expression** means that in order to understand what our interlocutor is trying to tell us, as well as attending to the actual words that they utter, we need to draw on our general knowledge of the subject under discussion and our expectations about what our interlocutor might have to say about it. In other words, the words that we read or hear act simply as a trigger for a series of cognitive processes whereby we use our knowledge of the world to fill in the rest of the missing information. For example, if I rang home and said 'I'm just passing the chip shop and was wondering if we had anything in for dinner', it would be up to my interlocutor to infer that I was suggesting fish and chips for dinner, and offering to buy them there and then. None of this information is explicitly given in the utterance, but would be inferred, based on his or her general knowledge

of what is available at the 'chip shop', the fact that fish and chips constitutes a meal, and so on. The knowledge that we draw on to understand
utterances such as these is referred to as **encyclopaedic knowledge**, and
is discussed in Chapter 4.

The **centrality of meaning** is a fundamental claim of cognitive linguistics. When new words and phrases enter a language, they tend to
do so as 'content' words, which means that they have concrete, lexical
meanings. Over time, through the process of **grammaticalization** (see
Hopper and Traugott, 2003), some of these words and phrases become
'function' words; that is to say, they acquire a more schematic, grammatical meaning which is different from, yet related to, their original lexical
meaning. For example, the original meaning of 'going to' in English
refers to movement and travel (Heine *et al.*, 1991). However, over time,
this phrase has acquired a much more common *grammatical* meaning as
an indicator of future action. Although the process of grammaticalization occurs in all languages, it does not always follow the same patterns.
So, for example, the use of 'going to' to indicate future action is not used
in Japanese. For native speakers of a language, grammaticalized expressions such as this have often lost their link with their original lexical
meanings. However, when we learn a new language, we are exposed
to different grammaticalization patterns, and the links to the original
lexical meanings of the items often seem more apparent.

One of the contributions that cognitive linguistics makes to second
language learning and teaching is to suggest ways in which the relationships between grammatical expressions and their original lexical
meanings can be made apparent in the language classroom to enhance
learning and memorization. This process encourages learners to explore
the deeper meanings of grammatical items, and to think about *why*
the target language expresses things the way it does. According to
Langacker (2008: 73), the learning of grammatical usage in this way
involves grasping the semantic 'spin' that the target language imposes,
which, he claims, is 'a far more natural and enjoyable process than sheer
memorization'. Cognitive linguistics thus posits a much closer relationship between form and meaning than more traditional approaches to
language, which, as we will see later in the book, has far reaching
implications for the way we look at language learning and teaching.

The above claims give rise to a number of key concepts in cognitive
linguistics, many of which are of particular relevance to second language
learning and teaching. Those concepts which are most relevant to the
field are: construal, categorization, encyclopaedic knowledge, metaphor,
metonymy, embodiment, motivation, and construction grammar. In

this book, I consider each of these concepts and look at how they relate to second language learning and teaching. As we will see later, some of these concepts give rise to possible new ways of teaching languages, whereas others provide further support for existing methodologies. The potential contribution that each can make to theories of second language learning and teaching is rich and varied, which is why one chapter is dedicated to each.

1.2   Key concepts in cognitive linguistics and their applications to second language learning and teaching

In this section, I introduce seven key concepts in cognitive linguistics and briefly say why I think they may be of interest to those who are concerned with second language learning and teaching. In doing so, I provide the outline for the remaining chapters of the book. Although these concepts are separated out for the purpose of writing this book, in many ways they are inextricably linked.

In **Chapter 2**, I introduce the concept of **construal**. A key claim in cognitive linguistics is that the words we use to talk about a particular phenomenon can never reflect a purely objective view of that phenomenon. We can only witness phenomena through human eyes and from a human perspective. While there may be default ways of describing situations, there is no completely neutral way of describing them. Because perspective is never neutral, the language we use is not neutral either, rather it reflects certain ways of viewing the world. For example, we can talk about driving *across* France, but we can also talk about driving *through* France. Both describe the same event, but with *across*, the focus in more on the length of the journey and the final destination, whereas with *through*, the focus is more on the country itself, and the *experience* of driving through it. Although we do have choices as to how we present our ideas, because of processes, such as grammaticalization, a language often contains ways of *conventionally* construing phenomena and events which sometimes differ from the way in which they are construed in other languages. Languages are no more and no less 'logical' than each other in this respect. They are simply different. The phrases that they contain represent particular ways of conceiving of a given situation. They may categorize things differently, highlight different elements of a situation, look at them from a different angle, or look at them more closely. It is because of these different construal patterns that learners of a second language sometimes comment that speaking the new language enables them to 'see things in different ways'.

Let us look at some examples of how languages construe things in different ways. We will see in Chapter 2 that there are four main ways in which our construal of phenomena or events affects how we talk about them. These are: attention/salience (the part of the phenomenon that stands out most, or in which we are most interested); perspective (the standpoint from which we view the phenomenon); constitution, (how fine-grained or 'close-up' our view of a phenomenon is); and categorization (how we divide phenomena up into categories). All four types of construal reflect differences in the way in which phenomena are viewed, which in turn affects the way they are talked about. For example, in an English park we might be told to keep *off* the grass, whereas in Japan we would be more likely to be told not to go *into* the grass.

Of these four areas, the one that has received the most attention from researchers is **categorization**. Language-specific categories provide a neat explanation for the fact that there are very few one-to-one correspondences between languages, so something we might describe as a *bowl* in English would not always be described as *un bol*. Thus, in French it is possible to 'verser le consommé dans une assiette' (literally-speaking 'pour the soup into a plate') as the word *assiette* can be used to refer to a wider variety of vessels than the word *plate*. In other words, the cut-off point between a *plate* and a *bowl* is different from the cut-off point between *une assiette* and *un bol*. In English it lies more towards the *plate* end of the continuum, whereas in French it lies more towards the *bowl* end of the continuum. Categories are said to be radial and to have 'fuzzy boundaries'. In other words, they have members that can be considered as more or less 'prototypical' and they overlap with each other. Early researchers in cognitive linguistics (e.g. Rosch, 1975) found considerable cross-linguistic variation in both of these areas. For example, for most British English speakers, the most prototypical comestible fish is probably *cod* or *haddock*, whereas for Spaniards, it is more likely to be *hake* or *sardines*. As an example of cross-linguistic variation in terms of where the 'fuzzy' boundaries lie, the type of footwear that comes above the ankle would tend to fall into the category of 'boot' in English, whereas in French it is more likely to be classified as a 'chaussure' ('shoe'). Categorization systems go beyond the noun, and can account for variation in other parts of speech, such as verbs, adjectives, adverbs and determiners. For instance, in English we divide objects into those that are countable (e.g. *houses*) and those that are uncountable (e.g. *sugar*). In Japanese this division does not exist, but objects have different determiners according to whether they are, for example, short and flat, long and thin, animate or inanimate and so on.

The fact that languages differ with respect to the ways in which they construe objects and events leads one to expect that this might well be a source of difficulty for second language learners. Indeed, as we will see in Chapter 2, Japanese learners of English, and English learners of Japanese do experience difficulties in the area of countable versus uncountable, and long thin versus short flat objects, respectively. Different languages conventionally construe things differently, and although we may not be consciously aware of it, it is likely that our cognitive systems will, to some extent, have been 'primed' by our first language (L1) in ways which might interfere with our learning of subsequent languages. We may be preconditioned in some ways to pay more attention to, or be more aware of those features of the world that are explicitly encoded in our language, and to be less aware of those that are not. In other words, we may develop 'cognitive habits' (Hunt and Agnoli, 1991) as a result of having acquired our first language, which may need to be broken or adapted in order to facilitate the learning of a second language (L2).

Comparing the respective construal patterns of a learner's L1 and L2 may thus get us some way towards predicting the types of problems that second language learners are likely to encounter. Indeed, it has been suggested (e.g. Taylor, 1993) that one of the main contributions that cognitive linguistics can make to theories of language learning and teaching is in the area of contrastive analysis. Under the contrastive analysis hypothesis (Wardaugh, 1970), which was popular in the 1970s, comparisons were made between the grammatical systems of different languages in order to predict the types of errors that language learners might make. The hypothesis fell out of favour, partly because other factors were found to influence L2 acquisition besides the nature of one's first language, and partly because of its over-emphasis on syntax. Taylor's point is that cognitive linguistics has a different view of language, in which 'meaning' rather than 'syntax' is central, and that cognitive linguistic tools such as construal and categorization provide us with better, more flexible tools that can be used for identifying important differences between languages. These differences can then be used to predict areas that are likely to present difficulties to language learners. Findings from cognitive linguistics can thus complement and extend earlier approaches to contrastive analysis which were much more static, and which relied upon more traditional 'grammar rules plus lexis' views of language. Indeed, findings from cognitive linguistics probably do have a great deal to contribute to contrastive analysis, and as we will see in Chapter 2, the construal patterns in a learner's first language can affect their ability to learn a second language. But cognitive linguistics can also address the remaining issues that were not covered by the contrastive analysis hypothesis. In other words, because of its focus on usage-based learning (which involves intention reading and pattern finding) it can tell us more about how other cognitive processes, such as noticing, over- and under-extension and probabilistic reasoning, play a key role in determining both the 'what' and the 'how' of second language learning.

Chapter 3 looks at **the construction of radial categories** (e.g. Lakoff, 1987; Taylor, 2003) in which categorization and related concepts, such as family resemblance, are applied to other linguistic phenomena, such as polysemy. Under this view, the various senses of particular words are also viewed as radial categories, with the more concrete, physical senses lying towards the centre of the category and the more abstract, metaphorical senses lying towards the periphery. The different senses are thought to be related through metaphor and metonymy. I explore the implications that this has for language learning and teaching. Then I go on to look at other areas of language that have been found to operate within radial categories, such as grammar rules, phonological features, and intonation. I explore whether and how flexible categories might be appealed to when teaching these areas of language. I argue that if teachers present language features as flexible categories they will give their learners a more accurate picture of how language really works and help them to understand why the 'rules' they may have learned have so many exceptions. A second aim of this chapter is to use corpus data to test some of the claims that have been made by cognitive linguists about the nature of radial categories, and to see how these claims stand up in the light of authentic language data.

In **Chapter 4**, I look at L2 vocabulary learning in more depth, focusing on **encyclopaedic knowledge**. The information we store in our minds extends well beyond the basic or 'denotative' meanings that words have, and includes all the connotations that have come to be associated with those words and expressions over the period during which we have been exposed to them. For example, the English words *bachelor* and *spinster* mean much more than 'unmarried man' and 'unmarried woman' (Fillmore, 1975). The word *bachelor* may connote ideas of freedom and licentious behaviour, whereas the word *spinster* may connote ideas of old age, a possible lack of desirability, and for some people it may even include idiosyncratic associations, such as the possession of a large number of cats. In recent years there have been attempts to reclaim the word *spinster* so that it has the free and independent sense of *bachelor* (see, for example, Weedon, 1999). Advocates of this reclamation object to the fact that the connotations of the word *spinster* clearly reflect society's inherently sexist and misogynist attitudes towards unmarried women. Despite their dubious provenance however, these positive and negative connotations are, for many people, as much part of the meaning of these words as the state of being unmarried, and thus will often form part of a person's 'encyclopaedic knowledge' for these words. In the terminology favoured by cognitive linguists, words and phrases act as 'access nodes' into a complex knowledge network (Langacker, 1987: 163). Thus, instead of thinking of them as expressing separate 'concepts' it is more appropriate to think of them as tools that cause listeners to 'activate' certain areas of their knowledge network, with different areas activated to different degrees, in different contexts of use. The encyclopaedic knowledge that is likely to be triggered by a particular word or phrase in a particular context is built up through repeated exposure to it in different contexts. The fact that we have encyclopaedic knowledge has huge implications for vocabulary teaching, and while the idea of encyclopaedic knowledge has been broadly taken on board in language learning contexts, cognitive linguistics has more to offer in this field. In this chapter I look at different types of encyclopaedic knowledge and at studies of word association patterns in the L1 and the L2 in order to gain a fuller picture of how encyclopaedic knowledge develops in the language learner and how teachers can help promote it.

Chapters 5 and 6 focus on two concepts which lie at the heart of human thought and communication: metaphor and metonymy. In very basic terms, metaphor draws on relations of substitution and similarity, whereas metonymy draws on relations of contiguity. In metaphor, one thing is seen in terms of another and the role of the interpreter is to identify points of similarity, allowing, for example, Romeo to refer to Juliet as 'the Sun'. In metonymy, an entity is used to refer to something that it is actually related to, allowing us to utter and understand statements such as: 'The White House has released a statement', where the White House stands metonymically for the American Government. Jakobson (1971) famously argued that metaphor and metonymy constitute two fundamental poles of human thought, a fact which can be witnessed through their prevalence in all symbolic systems, including language, art, music and sculpture. More often than not, metaphor and metonymy work together and are so deeply embedded in the language we use that we do not very often notice them. However, languages vary both in the extent to which, and the ways in which, they employ metaphor and metonymy, and this can have important ramifications for those endeavouring to acquire a second language.

Chapter 5 looks at the cognitive view of **metaphor** and its possible applications to second language learning and teaching. It then goes on to look at some recent developments in conceptual metaphor theory, such as the concept of primary metaphors and the relationship between phraseology and metaphor. I then move on to linguistic metaphor and the challenges it presents to language learners. I close the chapter with a discussion of the potential advantages and limitations of cognitive linguistic approaches for helping learners to meet these challenges.

Chapter 6 looks at the less widely studied area of **metonymy**, beginning with a discussion of cross-linguistic similarity and variation in linguistic and conceptual metonymy, and the challenges and opportunities that this presents to second language learners. I then go on to examine the functions of metonymy in discourse. In particular, I focus on its ability to serve as communicative shorthand, its use in building cohesion within discourse communities, and the role it plays in evaluating, hedging, relationship-building, distancing, and simplifying. Finally, I look at the role of shared knowledge in metonymy comprehension, and examine its contribution to vague language (Channell, 1994) and indirect speech acts. The discussion thus moves more towards pragmatics, as I look at how metonymy serves to reduce the directness or assertiveness of an utterance, or to prevent the speaker from sounding too pedantic. Despite its clear importance, and because there have been very few studies of the ways in which language learners understand, learn and use metonymy, I close the chapter by outlining some possible directions for future research.

Chapter 7 deals with **embodiment** (sometimes referred to as **embodied cognition**), which allows us to understand abstract concepts by relating them directly to our physical experience. Through embodiment, 'people's subjective, felt experiences of their bodies in action provide part of the fundamental grounding for language and thought' (Gibbs, 2006: 9). I begin by looking at the role of embodiment in understanding and learning a second language and then go on to look at the related area of gesture and at its role in second language learning and teaching. If language is truly embodied then one would expect the gestures that accompany it to be very closely related to the semantic and pragmatic content of the messages. Research has shown that this is indeed the case, but languages vary in terms of the way they use gesture. This variation makes for powerful arguments for paying increased attention to gesture in the language classroom. I examine the different communicative functions of gesture, and assess the extent to which the use of gesture can facilitate understanding and learning, as well as language production.

Chapter 8 looks at a concept which is very closely related to embodiment: **linguistic motivation**. Linguistic motivation is concerned with the non-arbitrary aspects of language form and structure. According to cognitive linguists, many aspects of language are 'motivated' in that they are explainable in terms of how they relate to our everyday experience of the world, a fact that has clear applications to language learning and teaching. In this chapter, I evaluate the effectiveness of teaching methods that exploit linguistic motivation through language play and related techniques. The chapter is structured around three types of motivation that have been identified by Boers and Lindstromberg (2006) as being of potential use to language teachers. These are: form–form motivation, form–meaning motivation, and meaning–meaning motivation. Form–form motivation refers to the fact that some words and expressions are salient, noticeable and thus learnable by sheer virtue of the fact that they alliterate or assonate. For example, students seem to be particularly good at remembering expressions such as *nitty gritty, mind your manners* and *tea for two*. Form–meaning motivation refers to the fact that the actual sounds of words can sometimes provide clues as to their meaning. For example, most learners would be able to hazard a pretty good guess at the meanings of *stodgy* cake, a *lump* of clay or a *flimsy* dress. Meaning–meaning motivation relates to the radial category structure of polysemy, and is concerned with how, through concepts such as metaphor and metonymy, abstract senses of words relate back to their more basic senses. So, for example, we can see that there are metaphorical relationships between the different senses of *under* in the following examples (1)–(3) from the Bank of English corpus. (The Bank of English, http://www.titania.bham.ac.uk/, is a 450-million word Bank of English monitor corpus, jointly owned by HarperCollins Publishers and the University of Birmingham. It contains a representative selection of written and spoken English and is regularly updated to provide a permanently up-to-date record of current English usage.)

   (1) ... others who live *under* their regime.
   (2) Today it stands at *under* thirty.
   (3) If I'm *under* pressure ...

and the more basic sense of *under* in (4):

   (4) My son was rolling ... *under* the chair (also from the Bank of English)

A substantial amount of research has already looked at the ways in which meaning–meaning motivation can be exploited for language teaching purposes, and more recently researchers have started to explore the potential of the other types of motivation mentioned above. In Chapter 8, I assess the benefits and drawbacks of exploiting all three types of motivation in the language classroom.

In **Chapter 9**, I introduce the concept of **construction grammar**, which concerns the tendency of words to group together to form 'constructions' that have meanings of their own. These meanings relate to everyday experience and exist in radial categories. For example, the meanings of the three sentences in (5), (6) and (7), all of which are taken from the Bank of English, can be seen as being somehow related, despite the fact that none of them contain the same words:

(5) He called me names and pushed me into the wall
(6) His own mother backed him into a corner
(7) They laughed him out of the door

This is because they all reflect the same underlying construction; in this case the 'caused motion' construction.

In first language acquisition, knowledge of constructions is acquired through interaction, and the language data that this interaction provides are thought to be analysed through pattern-finding and intention-reading skills. Although the data available to second language learners are different from those available to infants learning their first language, this usage-based account of language acquisition is likely to be of some relevance. In this chapter, I discuss the potential applications of construction grammars, and the theories as to how they are acquired, to second language learning, in both classroom-based and more naturalistic settings.

In **Chapter 10**, I provide an overall evaluation of the different ways in which findings from cognitive linguistics might be used in second language learning and teaching, and outline some of their limitations. I identify a number of areas where more research is needed, and conclude with a number of research questions concerning the relationships between language, thought and embodiment, and the implications these have for second language learning.

A criticism that has been levelled at cognitive linguistics is that it relies too heavily on artificial data and made-up examples, a practice which undermines some of its arguments. This book attempts to address this criticism by referring throughout to naturally occurring data from a wide variety of settings, ranging from language classrooms, learner corpora, university lectures, and workplace settings where native and non-native speakers have to engage in authentic interaction to communicate their ideas and accomplish their tasks. I use this data to examine carefully some of the claims made by cognitive linguists. At times, I show how some of these claims may need to be moderated or revised in the light of findings from real data. Unless otherwise stated, all the examples used in this book are taken from language corpora.

2

'I see less of the surroundings. The story feels different': Construal and Second Language Learning

2.1 Introductory comments

We saw in Chapter 1 that a key claim in cognitive linguistics is that the words we use to talk about a particular phenomenon can never reflect a purely objective view of that phenomenon, because pure objectivity does not exist. In this way, language reflects general cognition. When we observe a particular scene or event, we always observe it from a particular perspective. Some aspects of the scene will be more noticeable than others, either because of the position from which we are viewing it, or because we are perhaps more interested in those aspects. Language also provides different ways of directing attention to certain aspects of the thing that we are talking about, and reflects different viewpoints. In cognitive linguistics, this phenomenon is referred to as **construal**. The most salient aspect of the scene is referred to as the **figure**, and the rest of the scene is referred to as the **ground**. Construal is defined by Evans and Green (2006: 536) as:

> the way a speaker chooses to 'package' and 'present' a conceptual representation, which in turn has consequences for the conceptual representation that the utterance evokes in the mind of the hearer.

Construal operates at two levels. The definition offered by Evans and Green emphasizes the importance of speaker choice in the construal of events, and indeed we often have a degree of choice when choosing how to represent events. For example, when reporting an accident, it may be more in our interest to say 'one of the glasses got broken', rather than 'we broke one of your glasses'. However, at a second level, languages themselves have inbuilt, conventional ways of construing events and phenomena that are at times impossible to avoid. This means that even when we ourselves want to remain as objective as possible, the language that we speak will sometimes force us to emphasize certain aspects of the phenomenon more than others. It may also force us to describe the phenomenon from a particular perspective. In different languages, events and phenomena are conventionally construed – and therefore expressed – in different ways, which means that learning another language will often involve learning to see things in a different way, both physically and linguistically. Although the fact that we speak a certain language does not necessarily force us to *think about* phenomena in a certain way, it does mean that we tend to focus on, and *present* information in certain ways, which will always reflect certain standpoints. Thus, to some extent, learning a new language involves learning how to present phenomena from slightly different perspectives and an inability to do this will often result in very unnatural-sounding language.

We will see in this chapter that different phraseologies also represent different ways of construing the same situation, suggesting that to some extent learning a foreign language involves learning how to present and package information in different ways and from different viewpoints. The chapter looks at the different ways in which phenomena and events can be construed, at the effects this has on the way meanings are expressed in different languages, and at the implications this has for language learning.

Cognitive linguists have identified four sources of variation in terms of the ways in which phenomena or events can be construed, which in turn affect the ways in which we talk about them. These are: attention/salience (the part of the phenomenon that stands out most, or in which we are most interested); perspective (the standpoint from which we view the phenomenon); constitution (how fine-grained our view of the phenomenon is); and categorization (how we divide phenomena up into categories). Although I look at all four types of construal in this chapter, I devote most attention to **categorization** (in both this chapter and Chapter 3), as this is one of the most productive areas of work in cognitive linguistics. It also has the greatest number of potential applications to language learning and teaching. In the final section, I discuss the cognitive processes that have been found to be involved in second language acquisition more generally, and look at how these processes might be involved in the acquisition of L2 construal systems.

2.2 Attention and salience

When we are talking, we often refer to the most salient part of an event or phenomenon, using it as a kind of shorthand for the whole event or phenomenon. For example, when we talk about someone who 'fell asleep at the wheel', we know that 'the wheel' in question is in fact the steering wheel of a car, and that *falling asleep at the wheel* means falling asleep while driving. For the driver, at the time of falling asleep, the steering wheel is the most salient part of the car (a fact that is reflected if we ask people to mime the verb *drive*). On the other hand, someone writing about the car itself might talk about a 'nifty' or 'amazing' 'set of wheels' (Bank of English data). Indeed, corpus lines extracted from both the Bank of English and the British National Corpus appear to indicate that when the expression *set of wheels* is used to refer to the whole car, it is nearly always in the context of *purchasing* a car, or of positively evaluating a car. These examples show how we continually highlight some features of a phenomenon and leave others in the shade.

Different languages tend to construe different aspects of a phenomenon as salient, and background others, which presents a challenge to the language learner. For instance, in some languages it is more usual to introduce people by their first name, whereas in others the surname is used, and in some countries, such as Japan, other salient information is provided, such as the company the person works for: 'This is IBM's Mr Tanaka'. Differences in attention and salience are particularly apparent when we look at what information is obligatory in one language but not another.

There is an increasing amount of empirical evidence showing that linguistic differences in attention and salience do have an effect on cognition. For instance, in English, when we insert a CD in a CD player, we talk about putting one object *in* another. We use the same preposition, *in*, to talk about putting fruit *in* a fruit bowl. However, in Korean, the focus is much more on how *tight* a fit is involved. Because the CD is a relatively tight fit, they use the verb *kkita*, whereas when talking about putting fruit in a fruit bowl, they use the verb *nehta*, which reflects a looser fit (Choi and Bowerman, 1991). Thus in Korea, attention is drawn to the tightness of fit, whereas tightness of fit is less important and thus less salient in English. The fact that the Korean language makes these relationships salient means that Korean infants tend to be more aware of them than English-speaking infants, from a very early age (Bowerman and Choi, 2003). Choi and Bowerman (1991) and Choi (1997) found that, even in situations where no language was used, English-speaking children aged between 17 and 20 months systematically distinguished between actions involving containment and actions involving support, whereas Korean-speaking children of the same age systematically distinguished between tight fit, loose fit and loose contact events. Moreover, McDonough *et al.* (in press) found that English-speaking adults experienced considerable difficulties when asked to categorize actions in terms of closeness of fit, whereas Korean-speaking adults experienced no such difficulties. These findings suggest that the language we speak leads us to focus more on some aspects of scenes and events than on others. In cognitive linguistic terms, this is described as a form of **entrenchment**.

This raises questions as to how English-speaking learners of Korean or Korean-speaking learners of English are able to deal with these different foci of attention. Indeed, the picture becomes even more complicated when we look at the five Korean words which correspond to 'put on' or 'put in' in English, each of which highlights a different aspect of the 'put in/on' relationship. As we saw above, *nehta*, which roughly translates as 'putting something loosely in or around', can be used to talk about putting apples in bowls and books in bags. The second word, *kkita*, which means 'to interlock tightly', can be used to talk about putting a CD in its case, putting a ring on a finger, attaching a piece of lego to a model and adding a piece to a jigsaw. Korean also has a third word, *pwuchita*, which roughly means 'to juxtapose vertical surfaces', and which one would use to talk about putting a magnet on a fridge. The fourth word, *nohta*, roughly translates as 'to put on a horizontal surface', and would be used to talk about putting a cup on a table. Finally, the fifth word, *ssuta*, roughly translates as 'put clothing on the head' and would be used to talk about putting on a hat or a scarf. Are English-speaking learners of Korean ever going to be exposed to sufficient input to work out these different meanings for themselves, or do we have a case for some explicit teaching here? Although this area has not yet been investigated empirically, one would expect these differences to have an effect on second language learning. Later in the chapter we look at the issue of how second language learners learn from input, and at the role of explicit teaching. During that discussion it would be useful to think back about how an English-speaking learner of Korean might learn to distinguish between these five different areas of focus.

2.2.1 Attention, salience and manner-of-movement verbs: Slobin's thinking-for-speaking hypothesis

There is one area where cross-linguistic variation in terms of attention and salience patterns has been found to have a significant impact on second language learning. This is the area of 'manner-of-movement' verbs. When describing movement we can focus either on the direction of the movement or the manner of movement. Talmy (1985, 2000) categorizes languages into two types, in terms of the ways in which they habitually construe movement. According to Talmy, in 'satellite-framed' languages (such as English), the focus is on the manner; manner of movement is thus expressed within the verb, and the direction of movement is expressed through a preposition, as in *to dash in; to slip out; to creep up*, and *to eat away*. The reason why he claims that manner is prominent in this construction is that we usually understand (or 'parse') sentences by focusing first and foremost on the verb, then by working out how the rest of the sentence relates to the verb (Rost, 2002). The verb is thus the key constituent of a sentence, and any information contained within the verb can be considered paramount. As manner of movement is expressed within the verb in English, it occupies a central role in the message. In 'verb-framed' languages (such as Spanish), only the actual direction of movement is expressed in the verb, and the manner of movement is expressed as a non-finite verb as in 'entro en la casa *corriendo*' ('he entered the house *running*'); and 'Sali *corriendo* a la calle' ('I exited *running* into the street'). The focus in Spanish is thus very much on the direction of movement, rather than the manner. Thus verb-framed languages and satellite-framed languages vary in terms of where they place their attention.

Slobin (2000) suggests that speakers of satellite-framed languages are predisposed to cognitively encode motion events in a different way from speakers of verb-framed languages. As a test, he asked 14 Spanish speakers and 21 American English speakers to give an oral report on an English translation of a passage from Isobel Allende's *House of the Spirits*. As we can see below, the translation of the passage was a very literal one and thus contained very few English-style manner-encoded verbs:

He got off the train at the station of San Luca. It was a wretched place. At that hour of the morning there was not a soul on the wooden platform, its roof eaten away by inclement weather and ants. From there, one could see the whole valley through an impalpable mist that rose from the earth the night rain had soaked. He combed the landscape for the town of San Luca but was only able to make out a far off hamlet that was faded in the dampness of the morning. He walked around the station. There was a padlock on the door to the only office. There was a pencilled note tacked on it, but it was so smudged that he could not read it. He heard the train pull out behind him, leaving a column of white smoke. He was alone in the silent landscape. He picked up his bags and started to walk through the mud and stones of a path that led to the town. He walked for more than ten minutes, grateful that it was not raining, because it was only with great difficulty that he was able to advance along the path with his heavy suitcases, and he realized that the rain would have converted it in a few seconds into an impassable mud hole. Upon nearing the hamlet, he saw smoke in several of the chimneys and breathed a sigh of relief, because at the beginning he had the impression that it was so lonely and decayed that it was a ghost town. He stopped at the edge of the village and saw no one. (Slobin, 2000: 127–8)

When they provided an oral report of this passage, the American English speakers added a large number of manner-encoded verbs such as *stumble*, *stagger* and *trudge* to their reports, such as:

dodge occasional hazards in the trail; move *clumsily*; *rock* from side to side; *slosh* through; *stagger*; *struggle*; *stumble*, *sluggish* movement, *stumbling* over the rocks on the path; slowly *edge his way* down the trail; *slow* his pace; take each step *slow* and *difficult*, tiring and never-ending; *trek*; *trench* [sic] *through* a muddy path; *trudge*; slowly *hobbling*. (*ibid.*: 128)

Moreover, 95% of these respondents claimed to have mental images of various types of movement. They thus appeared to be focusing heavily on the manner of movement.

In contrast, the Spaniards' and South Americans' reports did not focus on the manner of the movement and only 14% reported having images of movement, although they did visualize the path, the physical details of the surroundings, the man's inner state, and his trajectory of movement. Typical comments from the Spanish-speaking informants were:

'I see him walking with difficulty, with care not to slip, making especially slow movements, as if it cost him special effort to move his legs or was carrying a weight in them. It was hard for him to walk through the mud hole. I don't picture him getting down from the train but rather standing still on the platform and I don't see him going along a very long trajectory in order to arrive at the village; rather I see him at a distance from it, looking at it. I repeat that I don't observe him moving in the direction of the village but rather as static images, more like photographs.' (Chilean) (*ibid.*: 129)

'It would seem that he moves, walks, but I don't see any sort of detailed action on his part. I know that he walks and must have his feet burdened with the stony ground but I see the stones and the path more than the manner in which he walks.... It would seem that he were floating at times as if he were seated in a cart.' (Mexican) (*ibid.*: 129)

Interestingly, there were a few bilingual subjects in the experiment who reported distinctly different imagery in their two languages, with more manner-of-movement imagery when reporting on the text in English than in Spanish, but still much less than the monolingual speakers of English:

'I'm still seeing very little manner of movement but I see more concrete walking and I can sort of make out a pace. I see less of the surroundings. The story feels different. There is less detail in regards to the scenery.' (Mexican bilingual) (*ibid.*: 130)

Slobin's findings suggest that the way in which one language encodes manner of movement has a significant effect on those aspects of the context that people perceive as being pertinent, and that they have difficulty envisaging those aspects of the context that are downplayed by their native language. Slobin's original study has inspired a significant amount of research into the differences between the ways in which speakers of verb-framed and satellite-framed languages construe motion events. Findings from these studies suggest that the language one speaks can alter the way in which manner of movement is construed, even amongst 4- and 5-year-olds (Ozcaliskan, 2007).

Slobin himself has an interesting take on the relationship between language and thought. In his **thinking-for-speaking hypothesis** he proposes a weak version of the linguistic relativity hypothesis. He argues that our minds are 'trained in taking particular points of view for the purposes of speaking' (Slobin, 1996: 91), and that this influences the way in which we encode information when we first encounter it, as we attend to those aspects of the information that are relevant to speaking. Thus although the language that we speak causes us to have different ways of construing phenomena, these are only activated when we actually attempt to put our thoughts into words or engage in private speech.

Different construals of events do not represent fundamental, immutable views of the world that are tied to the language we speak, but more superficial ways of seeing things that allow us to communicate and organize our ideas. Although the way in which a given language construes events will force speakers of those languages to perceive them in certain ways in order to communicate their ideas to others, it does not prevent us from seeing things differently if we want to. When we speak, the language we use simply highlights some semantic domains, whilst making others slightly less visible (Slobin, 2003). Thus the world does not present 'events' that are objectively encoded in language. Rather, experiences are filtered (a) through choice of perspective and (b) through the set of options provided by the particular language we are speaking, into verbalizable events. The speaker has to construct the necessary filters for organizing any experience into a verbal account of that experience – in accordance both with the communicative goals and the range of formal options that are available in the language (Berman and Slobin, 1994: 9, 12).

Slobin's thinking-for-speaking hypothesis is relevant to second language learning. Coping with new ways of 'thinking for speaking' will, according to Schmidt (1993:34) involve attending to features of the context that are either not relevant or are defined differently in the target language. It is therefore a matter of breaking 'cognitive habits' (see Chapter 1). The more deeply engrained the habits are, the more difficult it will be to learn a second language. This suggests that language learners may experience difficulties in those places where the target language construes things differently. Indeed, research has shown that the typological differences between satellite-framed languages and verb-framed languages do present significant difficulties to language learners. For example, manner-of-movement verbs in English have been identified as a significant source of difficulty for beginner-level Mexican learners of English (Ramirez, 2006). Looking at a different language pair, Choi and Lantolf (2008) found that Korean-speaking learners of English and English-speaking learners of Korean found it difficult to use L2 ways of expressing manner of movement and that the gestures they used when doing so indicated that they were still, by and large, operating within an L1 conceptualization of the scene. Research has also shown that the acquisition of a second language has an effect on the way in which manner of movement is encoded in one's first language. For example, Brown and Gullberg (2008) found that Japanese speakers who had reached intermediate levels of English used gestures when describing manner of movement in their L1 that were a mix of Japanese and English gestures (see Chapter 7, Section 7.4). A learner's stage of learning is likely to be of critical importance when looking at the impact of L1 construal systems on L2 production. Cadierno and her colleagues (Cadierno, 2004; Cadierno and Lund, 2004; Cadierno and Ruiz, 2006) investigated the issue of whether *advanced* L1 speakers of satellite-framed languages had problems expressing manner of movement when acquiring verb-framed languages, and vice versa. They found that for the learners in their studies, L1 construal systems had very little effect on the ability to express motion in both satellite-framed and verb-framed languages, and they conclude from their findings that there is a limited role for the L1 thinking-for-speaking patterns in advanced second language acquisition. Thus, it is more likely to be during the early and intermediate stages of learning that we might expect there to be a problem.

The thinking-for-speaking hypothesis may provide a partial explanation for the fact that, in general, young learners eventually overtake older learners in most areas of second language learning (Singleton, 1995) as their thinking-for-speaking patterns are not as deeply entrenched as those of adults. It may also explain why learners who are 'tolerant of ambiguity' tend, in some areas, to out-perform those learners who have a more rigid learning style (Ely, 1989). On a more positive note, learning new thinking-for-speaking patterns may have wider cognitive and social benefits. In the words of Gentner and Goldin-Meadow (2003: 12):

> language acts as a lens through which we see the world; it can provide us with tools that enlarge our capabilities; [learning a second language] can help us appreciate groupings in the world that we might not have otherwise grasped.

Thus the acquisition of a second or third language has the potential to extend and enrich the number of possible ways of perceiving, describing and structuring our realities. This is related to V. Cook's (2002) notion of multicompetence, whereby linguistic knowledge is restructured in the mind of a bilingual, leading to an integrated system which combines elements from both the L1 and the L2 to produce something new.

2.3 Perspective

Let us now look at a second source of variation in the way things are construed: **perspective**. Related to attention and salience, perspective refers to our own position with respect to the thing that we are talking about. In the physical world, the way we view things depends on where we are standing when we look at them, and this is reflected in language. For example, someone living in the North of England might talk about going 'down' to London because it lies to the south, which is 'down' on the map; whereas someone from the South would travel 'up' to London. However, if the person in the North is comparing where they live to London in terms of status, they might take the view that the North is somehow smaller, more provincial, and of lower status, and thus talk about travelling 'up' to London. Neither expression is more or less 'correct' than the other, rather they reflect two different perspectives on the same event. In fact, a search of the Bank of English reveals 161 instances of the phrase *up to London* and 204 instances of the phrase *down to London*, with relatively little variation in their collocations.

For language learners, this could be problematic, as different languages incorporate perspective in different ways. Indeed, where two languages lack a direct translation equivalent, this is often due to differences in the perspective from which they conventionally view a particular event or phenomenon. For example, languages vary in terms of the way they describe location. In most languages including English, it is possible to describe where objects are in relation to one's own position, or the position of some other object ('it's to the left of the tree'; 'it's on your right'), or in absolute terms ('it's to the north, south, east or west'). But there are some languages, such as Guugu Yimithirr, which is spoken in North Queensland, where it is only possible to use an absolute orientation (Levinson, 1996). Presumably, if a speaker of Guugu Yimithirr were to learn English, he or she would need to acquire a whole new system of perspective, which may not be that easy to do. Conversely, an English speaker of Guugu Yimithirr would need to acquire an excellent sense of direction!

Another example where perspective may present problems to language learners relates to the level of 'ego-centricity' in language. For example, in Japanese, perspective is said to be predominantly egocentric (Ikegami, 2000). This allows Japanese to drop the first person subject from the sentence as it is obvious that one is talking about oneself; for example, in (8):

(1) Asokoni Bigguben ga mieru
    Over there Big Ben (particle) see
    ('I see Big Ben over there')

The importance of the ego-centric perspective in Japanese is also shown in the use of the verbs *ageru* and *kureru* in (9)–(10), both of which mean 'to give'.

(2) *ageru*
Watashi wa kare ni puresento wo ageru
I (particle) him (particle) present (particle) give
('I give him a present')

(3) *kureru*
Kare wa watashi ni puresento wo kureru
He (particle) me (particle) present (particle) give.
('He gives me a present')

The use of *ageru* versus *kureru* depends on who is doing the giving. Although both verbs mean 'to give', the focus of *ageru* is on the giver, whereas the focus of *kureru* is on the receiver. Because Japanese is an ego-centric language, the focus of the sentence is on the speaker regardless of whether the speaker is the subject. Therefore, in example 1, *ageru* is used because the speaker is the giver, and *kureru* is used because the speaker is the receiver (Kuno, 1987). Learners of Japanese, whose first language (Chinese) is not predominantly ego-centric, have been found to experience considerable difficulties when learning *ageru* and *kureru* (Li Wei, 2003).

This subjective perspective of Japanese also manifests itself in the Japanese use of the verbs *iku* ('go') and *kuru* ('come'). In Japanese, *iku* is used when the movement is away from from the place where the speaker is present and *kuru* is used when this distance is towards one's present position, for example, in (11):

(4) Mother: Daidokoro ni kina-sai
Kitchen (particle) come-(imperative)
('Come into the kitchen')

Daughter: Ima iki-masu
Now go-(polite)
('I'm going')

The daughter in this example uses *iku* ('go') rather than *kuru* ('come') because the movement to the kitchen is away from the place where she is at the moment. Therefore one might hypothesize that Japanese students of English will over-use *go*, as in example (12):

(5) Are you coming to my birthday party?
    Yes, I will *go* to the party.

or that English speaking learners of Japanese will over-use *come* (Oe, 1975). Indeed, Japanese learners of English have been found to experience considerable difficulties in this area, and to show a degree of inflexibility when it comes to adopting the type of perspective that is conventional to speakers of English (Kusuyama, 2005).

Differences in the importance attached to perspective can have an impact on noun use as well as verb use. For example, in English we have a single word *corner* which we can use to describe the corner of a building or the corner of a square. However, in Spanish, there are two words for 'corner': *el rincon* (which roughly translates as 'the inside of a corner'), and *el esquina* (which roughly translates as 'the outside of a corner'). These two words reflect the speakers' different perspectives with respect to the corner. Because English does not see one's perspective as being central to the word *corner*, English-speaking learners of Spanish will not be 'primed' to notice the two different words in Spanish, and thus may initially find it difficult to work out the exact meaning of *el rincon* and *el esquina*, unless they have it explicitly pointed out to them. If learners use the wrong word when speaking to native speakers, this may result in confusion which will eventually lead to corrective feedback. This may make it a good candidate for the type of learning through interaction and feedback that is proposed by Gass (1997).

To take a final example, and another language pair, English and Turkish differ in terms of the importance they attach to the speaker's perspective when talking about an event that has been witnessed. In Turkish, if someone is describing an event, the way the language is constructed means that it is necessary to say whether or not the speaker actually saw the event, whereas in English it is possible to describe it in such a way that the interlocutor does not know whether the speaker was there or not (Gentner and Goldin-Meadow, 2003). Does this difference mean that Turkish speakers of English will want to indicate whether or not they were there at the time, or will they be happy with the ambiguity? When asked about this phenomenon, a native speaker of English (Richard Spiby, personal communication), teaching English at a Turkish university commented that:

With more sophisticated language users, the ambiguity in English may be felt more keenly. Fluent English speakers will sometimes ask whether the speaker had direct experience of an event. While speaking, they appear more likely to indicate that they were not present at an event when it happened, either by qualifying a statement in English or (when listeners include Turkish speakers) by concluding an English sentence with the Turkish verb ending 'miş', which shows that the information is second hand. This latter strategy can be amusing but does make for effective communication!

Given the aforementioned discussion on manner-of-movement verbs, it would be worth conducting a more systematic investigation into the ways in which Turkish-speaking learners of English and English-speaking learners of Turkish deal with this phenomenon both in their target language and in their mother tongue.

2.4 Constitution

The third component of construal, **constitution**, refers to how close we are to a particular phenomenon, and how fine-grained our description of it is. For instance, Croft and Cruse (2004) point out that we can use the words *leaves* and *foliage* to talk about the same thing, but they each reflect different constitutions. When they are seen from far away, leaves give the impression of being a mass of green, hence the uncountable noun *foliage*.

Research shows that the ways in which constitution is habitually construed in our language can affect the way we think about objects. For example, Lucy (1992) found that speakers of languages with grammatical number-marking (such as English) judge differences in the number of countable objects to be more significant than differences in the amount of non-countable substances. On the other hand, speakers of languages which lack grammatical number-marking (such as Yucatec) show no such preference. Nouns in Yucatec do not tend to denote bounded units, rather they represent 'stuff' or 'essence', so the word for 'banana' is used to refer to any entity that is banana-related (e.g. the tree, the leaf, or the fruit). Lucy found that on sorting tasks, English-speakers tend to sort by shape or function, whereas Yucatec-speakers tend to sort by the material out of which the item is made. Lucy also compared the behaviour of Japanese- and English-speakers on non-linguistic tasks involving constitution. Like Yucatec, Japanese is a non-plural-marking language and does not distinguish between countable and uncountable objects. Using a series of photographs, Lucy investigated whether English- and Japanese-speakers were equally likely to notice small increases in countable and uncountable objects. He found that English-speakers were significantly more likely to notice increases in countable items than they were to notice increases in uncountable items, when shown photos of the said items. Japanese-speakers were equally likely to notice increases in both types of items.

Lucy's findings were extended to Japanese learners of English by Athanasopoulos (2006), who compared monolingual English- and Japanese-speakers with Japanese speakers of English as a second language (L2). Athanasopoulos showed that intermediate Japanese learners of English behaved like Japanese monolinguals in that they were equally likely to notice increases in both countable and uncountable items when they were shown pictures of those items. In contrast, advanced Japanese learners of English behaved more like English monolinguals, and were significantly more likely to notice increases in countable items than in uncountable items. Athanasopoulos argues that these results provide support for the claim that grammatical representation may influence cognition in specific ways, and suggests that L2 acquisition may alter cognitive dispositions established by the L1. Thus advanced learners of a language behave more like native speakers of that language when they are asked to perform tasks that involve no language as such. This finding is important as it suggests that the learning of a second language has an impact on cognitive processing beyond language. This idea is discussed in more detail below.

2.5   Categorization

As we saw in Chapter 1, one of the key tenets of cognitive linguistics is that the development of language involves the same cognitive processes that we use for understanding the world in general. One of the first things that we do with information about the world is that we try and sort it into categories, and the language we use reflects this fact. Indeed, **categorization** has attracted a great deal of interest in cognitive linguistics, as it is one of the first things we do when we try to make sense of the world around us. Young children do this when they encounter new objects (Is it something I can eat? Is it something I can play with? Is it both?) and we do not stop categorizing things even when we reach adulthood, particularly when we find ourselves in a new environment, faced with unfamiliar stimuli. In this section, I begin by outlining some of the early cognitive linguistic work on categories. I then look at work that has been carried out into the ways in which different languages categorize space. In Chapter 3, I will look at more recent work on categorization, and discuss individual words, morphemes phonological features and intonation patterns as radial categories.

Most users of English would have little difficulty in accepting that cats, dogs, and sheep all fall within the category of 'animals'. However, the allocation of members to categories is not always as straightforward as this; categories are flexible, they have fuzzy boundaries, and some members are more prototypical than others. To illustrate the first of these features, let us take the category of 'pets'. Most people would argue that cats, dogs and goldfish are all pets. But could an elephant be a pet? In some circumstances it possibly could, but most people would argue that it is somehow less central to the category of 'pet' than a cat, a dog, or a goldfish. In the words of cognitive linguists, it is less 'prototypical' of the category of 'pets'. The category of pets can thus be said to be a 'radial category' as some of its members are somehow more central or prototypical than others. Let us think for a moment about where we might place 'cyberpets' (electronic pets that are popular with children) within this system. Are they a pet or are they a toy? They might be seen as being somehow on the outer fringes of the 'pet' category (Croft and Cruse, 2004). This tells us that categories do not have clear boundaries, but instead tend to be somewhat messy round the edges leading cognitive linguists to talk about 'fuzzy boundaries'.

All of this becomes interesting from a second language learning perspective when we look at variation in the ways in which different languages divide things into semantic categories. Although they may sometimes appear, to groups of native speakers of the language, to be the only rational and sensible divisions possible, categories are rarely entirely objective, and can sometimes be highly arbitrary. Coming back to the example given in Chapter 1, a 'shoe' becomes a 'boot' more quickly in English than in French, yet neither language is intrinsically more 'objective' or 'rational' than the other. Thus judgements as to where the boundaries lie are prone to linguistic diversity. Categories are formed around prototypes (e.g. the most 'typical' boot), although they are highly flexible, and are susceptible to change according to context. For the second language learner, the key lies in understanding how the target language categorization system works, and how it differs from their first language system. Under a dynamic systems theory perspective, one's existing system of categories and prototypes might be seen as an 'attractor state', which, as Larsen-Freeman and Cameron (2007) point out, is a period of temporary stability in the system. When language learners are exposed to new categories, they need to alter their categorization system and move towards new attractor states.

A particularly well-researched area of cross-linguistic variation in categorization patterns is that of countable and uncountable objects. In English, objects tend to be categorized as either countable or uncountable, and are indicated as such by different types of markers. Things such as flour, sugar, and salt are generally considered to be uncountable, whereas peas and beans are generally considered to be countable. However, in Japanese there is no such distinction; instead objects are divided into long thin objects (signalled by the marker *hon* or *pon*) and round flat objects (signalled by the marker *mai* or *pai*). In a revealing study, Imai (2000) presented a group of native English-speakers and a group of native Japanese-speakers with a number of objects including bags of sugar, plates of peas, pencils, tubes of sweets etc., and asked each group to divide the objects into two categories. The Japanese participants tended to divide them into long thin objects and round flat objects, and the English speakers tended to divide them into countable and uncountable objects, indicating that the categorization processes were, to some extent, real cognitive phenomena for these participants, and not just a matter of language. The difficulties that Japanese learners of English experience when grasping the concept of countable and uncountable nouns have been empirically documented (Nakao, 1998), and most Japanese-language textbooks written for speakers of English contain a section in the early chapters pointing out the difference between long thin objects and short flat objects in terms of the way they are counted, which suggests that it may be perceived of as being potentially problematic, at least by textbook writers.

There is some evidence to suggest that learning a new language enables us to categorize things in different ways. For example, in Japanese, it is normal to categorize objects according to substance, whereas in English we tend to categorize more according to shape. When they compared Japanese monolinguals with Japanese/English bilinguals, Cook *et al.* (2006) found that the bilingual subjects tended to use both English and Japanese systems to categorize objects, whereas the monolingual subjects were only able to use a single system. They argue that their findings provide support for the hypothesis that the minds of bilingual people are different from the minds of monolingual people. We will return to this subject below.

Languages also vary in terms of the number of categories that they split a particular phenomenon into. For example, in English we talk about *woods* and *forests*, and generally assume that the former are slightly smaller than the latter. In German, there is only one category represented by the word *Wald*, and no distinction is drawn between large and small versions. This means that German learners of English need to learn to split the category, whereas English learners of German must merge the category, and find other ways of conveying whether it is a small or large *Wald* (Walker, 2008a). To take another example, in English we have the single verb *to eat*, which in German, is divided into two separate verbs, depending on whether it is humans doing the eating, in which case the verb *essen* is used, or animals, in which case the word *fressen* is used. Distinctions such as these depend to some extent on the ways in which events are construed.

There is evidence to suggest that L1 categorization systems can exert an influence on a learner's sensitivity to naturalness in the L2. For example, Elston-Guttler and Williams (2008) looked at cases where a polysemous word in the L1 is represented by independent words in the L2. For example, the semantic space that is occupied by the German word *Blase* is occupied in English by the words *bubble* and *blister*. They asked a group of German speakers of English to spot any anomalous usages in English, some of which involved transfer from the German categorization system, others which did not. They found that the learners were consistently insensitive to unnatural-sounding English when the unnaturalness resulted from direct translations from German. The results were more marked for nouns than for verbs. Their findings indicate that the categorization systems that we build up due to our L1 cause us to form habits that are hard to break when we encounter a different language with different categorization systems. However, as we will see below, L1 transfer is likely to be just one factor among many when it comes to the acquisition of L2 categorization systems.

Things become even more difficult for language learners when a concept that is divided into two broad categories in their own language is divided into, say, three categories in the target language. For example, the concept of 'leadership' in business is expressed in English in three main ways. One can *run*, *manage* or *head* a department, whereas in German, this concept is covered by just two main verbs: *leiten* and *führen*. The task for the language learner is more difficult here than in the previous example. It is not just a case of merging or dividing categories, but of deciding which aspects of *run*, *manage* and *head* are covered by *leiten* and which are covered by *führen* (Walker, 2008a). This is likely to require considerable cognitive flexibility, as well as strong and astute 'noticing' skills (Schmidt, 1990).

2.5.1 Cross-linguistic differences in the categorization of space

A key area of experience that is subject to categorization, is **semantic space**. In other words, a single area of meaning can be divided up in different ways by different languages. For instance, Bowerman and Pederson (1992) and Bowerman and Choi (2001) show how different prepositions have different, but overlapping, senses in different languages. They studied 38 languages, and found significant variation in terms of how they divided a single semantic space that is covered in English by the prepositions *in* and *on*. For example, in English, we talk about cups being *on* tables, pictures being *on* walls and fruit being *in* bowls, whereas in Dutch, three different prepositions (*op, aan* and *in*) would be used to talk about these three different situations, and in Spanish just one preposition, *en* would be used to talk about all three. Finally, in Berber, the preposition *x* is used to talk about cups on tables and pictures on walls, but the preposition *di* is used to talk about handles on doors, and fruit in bowls. This variation can be illustrated as in Figure 2.1

Because they are susceptible to cross-linguistic variation, prepositions are very difficult for language learners to learn. Diagrams of the sort shown in Figure 2.1 may be useful to second language educators because they allow us to see in an instant how languages vary. They may also help us to make predictions about the types of difficulties learners may experience. For example, it might be that a Spanish learner of Dutch experiences more difficulties in this area than a Dutch learner of Spanish (who only has to learn one preposition). On the other hand, Bowerman's own research with L1 participants has shown that when they are learning their first language, children are more likely to over-extend

	A cup on a table	A plaster on a leg	A picture on a wall	A handle on a door	An apple on a branch	An apple in a bowl
	A	B	C	D	E	F
English	----------------------------On----------------------------					---In---
Japanese	---Ue---	----------------------Ni----------------------				-Naka-
Dutch	---------Op---------		---------------Aan---------------			---In---
Berber	-----------------X-----------------			----------------------Di----------------------		
Spanish	----------------------------En----------------------------					

Figure 2.1 Some cross-linguistic differences in terms of the way languages divide up spatial categories. Adapted from Bowerman and Choi (2001: 485) with the permission of the author and Cambridge University Press

large categories than small categories, so the picture may not be as straightforward as we may think. Another hypothesis is that learners will experience more difficulties at the boundary areas of the semantic space. For example, Dutch children learning their first language tend to have more problems with the *aan* category than with the other two categories. Indeed, Ijaz (1986) found that the use of the prepositions *on* and *over* by non-native speakers of English who spoke six different native languages, was strongly influenced by the ways in which these prepositions are used in their own languages.

Research into the effect of L1 categorization systems on L2 acquisition has shown that, in general, L1 categories exert strong priming effects that are then transferred into the L2 (e.g. Lucy, 1992; Lucy and Gaskins, 2003; Pederson *et al.*, 1998). However, the relationship is not always as straightforward as one might predict. A number of studies have looked at the ways in which second language learners juggle two semantic systems for categorizing a particular conceptual domain (Bowerman, 2008). Two studies in particular are interesting, as they show how second language learners merge their L1 categorization systems with those of the L2. These are Ameel *et al.*'s (2005) study of the acquisition of names for containers by Dutch and French bilinguals, and the study by Ervin (1961) of the acquisition of English colour terms by native speakers of Navajo. Ameel *et al.* looked at the ways in which French/Dutch bilingual participants categorized vessels such as cups, plates and dishes, and found that the naming patterns used converged on one common naming pattern that was somewhere between those used in Dutch and those used in French, but which resembled neither language. The category boundaries thus moved towards one another and diverged from the boundaries of the two 'first' languages. In other words, when people speak more than one language, these languages have an impact on each other, and their categorization systems are not the same as those in monolinguals. Ervin (1961) found evidence for the same phenomenon in Navajo learners of English.

Findings from these studies suggest that the second language learning process results in the formation of a blend between L1 and L2 categorization systems. This is in line with what recent work in the areas of bilingualism and cognitive linguistics would lead us to expect: when people speak more than one language, they do not develop two independent linguistic systems in their mind. Rather, the two systems overlap and exert a strong influence on each other, resulting in a blend from which new categorization patterns can emerge (Bialystok, 2002; Singleton, 1999).

It has also been found that people who speak two or more languages display greater cognitive flexibility than those who speak only one language. Even in non-linguistic tasks, bilinguals are able to switch more easily between different types of information, and focus on that information which is most relevant to the task (Gass, 2008). In other words, they develop certain cognitive capacities, beyond language, that monolingual people do not possess. It has been found that bilingual children are better than monolingual children at *non-linguistic* tasks that involve shifts in their categorization systems. For instance, Bialystok (1999) reports a study in which pre-school children were required to conduct a task developed by Zelazo and Jacques (1996) in which they were asked to sort cards into two compartments, each marked by a target stimulus, for example, a red square and a blue circle. The set of cards contained instances of shape–colour combinations that reversed the pairings, in this case, blue squares and red circles. The children were first told to sort by one dimension, such as colour; then they were asked to re-sort the same cards by the opposite dimension, shape. Monolingual children were found to persist in sorting by the first dimension (colour) even after they had been given the second instruction (shape), whereas bilingual children were able to adapt to the new rule and solve this problem significantly earlier than the monolinguals. These findings suggest that by learning to speak another language, we develop more flexibility in our categorization systems, providing strong support for the link between language and more general areas of cognition, a theory that underlies much work in the area of cognitive linguistics. Returning to the subject of language, research by Slobin (2000) suggests that when people speak two languages that construe events differently, they are able to store both types of construal within a single system, and that they can switch between the two with ease.

We have seen from the above discussion that L1 construal patterns are likely to exert an influence on L2 acquisition, but as already indicated by some of the findings mentioned above, the development of L2 construal patterns within the mind of a learner is likely to be a much more complex process than this. When people learn a second language, they do rely to some extent on their L1, but they do much more than this. They also attempt to learn new rules, and when they have learned those rules they need opportunities to interact in the target language, in a relatively non-threatening environment in order to try things out and develop a feel for how far these rules apply (see, for example, Block, 2003; Gass, 1997). The development of L2 knowledge thus relies on multiple factors, such as the language that they happen to encounter, the context in which they encounter it, and their own language learning styles and capacities. In other words, the ability to perceive and change L1 construal patterns is only one process among many that are involved in second language learning (Kaufman, 2004; Lantolf and Appel 1998; and Larsen-Freeman 2006).

2.6 Beyond transfer: other cognitive processes that influence the acquisition of L2 construal patterns

So far, this chapter has focused mainly on the ways in which languages vary in terms of how they construe scenes and events, and has made predictions about how L1 construal patterns might influence L2 acquisition. Although a number of findings have been reported that provide evidence for the role of L1 transfer, the complete picture is likely to be much more complicated than this, and contrastive analysis accounts of second language acquisition will only ever provide us with part of the explanation. In subsequent chapters I discuss other concepts from cognitive linguistics, besides construal, that have an important bearing on how second languages are learned; but first, in this section I focus on other cognitive processes, besides transfer, that are likely to influence the acquisition of L2 construal patterns in naturalistic learning settings.

In both cognitive linguistic theory and second language acquisition research there has been increasing recognition of the extent to which language learning is usage-based. That is to say, it is derived from and informed by language use. Cognitive linguists (e.g. Tomasello, 2003) have shown how children learning their first language are able to extract expressions from the language that they hear around them. They use their intention-reading skills (i.e. their ability to work out from the context what meaning the person talking to them is actually trying to convey) to infer form–meaning pairings, and their pattern-finding skills to infer relationships between different sorts of expressions. Thus, as there is no pre-existing 'universal grammar' in the mind of the child, the acquisition of 'grammar' is a bottom-up phenomenon consisting of the patterns that children have found in the language data to which they are exposed.

There is no reason why the types of pattern-finding skills that L1 learners employ should not still be available to *second* language learners, so many of Tomasello's findings are likely to apply to second language learning too. I explore these in relation to *construction* learning in Chapter 9. But it is important to bear in mind that second language learning is different from first language learning in two important respects: firstly, second language learners already speak one language, and secondly, they have already acquired many of the concepts or 'world knowledge' that first language learners are having to acquire at the same time as learning the language. One would therefore expect them to use this existing linguistic and conceptual knowledge to help them learn the second language. Indeed, it has been shown that in the early stages of learning, a second language is likely to bear a close, even parasitic relationship with the L1 (Ellis, 2006c; MacWhinney, 1997). As exposure to the second language increases, other processes, that do not rely on L1 influence take on a more prominent role.

A good account of the sorts of cognitive processes that are used by second language learners to turn L2 input into acquisition is given by Nick Ellis (2002, 2006a,b,c). Some of these processes are particularly relevant to the learning of L2 construal systems. These are: entrenchment, interference, over- and under-extension, probabilistic processing, contingency learning, learned (in)attention, salience, and perceptual learning. In this section, I look at each of these processes in turn, and assess how they relate to the formation of new construal systems that are necessary for successful L2 acquisition. As we will see below, all of these processes can easily be related to a usage-based view of second language acquisition, as they have all been studied in the context of non-educational learning settings. Later in the book, I will consider classroom-based learning.

Ellis's first two factors (entrenchment and interference) relate closely to the discussions of transfer that we saw in the previous section. We saw above that because of the way their first language works, people tend to become used to focusing on phenomena in different ways, from different angles, and dividing them up in different ways. This leads to the strengthening of certain memory traces through repeated activation, a process which is referred to by cognitive linguists as **entrenchment**. As we have already seen, to some extent, learning a second language involves focusing on different aspects of scenes and events, or dividing them up in different ways and overcoming L1 entrenchment patterns.

Interference refers to the effect that entrenchment patterns that have originated in the L1 can have on the L2. Types of interference can range from phonological interference through to pragmatic interference. In the previous sections we saw a number of examples of how differences in construal patterns might predict, but not fully account for, the types of difficulties experienced by language learners. The challenge for second language learners thus involves overcoming what Odlin (2005: 17) refers to as the 'binding power' of L1 construals and breaking the 'cognitive habits' that were discussed in Chapter 1. It should be noted however that transfer from the L1 can be both positive and negative, and that 'influence' might therefore be a better word than 'interference'.

But as we have already said, overcoming L1 entrenchment patterns is only one part of the language learning process – we need to look beyond L1 transfer in order to account more fully for L2 acquisition patterns. It is for this reason that we now turn to some of Ellis's other factors that are likely to impact upon second language acquisition. First, Ellis argues that second language learning is likely to involve the cognitive processes of **over- and under-extension**. The phenomena of over- and under-extension have been well reported in the literature. For instance, when a learner of English has learned that past participles end in the morpheme -*ed*, he or she may **over-extend** this to all past participles, not realizing that some are irregular. The notions of over- and under-extension may also apply to vocabulary learning; for instance, the following use of the word *considerable* by a Polish learner of English, taken from the Polish section of the International Corpus of Learner English (http://www.staff.amu.edu.pl/~ przemka/picle.html), suggests that the learner is aware of the meaning that *considerable* has in English, but that he or she has over-extended the meaning to encompass notions of computer power:

> A genius has decided that people wait too long at supermarket check-outs, and so he has developed a *considerable* computer to make people's lives easier . It all involved weighing, tearing off special little tags from each item one buys, and feeding them into a machine and weighing again.

Although discussions of over- and under-extension have traditionally centred on the acquisition of grammar and vocabulary, the same arguments can be applied to the acquisition of L2 categories. As well as transferring their own L1 categories learners may also over- or under-extend L2 categories in the process of acquisition. For example, once an English-speaking learner of Dutch has understood that the word *aan* occupies a large part of the semantic space for prepositions, the learner may start to use it in places where *op* or *in* should be used. Alternatively, he or she may **under-extend** the usage of an L2 category. For example, with reference to Figure 2.1 above, an English-speaking learner of Berber might under-extend the preposition *di*, using it to talk about an apple in a bowl or on a branch, but not a handle on a door. A Japanese learner of English who has learned that items can be categorized as countable or uncountable may over- or under-extend the number of items that fall into either of these categories.

Ellis's next factor, **probabilistic processing** refers to the remarkable sensitivity that learners have regarding the relative frequency with which certain forms are used in particular contexts in the input they receive, and their ability to match their output according to what they think might be appropriate. In other words, probabilistic processing can be seen as a kind of 'intuitive statistics'. In terms of construals, the argument here would be that learners gradually attune themselves to the construals preferred by the target language, and match them to the situations in which they encounter them. They are thus able to learn to use them appropriately without being fully aware of the fact that they are doing so. This may account for Cadierno's (2004) findings with respect to manner-of-movement verbs that were discussed in Section 2.2.1. Here, advanced learners appeared to have picked up the new construal pattern on the basis of evidence in their L2 input, without having been explicitly taught it.

Related to probabilistic processing is **contingency learning**. This refers to the fact that the more often a particular morpheme corresponds to a particular meaning, the more quickly it will be learned. For example, the plural -*s*, which sounds different every time one hears it, scores low on contingency, and is thus learned more slowly. The same can be said for the definite article (which is used for many different reasons in English) and highly polysemeous words such as prepositions. Thus Ellis argues that the polysemy of prepositions means that they do not lend themselves well to contingency learning. In terms of construal systems, this would mean that if a particular form is regularly associated with a particular way of construing a scene or event, then this will be more readily learned than a form that corresponds to several different construal patterns. I return to the issue of contingency learning in Chapter 9, when I look at the acquisition of L2 constructions.

One of Ellis's processes that is particularly relevant to the acquisition of L2 construals is **learned (in)attention**. The fact that L1 construal patterns are so deeply embedded and entrenched means that, in many cases, learners will simply not notice the new construals in the target language. For example, an English-speaking learner of Spanish, who is not used to distinguishing between the two sides of a corner, may simply infer that there are two words for *corner* in Spanish and that they are interchangeable. Learners of Spanish whose L1s do make this distinction will be more predisposed to noticing it in Spanish. The issue of **noticing** is very important in second language learning and teaching, and I return to it later.

Related to noticing is the issue of **salience**. According to Ellis, salience refers to how *noticeable* a particular morpheme is and how *useful* it is to the learner. The more salient and the more useful it is, the more likely acquisition becomes. Salience (or lack of salience) is an important consideration in the acquisition of L2 construal systems. Differences in construal systems, particularly those that involve perspective and categorization, are often difficult to spot, a fact which is emphasized in Kellerman's (1995) 'transfer to nowhere' principle. Kellerman argues that it is extremely hard for learners to acquire L2 construal patterns because they are very difficult to perceive, as there is no single piece of tangible evidence for them. He argues that:

> learners may not look for the perspectives peculiar to the (target) language; instead they may seek the *linguistic* tools which will permit them to maintain their L1 perspective. Such cases represent 'transfer to nowhere', an unconscious assumption that is subject to between-language variation. (Kellerman, 1995: 141)

For these reasons, as I will argue below, second language learners may benefit from having some L2 construal systems explicitly pointed out to them in class.

Perceptual learning is closely related to salience but is more concerned with the ability to perceive particular words and sounds in spoken discourse. Some words tend not be stressed as strongly as others, and will thus be less perceptually salient to the learner, which may make them more difficult to learn. The issue of perceptual salience is particularly relevant to the acquisition of phonological categories, which we will explore in Chapter 3.

All of these processes are likely to be brought to bear on the learning of target language construal patterns. Specific memory traces will become more or less entrenched, depending on the degree and nature of exposure. However, complex systems theory predicts that Ellis's factors are likely to interact in a way that is neither linear nor predictable (Ellis and Larsen-Freeman, 2006; Ellis, 2008), which accounts, to a large extent, for the fact that language learners rarely seem to 'learn what they are taught'. Ellis's ideas will be returned to periodically throughout the rest of this book as we look at other concepts from cognitive linguistics besides construal, and assess how they relate to second language learning.

2.7   The role of explicit teaching in the learning of L2 construal patterns

Much of the above discussion has focused on implicit learning, but it is also important to think about what we as language teachers can do to facilitate learning. Form-focused instruction is nearly always more effective than mere exposure to L2 input (Doughty, 2003) but it is not always clear what aspects of the language we should focus on in these form-focused instruction sessions. De Bot *et al.* (2005: 85) provide a partial answer to this question when they say that: 'The role of explicit instruction is... to "prime" for noticing and to make clear those rules that cannot be [deduced] easily without instruction'. This implies that L2 construal patterns are a good candidate for explicit teaching. Findings from the research presented in the previous sections suggest that learners are often primed by their entrenched L1 construal patterns not to notice new L2 construals. Construal may thus be one area of second language learning where learners benefit from explicit instruction.

Research into the acquisition by language learners of L2 categorization systems suggests that learners do indeed learn them better if they are in some way primed to notice them. For example, in order to investigate the learning of category formation in English by students with a range of first languages, Williams (2005) devised a study in which a group of learners of English were presented with a 'new' version of English in which there was a gender system where the gender of a noun depended upon whether or not that noun was animate or inanimate. The participants were not made explicitly aware of this distinction but were shown lots of examples where this was the case. The participants were then given a test in which they had to choose between the two genders for a set of nouns. In this test, they chose the one that was appropriate to the noun's animacy at significantly above-chance levels, even though these particular nouns had not been encountered during the training. Williams concludes that the participants were able to set up a new categorization system without awareness. Interestingly however, he found a correlation between test performance and previous knowledge of languages that encode grammatical gender, which shows the importance of prior knowledge in implicit language learning. Williams' study suggests that although language learners may eventually notice differences in categorization systems between their own and the target language, acquisition is likely to be accelerated if they have prior knowledge of such a system. Following on from this, we might conclude that one role for explicit teaching could be to make learners aware of those categorization and construal systems that exist in the target language but not in their first language.

The question is: what form might such explicit teaching take? From a practical point of view, diagrams such as those in Figure 2.1 may be useful for teaching purposes, as the learners can see at a glance how the target language divides up the semantic space, in comparison with their own language. New European Union policies that involve the teaching of several languages at once might also benefit from this contrastive approach. Also useful are the three-dimensional diagrams proposed by Majid *et al.* (2007) for showing how the semantic area of cutting and breaking is divided up along different axes in different languages. These diagrams would be even more useful if they could be displayed dynamically in three dimensions, allowing the learner to view them from different angles. With current developments in information and communications technology (ICT), we may soon see these sorts of diagrams appearing in language teaching materials of the future. Indeed, ICT probably has a great deal to offer in this area as it can show interactive scenes that can be presented from different perspectives. It also provides opportunities to zoom in on particular features of a scene in order to raise awareness of its constitution, and it can be used to highlight different aspects to show attention and salience, and to show how things are divided up into categories. I will return to the subject of explicit teaching in the next chapter, when I discuss the relationship between categorization and grammar.

2.8 Concluding comments

This chapter has looked at how different languages construe objects and events in different ways, and we have considered the implications that this has for language learning and teaching. We have seen that the acquisition of a second language requires a flexible approach to construal, and an understanding of the fact that other languages incorporate other ways of seeing things that are just as valid as those in one's own language. This may partly explain why, when a learner acquires another language, they tend to develop higher levels of cognitive flexibility, which then make it easier for them to learn subsequent new languages. We have seen that entrenched L1 construal systems can affect a learner's ability to acquire new construal systems in the L2, but that transfer is just one process operating in a complex system alongside other cognitive processes, such as, for example, over- and under-extension, learned attention and probabilistic processing. I have also tentatively suggested that explicit presentation of L2 construal systems is likely to be beneficial to language learners.

Future studies could usefully examine the ways in which new construals are learned when they appear in both non-negotiated L2 input and in interactional settings, and could explore how this data fits with existing models that attempt to explain the interaction between L1 and L2 knowledge (e.g. MacWhinney, 1997). Further research is needed to evaluate the relative success of the various attempts that have been made to explicitly address the issue of categories and prototypes in second language teaching.

The next chapter remains with the theme of categorization, but looks at work that views all aspects of language, such as words and morphemes, phonology and intonation patterns as operating within flexible radial categories. I will show how this approach accounts for aspects of language such as polysemy and the fact that traditional grammatical 'categories' tend not to behave themselves or conform to any sort of single, easily described system.

3
More on Categories: Words, Morphemes, 'Grammar Rules', Phonological Features and Intonation Patterns as Radial Categories

3.1 Introductory comments

In the previous chapter we began to look at cognitive linguistic approaches to 'linguistic categories'. In recent years, the concept of linguistic categories has been used to account for the polysemous nature of individual words, morphemes, parts of speech, and even intonation patterns. According to cognitive linguists, the different senses of a word operate within a radial category, and they are linked through processes such as metaphor and metonymy.

Knowledge of the different senses that a word can have is an important measure of vocabulary depth (Read, 1993), which is an important aspect of language learning. As I have argued before (Littlemore and Low, 2006a) it is important for language learners to be aware of the conventional ways in which word meanings are figuratively extended in the target language. For example, most learners of English will learn fairly early on that the word *hand* refers to a part of the body. It is only later on that they will encounter this word in other contexts where its meaning is extended metaphorically to refer to the 'hands of a clock' or of a compass, or metonymically when someone might ask them to 'hand them a pen', or 'give them a hand'. The cognitive linguistic view is that all these possible senses of *hand* are related to one another in a single radial category, with the basic sense of *hand* serving as the prototype.

41

As we saw in Chapter 2, the human mind has an innate tendency to categorize incoming stimuli in order to make sense of them and relate them to prior knowledge. The categories that we form are flexible and radial in nature, in that some members can feel more central than others. We will see in this chapter that this has significant implications for language learning, as the concept of flexible categories applies not only to individual words and morphemes, but also to 'grammar rules', phonological features, and intonation patterns. To keep things simple for now, let us begin with *individual words*.

3.2   Individual words and morphemes as radial categories

In cognitive linguistics, the senses of individual words are thought to constitute radial categories, with the most basic senses lying towards the centre, and more figurative senses radiating out towards the edge (Taylor, 2002). For example, if we look at the word *through* in the following citations taken from the Bank of English (Figure 3.1), we can see a gradual cline from more central or 'prototypical' uses (such as citations 4, 5, and 18) to more peripheral or abstract uses (such as citations 1, 2, 14 and 20).

It can be seen that many of the uses of *through* in Figure 3.1 are metaphorical or metonymic. Indeed metaphor and metonymy are the two main processes through which meanings are extended. I look at metaphor and metonymy in depth in Chapters 5 and 6. For now, let us remain with categories. A possible radial category representing the examples in Figure 3.1 is shown in Figure 3.2.

Languages vary considerably in terms of the ways in which senses are conventionally extended. Thus, although the basic senses of many words are highly similar, the figurative senses, which lie towards the periphery of the category, will often be very different. For example, Littlemore and MacArthur (2007a) conducted a detailed corpus study of the words *thread* (or *hilar*) and *wing* (or *aletear*) in English and Spanish and found evidence to suggest that both words operate as radial categories in both languages but that the nature of the categories is very different. We found that in the English corpus (the Bank of English), the manner-of-movement verb *to thread* was often used transitively to talk, for example, about a footballer 'threading' a pass between several opponents. It was also used to describe paths 'threading' their way through a forest, and it was used in a very abstract sense to talk about literature: 'threading the nostalgia with reflections on friendship and

1	as a 'recovery" movement sweeps	through	the talk shows of middle America.
2	of thinking about values comes	through	in this quote from Kohlberg (1984,
3	of intercultural understanding	through	games and multicultural
4	including Barents, on the way back	through	what is now called the Barents
5	and are quite capable of diffusing	through	metal films. Because it is so readily
6	by decree. <p> Valdema Veronin:	(Through	translator) We've already had
7	pledged to help the Soviet Union	through	the upcoming difficult winter, but
8	so schmaltzy that you have to wade	through	it with hip boots." It's typical
9	There are efforts ongoing	through	the good offices of Ambassador
10	Repeated </subh> Henry was eased	through	by a cunning flick from Kanu but
11	Chelsea's dominance. <p> By mid-way	through	the second half, Chelsea were in
12	we showed sheer determination right	through	to the end." <p> Ferguson was
13	HQ. <p> The letters were dropped	through	the front door of Chris's Surrey
14	Brown is now out for a month	through	injury so Cregan is trying to get
15	the end of November. But he played	through	the pain barrier in a vain bid to
16	Skopje -- said: 'We have been	through	the worst experience of our lives.
17	as cheeky Tony charmed viewers	through	the years. His joy at becoming a
18	raced in and fired a drive that spun	through	the air, round the wall and curled
19	bit. 'You mean - she'll have to read	through	all those? Why?" <p> Don't you
20	trying several times I failed to get	through	to either of them. <p> Desperatio

Figure 3.1 Different, yet related, senses of *through* shown by the Bank of English data

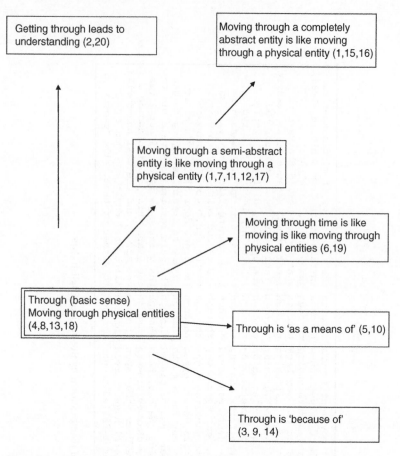

Figure 3.2   An example of a radial category diagram for *through*, based on the corpus data in Figure 3.1 (the numbers in brackets refer to the citations in the figure)

cruelty, innocence, memory'. In the Spanish corpus (The Corpus de Referencia del Español – 'CREA' – http://corpus.rae.es/creanet.html) many instances of *hilar* ('to thread') were found to involve the idiom *hilar fino*, which roughly translates as 'to thread very finely' and which means to do things carefully. The word *hilar* is often used in Spanish to refer to the connection between actions or events occurring one after another; a meaning which is much less frequent in English. As this small corpus study shows, although there is sometimes overlap between the figurative senses of words in different languages, there is often a great deal of variation. In Section 3.2.1 below, I look at the extent to which this variation is problematic for language learners, and suggest ways of helping them to deal with it.

In the Littlemore and MacArthur (2007a) study, we also found that the more figurative uses (which might be seen as lying at the periphery of the radial category) had very marked phraseologies. These phraseological patterns correlated strongly with particular meanings. For example, there were numerous examples in the Bank of English of fictive motion (where a stationary object, such as a path, is described as if it were moving), many of which were signalled by the phrase *its way through* (e.g. 'The river threaded its way through the hills'). An abbreviated form of this particular phraseology often indicated an abstract extension of fictive motion (e.g. 'Slavery threaded its way as an issue, a concern, and eventually a threatening problem through the fabric of American democracy'), and another abstract usage was marked by the use of *together* (e.g. 'He manages to thread his ideas together'; 'Threading two words together'). Another way of marking abstract usage is to use the passive voice (e.g. 'The novel is threaded with the effects of slavery'; 'Threaded into the book is the sense that...').

These findings concur with Deignan's (2005) observation, based on corpus data, that figurative use is often signalled by particular phraseology. Gries (2006) notes that the more prototypical senses, which lie at the centre of a category, are less likely to exhibit these fixed phraseological patterns. As we will see below, the finding that the more abstract senses that lie towards the periphery of the category tend to have fixed phraseologies also has important implications for language learning and teaching.

As well as entire words, individual morphemes also operate within radial categories. As Evans and Green (2006) point out, the Italian diminutive has a variety of related senses. They all carry a sense of lessening, but the actual senses vary depending on which word the diminutive is being attached to. For example, when attached to the Italian word for 'to sleep' (*dormire*) it has the meaning 'to snooze' (*dormicchiare*); when attached to the word for 'to work' (*lavorare*) it has the meaning 'to work half-heartedly' (*lavoricciare*); and when attached to the word for 'to speak' (*parlare*) it has the meaning of 'speak badly' (*parlucchiare*). Thus it would be unhelpful for a language learner to attempt to identify a single meaning for the Italian diminutive. It would also be inappropriate for them to see it as having a set of entirely unrelated meanings. The most useful way of viewing the Italian diminutive, from a language learning perspective, is as a radial category. Thus, all of its senses are to some extent (but not entirely) motivated by the idea of smallness or reduction.

The morpheme *hon* (meaning long thin object) in Japanese also operates as a radial category. We saw in Chapter 2 that in Japanese, long thin objects constitute a category. Here we can see how the category *'hon'* is figuratively extended from its basic sense to include more 'metaphorically' long thin objects. Lakoff (2007) lists, among other things, the following objects, all of which can be indicated by this morpheme:

Pencils
Judo fights
Hits in baseball
Shots in basketball
Rolls of tape
Telephone calls
Radio and television programmes
Films
Medical injections

Of all these objects, only pencils are prototypically long and thin. All the others require some sort of metaphorical or metonymic extension process in order to understand them as being long and thin. For example, films used to be on a long piece of tape (and presumably this construal is extended to radio and television programmes), telephone calls go along a long thin wire, and medical injections involve a long syringe. Judo fights and radio programmes are perhaps *'hon'* in that they have a beginning and an end. Interestingly, according to the Kodankan Judo Institute Niigata, Judo fights used to be much longer than they are now, sometimes lasting up to two hours which gives a historical perspective on the use of *hon* in this context. We will look in more detail at the processes of metaphor and metonymy in Chapters 4 and 5, as they are key cognitive processes that we use in order to form and hold together radial categories. They also form a core component of the type of cognitive flexibility that we need in order to understand categorization systems that are new to us.

A note of caution is sounded by Taylor (2008), who is somewhat sceptical about the idea that *all* words can be seen as radial categories with identifiable prototypes. He cites the example of *cardinal*, which has evolved from an original sense of 'principal' (as in 'cardinal sins') through to a church official, then to the deep red colour of his robes, and finally to a butterfly of that colour. Taylor points out that it is unlikely that all these senses exist in a psychologically real single category for native speakers of English. The senses of the word *cardinal* only constitute a radial category if viewed from a diachronic, rather than a synchronic, perspective. It would not be very easy for a language learner to use the original sense of the word to work out the meaning of one of its other senses. On the other hand, as we shall see below, there are many other words that do have clear relationships between the different senses, and which meet the criteria for being described as a radial category. Indeed, cognitive linguistics would predict that some words are better described as radial categories than others, as radial categories themselves can be found in more and less prototypical forms.

A second problematic case cited by Taylor concerns the word *long*, which has both a physical sense and a temporal sense. For Taylor, both of these senses are likely to be equally important and central for speakers of English, and there is unlikely to be a 'psychologically real' category which contains them both. Rather, he suggests, the two senses are likely to form separate but equally important categories. Indeed, the vast majority of uses of the word *long* in the 1,848,364-word Michigan Corpus of Academic Spoken English (MICASE) (http://quod.lib.umich. edu/m/micase/), which includes English spoken by both native and non-native speakers, relate to time rather than distance, so it may be somewhat artificial to view these two senses as operating within a single category. This supports Taylor's suggestion that people may form 'local' prototypes, which are conventional in their own right. This last criticism has some bearing on Lakoff's analysis of the word *hon* above, as there could be more than one category at work here. Some of the examples cited above refer to things that are physically long, things that are temporally long, and things that are both. Although the case of *long* highlights a potential problem with the concept of words as radial categories, it is perhaps best seen as a special case. As we shall see below, there are many other examples of words that do indeed appear to cluster round a single prototype.

3.2.1 How might the idea that words and morphemes operate within radial categories help second language learners and teachers?

We can conclude from the previous section that under the cognitive linguistic paradigm, words and morphemes tend to operate within radial categories with basic, prototypical senses lying towards the centre, and figurative senses lying towards the periphery. Among the most regular principles motivating meaning extension are metaphor and metonymy. So what does this mean for second language learners, and how might radial categories help them learn the language?

It has been noted that non-native speakers tend to avoid using metaphorical senses of words, preferring to stick to more literal uses, which in cognitive linguistic terms would be those lying at the centre of the categories (Danesi, 1992). Indeed, if we look at the use of the word *saw* in the MICASE, and compare its use by native and non-native speakers, we see that native speakers make far more use of peripheral, figurative senses, such as:

the way I	saw	it we'd have it all
so one department	saw	'em as a threat and
or administration	saw	as its purpose? was it
and then the sixties	saw	a great effort to, to
and the United States	saw	a series, of economic developments

In contrast, uses of *saw* by the non-native speakers tend to be far more literal:

plantations, like the one you	saw	before, but the actual location
the plantation that you just	saw	is in this side here
in that circle that you	saw	drawn here ... okay and uh
of an electron we actually	saw	a muon etcetera, other particles
a very exciting time you	saw	these pictures coming you would

This is interesting, given that the non-native speakers in this corpus are, for the most part, advanced-level students, studying at a US university, surrounded by native-speaker input on a daily basis. Perhaps what we have here is a case of learned inattention (see Chapter 2). Despite the fact that the students are surrounded by data telling them that *saw* is most often used in a figurative sense, they do not seem to notice it, which suggests that for some reason it is not perceived as salient in their input. Alternatively, it could be that they understand these figurative uses but that they lack the confidence to use them themselves. Either way, figurative extensions of word meaning appear to be a good candidate for explicit teaching.

There is some empirical support for the contention that language learners tend to steer clear of figurative senses, and that they favour prototypical senses. For example, in his corpus-based study, Alejo (2008) found that even advanced learners of English living and working in a target-language environment tend to rely on prototypical senses significantly more than native speakers do. His findings also suggest that L1 transfer is a significant factor. He used the MICASE learner corpus (see above) to compare patterns of phrasal verb usage by learners of English whose native language is satellite-framed (like English) with speakers whose native language is verb-framed (see Chapter 2). His focus was on phrasal verbs with *out*. He found no evidence of avoidance of these phrasal verbs among those learners whose first language was satellite framed, but significant evidence of avoidance among those learners who spoke verb-framed languages. Thus one's first language appears to be a major factor influencing this aspect of L2 production. However, when he looked more closely at the types of phrasal verb used, their collocations and the meaning of the particle, he found that the non-native speakers (regardless of their L1 background) all tended to favour the prototypical (locational) meaning and that they used fewer types of this phrasal verb than the native speakers. This suggests that even advanced learners of English who are surrounded by English in their daily lives tend to avoid operating at the periphery of categories. In addition to transfer, it would be interesting to investigate the importance of learned attention and frequency effects as potential variables influencing the acquisition of this type of language.

In some ways, the fact that language learners operate more towards the centre of radial categories than native speakers is not surprising, given that in a usage-based system, native speakers build up knowledge of the semantic extension potential of the words in their language through encountering them in multiple discourse situations. It is hardly surprising that language learners, who do not have access to such frequent, meaningful and varied types of communicative interaction, will have relatively impoverished knowledge of meaning extensions. In a recent study, (Littlemore and MacArthur, forthcoming) we found that even advanced learners of English have lower levels of awareness than native speakers of senses that lie towards the periphery of a category. In this study, we investigated the intuitions that both native speakers and learners of English and Spanish had of the categories of senses associated with the words *thread* (including *threaded* and *threading*) and *wing* (including *winged* and *winging*). We compared these intuitions with each other, and with our findings from the corpus-based study. Our initial findings suggest that:

- even advanced learners have very limited knowledge of the senses that lie towards the periphery of this category compared with that of native speakers;

- compared with the corpus data, intuitive data for both native and non-native speakers are relatively impoverished;
- even among the native speakers there was considerable variation, with younger speakers exhibiting much less knowledge than older speakers;
- different word forms trigger different senses and phraseologies in both the corpus data and the intuitive data;
- the intuitive data for the native speakers largely reflect the backgrounds of the participants;
- popular culture has a strong influence on the intuitive data, suggesting that this knowledge is dynamic and unstable;
- fixed phraseologies appear to help native speakers access more meanings.

These findings indicate that radial category knowledge is something that builds up over a lifetime. People are able to access this knowledge much more readily in natural communicative contexts than they are in decontextualized, controlled settings, which underscores the usage-based nature of language processing and production. It is also important to bear in mind that, like all areas of the lexicon, radial category knowledge will be subject to considerable fluctuation over time. It is therefore not surprising that learners lack this knowledge, even when they reach quite advanced levels.

Detailed corpus work has revealed that it is not simply the senses that lie towards the periphery of the category that learners tend to avoid. Sometimes learners will avoid a whole branch of senses. In an in-depth study of the use of the word *out* by native and non-native speakers in MICASE, Mahpeykar (2008) found that not only did the non-native speakers make significantly less use of the figurative/peripheral senses of *out*, but that there was also considerable asymmetry between the categories of senses that were used by the native and non-native speakers, and that some senses were missing from the non-native speaker data altogether. The aim of her study was to use corpus data to test the categories of senses of *out* that were originally proposed by Rudzka-Ostyn (2003), proposing her own set of categories that are slightly different from those proposed by Rudzka-Ostyn. Mahpeykar's new categorization system and statistics showing the relative use made by native and non-native speakers of English of these different categories are shown in Figures 3.3(a, b). In this figure, Mahpeykar makes use of the cognitive linguistic terms 'trajector' and 'boundary'. These refer respectively to the thing that is leaving, and the edge of the container that it is leaving.

Semantic categories of *out*	Schematic images
1. The basic sense of *out*: entities moving out of physical, concrete containers e.g: *come out, take out, pop out* 1(a) metonymic extension: e.g *hew out, carve out* 1(b) metonymic extension of (1a): *print out, make out*	
2. People moving from inside to outside a container e.g: *go out, invite out*	
3. Sets, groups are conceptualized as containers e.g: *filter out, take out, pick out*	
4. Bodies, minds, mouths are viewed as containers e.g: *say out loud*	
5. States/situations are viewed as containers e.g: *come out* (of a situation)	
6. Act of appearance and visibility is *out*. e.g: *check out, find out, make out*	
7. Trajectors increasing to or beyond maximal boundaries e.g: *sent out, put out, splash out* 7(a) boundaries are occupied, but not surpassed. e.g: *draw out, fill out, write out*	
8. Trajectors decreasing to or beyond minimal boundaries e.g: *run out, cancel out, phase out*	

Figure 3.3(a) Senses of *out*

Category	1	2	3	4	5	6	7	8
Non-native speakers	23%	5%	14%	1%	3%	38%	11%	5%
Native speakers	11%	1%	4%	11%	4%	35%	30%	4%

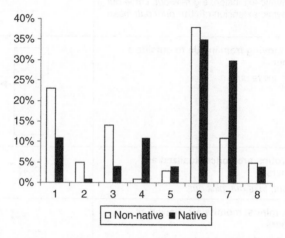

Figure 3.3(b)   Statistics showing the relative use made by native and non-native speakers of English of these different categories of *out* (Mahpeykar, 2008), reproduced with the permission of the author

It is interesting to note that the non-native speakers in Mahpeykar's study tended to make much more use of the basic sense, as well as sense 2 (people moving from inside to outside a container) and sense 3 (where sets and groups are conceptualized as containers) but that they made much less use than native speakers of senses 4 (where bodies, minds and mouths are viewed as containers) and 7 (where trajectors increase to or beyond maximal boundaries). Unfortunately, Mahpeykar does not provide information concerning the statistical significance of these findings but the differences she identifies are certainly sufficiently marked to warrant further investigation. The facts that the native speakers in the study did make use of these categories, and that the data are taken from the same settings, indicate that the non-native speakers were certainly exposed to them on a fairly regular basis. In Ellis's terms (Ellis, 2006 a, b, c; see Section 2.6 of this book) they would have had sufficient data to engage in probabilistic processing and contingency learning. Therefore, in order to find out why certain senses were relatively under-used in this corpus, we would need to consider the role of some of Ellis's other factors, such as learned (in)attention, L1 interference, and entrenchment. Of course, it is always possible that these senses existed in the learners' receptive vocabulary but that they had not yet moved across to their productive vocabulary. This too would be worthy of further investigation as part of a case study into the reasons why learners acquire some senses of English prepositions but not others.

Mahpeykar's findings may be partly due to L1 transfer. In all languages, words can figuratively extend their meanings, although the figurative extensions of a term in one language may not be possible for the equivalent word in another. The fact that the advanced learners studied by Mahpeykar tended to avoid certain senses of the word suggests that these senses may not be present in the first languages of the speakers in the corpus. More research is needed to establish whether or not this was indeed the case. Whatever the cause of the problem, her findings indicate that when learners have been living and studying in the L2 culture for some time, they do not automatically pick up on all of the senses in the category, and that some senses are systematically avoided. This implies that there may be a role for explicit instruction to develop learners' sensitivity to the fact that L2 words and morphemes operate within flexible and radial categories, and to help them explore the senses within these categories in more detail.

One way in which radial categories might be explicitly incorporated into second language teaching materials is through an overtly grammatical syllabus that starts with the prototypical representations and gradually moves towards real-world language that sits towards the periphery of the categories (Shortall, 2002). In other words, beginner-level students could be introduced to the prototypical senses of words and their syllabus could then be systematically extended to include less central senses of a word. In some ways, it makes sense to introduce the basic, or prototypical senses first, and then move out towards the edges of the categories. Exceptions would need to be made for highly frequent senses that happen to lie towards the periphery of a category, and useful set expressions that are not prototypical.

Although the idea of developing a syllabus which starts with the prototypical senses of words and then moves out towards the more peripheral uses may be beneficial, in practical terms it is very difficult to imagine how this might be done, as presumably every word or construction would need to be presented in this way, leading to some very artificial-sounding texts. Moreover, corpus linguistic research shows that categories develop around morphemes rather than individual words, so that, for example, the pattern of senses associated with *eye* is very different from the pattern of senses that is associated with *eyes*. Controlling for this level of detail would probably be a monumental task for even the most committed cognitive linguist course designer. More importantly, Shortall's idea rests on an assumption that the different senses of a word sit along a single continuum. Corpus studies of polysemous words have, however, revealed that this is not necessarily the case and that senses extend in different directions with a fair degree of overlap between them. For example, in our study (Littlemore and MacArthur, 2007a) we identified patterns of senses for the word *threading* in English, as shown in Figure 3.4. Although the senses in Figure 3.4 are very much related, they do seem to develop in parallel along distinct branches that would be difficult to accommodate within a strictly linear syllabus. Thus, rather than attempting to identify some sort of 'order' in which senses develop and then introducing learners to these senses one at a time, it might make more sense to introduce them to several senses at once, and to get them to work out the metaphorical and metonymic relationships between those senses for themselves. The idea of radial categories could thus be useful for explaining the relationship between concrete and more abstract or figurative senses of words. It could also be used to illustrate how figurative uses tend to be accompanied by certain fixed phraseologies. This is an idea that I have suggested in earlier work, particularly in relation to the teaching of the words *this* and *that*. In Littlemore and Low (2006a), we suggested that several uses could be presented together and that the basic senses of closeness and distance can be exploited in the classroom to explain abstract and figurative expressions such as 'what's that?', 'that was delicious', 'you're going to love this', and so on. Indeed, research shows that introducing learners to the prototypical sense of figurative words results in better long-term retention than comparable methods that focus on contextual cues (Boers, 2004), and that it is better to give learners the prototypical sense to work with rather than one of the other figurative senses that the word has (Verspoor and Lowie, 2003).

Tyler and Evans (2004) offer a practical description of how this might be done with the radial category of *over*. They argue that the prototypical sense should be presented first and that diagrams and physical actions can be used to demonstrate the relationship between this prototypical sense and the other senses in the category. This, they argue, should help to overcome the tendency of language learners to avoid using phrasal verbs. Indeed, findings from several studies do appear to confirm their predictions (e.g. Kövecses and Szabo, 1996). Learners who have been exposed to the entire category do appear to retain the meanings of the

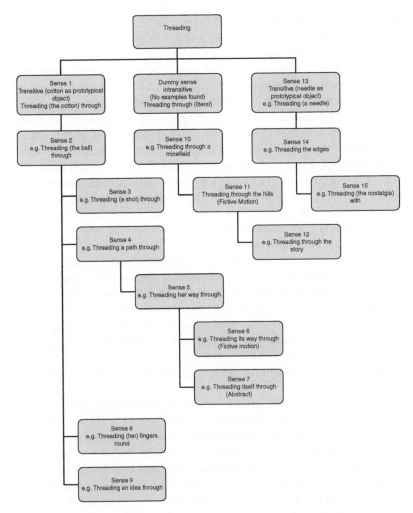

Figure 3.4 Senses of *threading* found in the Bank of English (from Littlemore and MacArthur, 2007a)

phrasal verbs for longer than those who have been taught the verbs through more traditional approaches. Unfortunately, the approach is less effective at teaching the phraseological aspects of phrasal verbs. For a more detailed discussion of this whole area, see Littlemore and Low (2006a).

Another way of introducing learners to all the senses at once is through the use of language corpora. This approach, sometimes described as 'data-driven learning' (Johns, 1991, 1994), involves showing learners multiple exemplars of a target language item taken from a corpus of authentic language, and asking them to develop their own ideas (and here I deliberately avoid using the word 'rules') about the possible meanings of that item. For example, by looking at the corpus data for the word *through* in Figure 3.1, a learner may come up with a radial category diagram such as the one shown in Figure 3.2, or they may come up with their own slightly different diagram. It would probably be better if students were encouraged to create their own diagrams, rather than being shown them by the teacher. There is no right or wrong way of doing these diagrams and a personal, idiosyncratic diagram (as long as it reflects the true senses of the words) is likely to be far more meaningful, and therefore memorable, for a language learner than one that has simply been shown to them by a teacher. The use of language corpora in the language classroom to help learners build up their categories in this way may speed up the acquisition of category knowledge, as it would provide opportunities for learners to encounter a single word in all its guises at once and may promote a flexible approach to understanding and an ability to move between its different senses. Research is needed to investigate whether the language that is learned through this explicit approach can easily be transformed into implicit knowledge (see Section 3.3.1).

MacArthur and Littlemore (2008) studied the effectiveness of this corpus-based approach for familiarizing learners with denominal verbs (i.e. verbs that originate from a noun) in English and Spanish. The reasons why denominal verbs were chosen were that they are highly polysemous and that the relationships between the different senses are overtly metaphorical or metonymic. Metaphor and metonymy are two of the basic processes of meaning extension in polysemous words (Verspoor, 2008). In the study, we selected a number of denominal verbs in English and Spanish and asked two small groups of upper-intermediate students (11 learners of English and 6 learners of Spanish) to look them up in a corpus. The students were then asked to use the corpus data to work out the meanings of the denominal verbs. The students of Spanish were asked to use the CREA Reference Corpus of Contemporary Spanish to work out the meaning of verbs such as *monear* ('to monkey', meaning 'to climb'), *torear* ('to bull', meaning 'to dodge') and *ningunear* ('to nobody', meaning 'to ignore'). The students of English were asked to use the British National Corpus (http://www.natcorp.ox. ac.uk/) to work out the meanings of verbs such as *to snake, to worm* and *to mushroom*. We were interested in looking at how the students used the corpus examples to work out the various meanings of these words, and at the factors that aided retention. Because of the smallness of the groups and the non-parallel nature of the examples, its findings cannot be said to have a broad application; however, the qualitative data provided by the study were very rich, and told us a great deal about how these students responded to the corpus data. Our main findings were that in many cases students were able to use the basic sense to work out the meanings of the more peripheral senses, and that the corpus data sensitized them to the particular phraseologies that accompanied the peripheral senses. More work is needed in this area to investigate whether indeed exposure to L2 corpora helps learners acquire the sort of flexible categories that tend to result from implicit learning.

To close this section, I would like to quote from the self-study book *Spanish in Three Months* by Isabel Cisneros (1992). In this book there is a section on Spanish augmentatives and diminutives, which, like their Italian equivalent mentioned above, operate within radial categories with clear relationships between the different senses. Cisneros introduces this section with the words (p. 136):

> Certain augmentative and diminutive endings are added to nouns, to qualify their meaning. As the use of these terminations can present considerable difficulties, without a thorough knowledge of the language, the student is advised to employ adjectives instead.

This is a rather depressing way to introduce the subject, as the student is encouraged to give up before he or she has even started. A better approach might be to present the various endings as overlapping radial categories, or to provide opportunities for the students to work this out for themselves. This would be a far more motivating and stimulating approach than simply saying 'here's a list of them, but you'll probably find them too hard to learn, so I wouldn't bother if I were you'. As language educators, we can do better than this.

3.3 'Grammar rules' as radial categories

For cognitive linguists, the concept of radial categories also operates at the level of 'grammar'. This should not come as a surprise, as grammar and lexis are considered to be inseparable by both cognitive and corpus linguists. The fact that grammatical features operate as radial categories is largely due to the fact that many, if not all, grammatical items originally entered the language as lexical items and through a process of 'grammaticalization' have become de-lexicalized, and more grammatical in meaning, an idea that is discussed in depth in Chapter 8.

As an example of a 'grammar rule' operating as a radial category, let us look at Lakoff's (1970) example of transitive verbs. Transitive verbs are thought to have at least three defining characteristics. Firstly, they can often be nominalized, so *drive* leads to *driver*, *teach* leads to *teacher* and *write* leads to *writer*, and so on. Secondly, they can often feature in VERB(-able) constructions, such as *readable, countable, manageable,* and so on. Thirdly, most can undergo passivization, leading to sentences such as 'her great uncle was eaten by cannibals', 'nothing has been delivered yet', and 'the proposal was attacked by the unions' (Bank of English examples). Those transitive verbs that have all three of these characteristics are more likely to be found at the centre of the category. As with all radial categories, those verbs are also likely to be the most concrete and literal.

Lakoff argues that not all transitive verbs are equally open to these processes, and that some transitive verbs (i.e. those that lie more towards the edge of the category) cannot undergo them. He gives the following examples, numbered here as (13)–(15), which he argues are 'impossible' in English:

(13) *(sic) John was the knower of that fact (Lakoff, 1970: 20)
(14) *(sic) The lighthouse is spottable (Lakoff, 1970: 32)
(15) *(sic) Two pounds are owed by John (Lakoff, 1970: 19)

Lakoff's claim is potentially of interest to language teachers as it provides a way of introducing transitivity in English. It illustrates how transitivity is a matter of degree rather than being an 'either/or' issue. However, we need to exercise a degree of caution here. Although Lakoff's claims do have validity, there is a problem with the artificial examples that he uses to support them. Corpus data suggest that usages of this type do in fact exist, but that the resulting senses are somewhat narrower than those that we might expect. For instance, *knower* appears 54 times in the Bank of English. Of these, at least 30 appear to relate to religion or philosophy, the 'knower' being the person who somehow understands, or is close to God. Of the remaining 24 instances, three appear to relate to the world of business, two to teaching, five are to do with ways of describing grammar and the remaining 14 are general. So, it appears that rather than being 'unacceptable' in English, the noun *knower* has a somewhat restricted usage and belongs mainly to a particular area of discourse. This narrowing of meaning corresponds in many ways to **stereotypical narrowing**, an idea that is proposed by relevance theorists (Wilson and Sperber, 2004). When stereotypical narrowing occurs, words acquire a particular sense in some contexts which is more limited than their basic sense. For example, in some contexts, the exclamation 'I'm dying for a drink' means that the speaker is in need of an *alcoholic* drink, and he or she would not be pleased to be offered a glass of orange juice. Interestingly, the French verb for 'to know' (*connaître*) also undergoes a process of stereotypical narrowing when it is converted into the noun form: *connoisseur* also has a restricted, yet different sense of being an expert in something. Thus it would seem that words can undergo a stereotypical narrowing process when their form changes, but, and this is crucial for language learners, the direction of the narrowing may well vary from language to language. This is something that language learners need to know about.

Lakoff's second example, *spottable* also appears in the Bank of English, although only twice. Both instances relate to the ease with which things can be spotted, but the fact that there are only two instances cannot be taken as evidence for stereotypical narrowing.

> (16) under government control, or easily spottable. Mr Irwin cites Singapore, a
> (17) greenhouse effect should still be spottable. But there is no denying that if

However, a Google search for the word *spottable* results in 6,950 hits. Even allowing for the fact that some web pages will be duplicated, and that some of the hits appear to be about the word *spottable* itself, this is still a large number of hits, which we can take to indicate that the word *spottable* is used in English. A brief survey of these hits indicates that there is a strong collocation with the word *easily* and so a process of stereotypical narrowing may have taken place here as well, although it is much less marked than in the *knower* examples.

Other instances of word class change of this type exhibit stronger evidence for what might be seen as a stereotypical narrowing process, or at least a meaning change of some description. For example, the verb *consider* gives rise to the construction *considerable* which clearly does not mean the same as 'able to be considered'. Rather it means 'large' or 'substantial'. Again, this meaning change may be a product of the fact that *consider* lies towards the edge of the radial category of transitive verbs.

The third example, as in (18):

> (18) *(sic) Two pounds are owed by John

```
after almost $ 2 billion it claims   are owed by   the developers of the cancelled
        substantial" grant payments   are owed by   the US multi-national to the
afford to wipe out the debts we       are owed by   Third World countries. <subh>
venue. So two big thank-yous          are owed by   us. First, to Graham Henry,
on&hellip # What karmic debts         are owed by   hellip Then the rune is white.
that the East Timorese think they     are owed by   the world. Indonesian troops have
like Russia, to whom large sums       are owed by   former Soviet proteges, such as
that they will get all that they      are owed by   this method. One way that
        is at least paid what they    are owed by   law, you are making a significant
money he believes he and others       are owed by   Holly. Holly has moved to dismiss
made me remember how much they        are owed by   most of those who have surfed
```

Figure 3.5   Citations for the string *are owed by* in the Bank of English

which Lakoff uses to support his argument that not all transitive verbs lend themselves equally well to passivization, is also problematic. The construction may sound strange in this rather artificial context, but a Bank of English search for the string *'are+owed+by'* produces the 11 citations in Figure 3.5. What seems to be happening in Figure 3.5 is that the passive construction *'are+owed+by'* is only used when referring to approximate or vague amounts. Again, this may be seen as a subtle instance of stereotypical narrowing, resulting in a more specific meaning.

Thus in all three cases, the situation appears to be more complex than Lakoff would have us believe. Rather than thinking of these syntactic changes as being 'impossible' for these particular words in English, it is perhaps more appropriate to say that a semantic change (which often entails stereotypical narrowing) takes place when we try to change the syntactic form of peripheral members of the category. Although Lakoff's view of transitivity as a radial category is somewhat problematic when we look at it in detail, in the main this sort of approach could be a very useful resource for language teachers. It could be useful for learners to be sensitized to the fact that some verbs are more prone to transitivity than others, and that it is not an 'either/or' issue. The findings on stereotypical narrowing are also of potential interest as this appears to be one of the areas where languages differ significantly. Moreover, differences in meaning at the periphery of grammatical categories also appear to be a feature of discourse community-specific language, and should therefore be of interest to learners of languages for specific purposes (Littlemore, forthcoming). These may well be features of the language that learners pick up naturally through exposure and probabilistic processing; however, as we will see below, there may also be a case for explicit teaching.

3.3.1 How might the idea that 'grammar rules' operate within radial categories help second language learners and teachers?

Traditionally when a grammar rule is taught, it is presented as an overarching rule which is then accompanied by a list of so-called 'exceptions'. There is rarely any principled explanation as to why these exceptions might exist and they are largely seen as arbitrary and therefore suitable for rote memorization. Language learners may find it more beneficial to have grammar 'rules' presented to them as radial categories. If the existence of radial categories could be made apparent to language learners, this might help them come to grips with aspects of the target language that have traditionally been seen as difficult to grasp.

In language teaching methodology, there has sometimes been tension between, on the one hand, the idea that languages can be taught through grammar rules and exceptions and, on the other, the idea that rules don't work and that languages are best learned through the acquisition of prefabricated chunks. These are two extremes of a debate that has lasted over forty years. The idea that grammar rules operate within flexible radial categories with fuzzy boundaries is useful as it provides a kind of mid-point between these two views. It suggests that there are indeed 'rules' at work in language, but that these rules encompass flexibility and change. According to Maldonado (2008), radial categories are particularly useful for teaching the 'small' rules of language that are often the most difficult ones to learn. We will see in Chapter 9 that the concept of radial categories also applies to lexicogrammar, which has far-reaching applications for language learning and teaching.

Another reason for evoking radial categories when introducing 'grammar rules' in the language classroom is that they can be used to explain those learner utterances that are 'not exactly wrong but not exactly right'. Most language teachers would agree that their students sometimes produce utterances which sound a bit wrong, but they are unable to tell these students exactly why they are wrong. These sorts of utterances are most likely to occur with items that lie at the edges of radial categories, where strange things start to happen, and subtle changes in meaning (such as the stereotypical narrowing mentioned above) result from apparently straightforward changes in syntax. There is thus an argument for making language learners familiar with radial categories, and with the factors that make certain words or usages more or less central to those categories. If learners were more aware of the way languages work at the periphery of categories, they might be more tolerant of the perceived 'arbitrariness' of language, for behind this apparent arbitrariness there is indeed a system, albeit a highly flexible one.

Verspoor (2008) provides a good example of how a radial category approach might be used to teach a grammar point. She shows how the definite article (an aspect of language which, according to, Ellis (2006, a), does not lend itself well to contingency learning) could be taught through such an approach. She suggests that learners could be introduced to the idea that the definite article system constitutes a radial category and that members of the category that lie towards the centre tend to score fairly highly in terms of 'known-ness and uniqueness'. Learners could first be introduced to the more prototypical members of the category, whose definiteness is apparent to both speaker and hearer (e.g. the sun, the moon) and then gradually they could be introduced to more peripheral members whose definiteness is not necessarily identifiable to both the speaker and the hearer, but where the hearer can infer that the speaker is referring to something that is unique in his or her mind (e.g. Beware of the dog!). Learners might even benefit from a visual representation of the category. However, as Verspoor herself points out, the effectiveness of this approach has not yet been empirically tested.

However we decide to do it, there is a need for change in the way explicit language teaching is structured in the classroom, from a traditional rigid, 'rules plus exceptions' approach to a more flexible, realistic 'rules as radial categories' approach. Roehr (2008) identifies a fundamental problem with current approaches to grammar teaching. As a basis for her argument, she makes reference to the two types of learning and knowledge that have been identified in second language acquisition (SLA): second language knowledge can be implicit (i.e. knowledge of the target language of which the learner is generally not consciously aware) and/or explicit (i.e. declarative knowledge of the language that the learner is usually aware of and can describe if necessary). Explicit knowledge is knowledge about the language that the learner has, and which he or she can draw on during tasks that allow time for reflection. Implicit knowledge tends to be more procedural, and learners are not consciously aware of the fact that they possess this knowledge, nor can they verbalize it if asked to do so. It is when explicit knowledge is brought to bear on implicit knowledge and vice versa, that lasting learning effects are most likely to result (Ellis and Larsen-Freeman, 2006).

Roehr argues that learners may have implicit knowledge of the flexible, prototypical nature of L2 categories, which are acquired probabilistically through exposure to numerous exemplars to which they apply processes of comparison. This linguistic knowledge results from the usage-based learning of the sort cognitive linguists describe, and results in the creation of flexible, exemplar-based, radial categories. In contrast, their more explicit, metalinguistic knowledge tends to consist more of fixed categories, rules, and exceptions. This is learned through the acquisition of 'rules', and the resulting categories are stable, discrete, clearly delineated, and most importantly, largely artificial as they do not reflect language as it really is. Roehr also argues (2008: 68) that there are fundamental differences in the ways in which explicit and implicit knowledge of language are represented and accessed in the mind:

> While implicit linguistic knowledge is stored and retrieved from an associative network during parallel distributed, similarity-based processing, explicit metalinguistic knowledge is processed sequentially with the help of rule-based algorithms.

Learners who have learned predominantly through explicit instruction may therefore experience difficulties with categories containing many items at the periphery, and with senses that change radically across different contexts. Roehr postulates a number of hypotheses concerning the relationship between implicit and explicit knowledge, based on the assumption that teachers will continue to teach these 'rules'. Her main argument rests on the premise that in order to be useful, knowledge of 'grammar rules' requires conditions of stability and discreteness that are rarely available in real language.

Although Roehr's hypotheses are interesting and worthy of investigation, they seem to assume that explicit grammar teaching will continue to take the form of a 'rules plus exceptions' approach. A better approach might be to abandon this way of teaching altogether and to find a better way of presenting grammar in the form of radial categories in the first place. Rather than being viewed as rigid, inflexible things, which are accompanied by lists of exceptions, the grammar rules themselves could be presented to learners as flexible radial categories that are sensitive to context. This would be a more accurate way of presenting language, which would better prepare learners for the semi-predictable ways in which language tends to behave.

3.4   Phonological features as radial categories

The principle of radial categories also operates at the level of phonology. By the end of their first year, infants have organized their pattern of speech-sound discrimination in line with the phonetic structure of their native language, and have lost sensitivity to some of the contrasts their language does not use (Werker and Tees, 1999). For example, whereas speakers of English have two separate categories for the sounds /l/ and /r/, speakers of Japanese merge these sounds into a single category. Japanese learners have been found to experience difficulties discriminating between the two sounds, and the older they get, the harder it becomes for them to do so (McClelland *et al.*, 2002). This finding is in line with research suggesting that when a second language is acquired in later life, it is more likely to bear a close, even parasitic relationship with the L1 in the early stages, as discussed in Chapter 2 (N.Ellis, 2006c; MacWhinney, 1997) and is thus likely to be more heavily influenced by it.

Research suggests that when infants learn their first language, they have organized their sound systems around a set of L1 prototypes, which in many ways act as attractor states (see Chapter 2, Section 2.5), and affect their ability to discriminate between sounds in the L1 as well as between sounds in foreign languages. In a review of research in the area, Bohn (2000: 9) asserts that: 'The research summarized so far has shown that dramatic and profound changes in perceptual patterns make infants language-specific perceivers for most aspects of speech before the end of the first year of life.' Kuhl *et al.* (1992) found a *perceptual magnet effect* in English-learning infants' discrimination of English /i/ (as in 'eat') tokens and in Swedish-learning infants' discrimination of Swedish /y/ tokens, but identified no such effect in the within-category perception of 'foreign' vowels. In other words, when a sound is particularly prominent in a given language it becomes a kind of prototype, and similar sounds are perceived as being identical to the prototype. Speakers of that language are thus less able to distinguish between sounds that are near the prototype than speakers of languages which do not have that particular prototype. Taylor (2008: 53), discussing these findings, concludes that 'with ongoing exposure to the ambient language the vowel space is restructured or warped'. Thus exposure to our first language forces us to categorize sounds in a particular way, which will need to be unlearned, or at least perceived as only one way of dividing up sound, if we are to successfully master a second language.

Some phonetic categorization has been found to occur later in life. For example, Butcher (1976) found that the perceptual space for some vowels changes between late childhood and early adulthood. When he asked native speakers of English and native speakers of German to assess the perceptual difference between the vowels /ɛ/ (as in 'bet') and /ə/ (as in 'about'), he found that the speakers of English tended to perceive a larger difference than the speakers of German, He thus concluded that the arrangement of English vowels in the vowel space *sensitizes* native English speakers to differences among low front vowels, whereas the arrangement of German vowels *de-sensitizes* native German speakers to differences among low front vowels. In his wide-ranging survey of the area, Bohn concludes that the L1 vowel system tends to stabilize in infancy but that minor adjustments are possible throughout adulthood:

'Selective (phonological) attention is highly over-learned and indispensable for accurate and efficient perception of speech sounds in the L1, but may entail inattention to those acoustic dimensions and patterns that non-native languages employ to classify phonetic segments into functional categories' (Bohn, 2000: 15).

3.4.1 How might the idea that phonological features operate within radial categories help second language learners and teachers?

Much of the above discussion is relevant to second language learning and teaching. Teachers sometimes complain that their students 'can't seem to hear what I'm saying'. This is an interesting point. Can learners actually hear differences that they are not used to attending to? To a large extent, the difficulties experienced by adult learners are not sensory but attentional (Werker and Tees, 1984). That is to say, the difficulties that adult foreign language learners experience when trying to learn L2 pronunciation do not have a clear physiological basis; they are more to do the fact that adults have become used to noticing particular features, and ignoring others. Learning a second language requires them to attend to sounds that they may otherwise ignore.

The phonetic system that we acquire as a result of our first language is thus likely to exert an influence on the way we acquire the phonetic system of a second language. On the other hand, transfer is unlikely to be the only factor influencing one's acquisition of the L2 phonetic system. Other factors, such as the amount of exposure to the L2, one's capacity for perceptual learning, and one's attitude to the L2 speech community, have also been found to exert an influence (Rost, 2002). An important factor is likely to be the degree of similarity between the L1 and the L2. When he looked at the ability of German learners of English to acquire the English phonological system, Flege (1995) found that they experienced far more difficulties with sounds that were similar to those in German than they did with sounds that had no equivalent in German. He thus concluded that perceptual learning of the L2 phonology can be blocked by the existence of near-equivalents in the L1, and that contact with the L2 is most likely to result in perceptual learning if the L2 contrast is 'new', and has no easily identifiable counterpart in the learner's L1. Flege goes on to propose a 'speech learning model' which claims that the more similar an L2 sound is to an L1 sound, the more difficult it will be to learn. This model is supported by findings by Aoyama *et al.* (2004) that even advanced Japanese learners of English find it more difficult to produce and perceive the /l/ sound than the /r/ sound, as the /l/ sound has a closer equivalent in Japanese.

As we saw in Chapter 2, one factor that is likely to influence acquisition is perceptual salience. Pisoni and Lively (1995) showed that Japanese learners of English are more likely to perceive the /r/–/l/ distinction in post-vocalic position than in pre-vocalic position. This is because the preceding vowel significantly affects the way in which the phoneme is pronounced. A further factor is the attention strategy employed by the learner. When asked to explain the /i/–/ɪ/ contrast, Flege *et al.* (1997) found that native speakers of English differentiated on the basis of actual sound or 'spectral' differences, whereas German, Korean, Mandarin-speaking Chinese and Spanish learners of English differentiated only on the basis of duration of the vowel. In other words, whereas the English speakers heard a distinct sound, the non-native speakers simply thought that the /i/ sound was more stretched than the /ɪ/ sound. As none of the first languages of the non-native speakers differentiate vowels on the basis of duration, Flege *et al.* concluded that attention to duration is likely to be a language-independent strategy employed by language learners, rather than native speakers.

The implications that this has for language learning are that we should draw learners' attention to the L2 prototypes which will usually be different from their L1 prototypes. An intriguing, but as yet untested, way of doing this is proposed by Paganus *et al.* (2006). They have developed computer-based vowel charts which are shaded to show how, in a particular language, the entire vowel space is divided into prototypical categories. When a language learner produces a particular sound, the vowel chart lights up to show where the sound that they produced is in relation to the prototypical sound in the target language. This activity could provide focused practice that might then accompany more communicative approaches. However, as Paganus *et al.* themselves admit, the effectiveness of this technique remains to be tested, and much needs to be done to incorporate different pronunciation styles and the sorts of sound variations that are apparent in continuous speech.

3.5 Intonation patterns as radial categories

Given that these other areas of language operate within radial categories, it should come as no surprise that intonation patterns also exhibit this sort of behaviour. The fact that intonation patterns have meanings that vary according to context has been demonstrated by Brazil (1985). Brazil argued that intonation is inherently meaningful and that the intonation choices that speakers make depend on their perception of the knowledge that they share with their interlocutors: these understandings relate to their shared histories, and to the perceived purposes of their communication in a given context.

Therefore one might expect intonation patterns to behave very much in the same way as lexical items, and this does in fact appear to be the case. For example, Cruttenden (1981, quoted in Taylor, 2003) looked at the different senses that are related respectively to falling and rising intonation and found that they represented sets of different yet clearly related senses. Falling intonation is associated with statement, finality, and assurance, whereas rising intonation is associated with questioning, openness and conciliatoriness. Some of these senses (such as finality for falling intonation and questioning for rising intonation) appear to be more prototypical than the other senses, and they are metaphorically related to the physical processes of falling and rising. Therefore, it would not be surprising to find that the senses that are associated with different intonation patterns exist within flexible, prototypical categories that have fuzzy boundaries. This view of meaning helps to explain the rising intonation pattern which is common in Australian English, and which has since entered some varieties of British English. Here the rising intonation does not correspond to a question so it is not a prototypical usage. In Guy and Vonwiller's (1989: 30) words:

> it seems to us that Australian Questioning Intonation (AQI) is best understood as an extension of a high-rising-tone-in-declarative as a device for asking questions.... Instead of questioning propositional content, AQI questions the listener's state of understanding.

By showing concern for the interlocutor this intonation pattern serves an important relationship-building function for those who are members of the discourse community that uses it. Questioning of understanding is related to questioning of content, and seems to be as good an example of radial category extension as any.

3.5.1 How might the idea that intonation patterns operate within radial categories help second language learners and teachers?

Teaching intonation patterns as radial categories is likely to bring the same benefits as for the other linguistic phenomena that have been discussed in this chapter. Rather than looking for clear-cut relationships between certain intonation patterns and their corresponding meanings, learners should be made aware of the fact that different, yet *related* meanings can be conveyed through a single intonation pattern. Contextual factors will determine which meaning is to be selected. Diagrams showing areas of overlap and variation between L1 and L2 intonation patterns could be useful if they are accompanied by auditory aids.

In terms of SLA that takes place in non-classroom settings, the acquisition of intonation patterns is likely to resemble the acquisition of other types of language in that the acquisition of form–meaning mappings is related to factors such as frequency, salience and attention. Indeed, in first language acquisition research, it has been noted that infants often understand, from a very early age, the communicative function of different intonation patterns, and are able to use these patterns effectively, even without all the words being present; it is only in the later stages of learning that they actually fill in all the words in the pattern (Peters, 1977). This finding led to research into formulaic sequences (Wray, 2002), and more recently into constructions, which are often accompanied by their own characteristic intonation patterns. These are discussed in Chapter 9.

3.6 Concluding comments

In this chapter we have looked at how words and morphemes, grammar rules, phonological features and intonation patterns operate within radial categories, and we have considered the implications that this has for second language learning and teaching. The general conclusion is that instead of presenting these aspects of language as fixed categories that are accompanied by lists of exceptions, it may be more useful and accurate to present them as flexible radial categories, which exhibit substantial variation according to context. This approach would strike a balance between the overly rigid, analytical 'grammar-translation' approach (with its lists of rules that don't always work) and the slightly overwhelming, memory-based 'lexical' approach (with its lists of set phrases that simply have to be memorized). The flexible radial categories approach shows us that language is systematic, but that within this system there is considerable flexibility. What this chapter has not done is to state explicitly how radial categories should be presented. A few suggestions have been made and references given to exploratory work in the area. However, much more needs to be done to test the applications of this area of cognitive linguistics to second language learning and teaching. Finally, although this chapter has treated each area of language independently, it is important to remember that words and morphemes, grammar rules, phonological features and intonation patterns do not operate as discrete linguistic systems. Rather, these different areas of language interact and are mutually dependent upon each other, and they cannot be taught independently. It might therefore be useful to make language learners aware of the pervasiveness of radial categories, and of the fact that they apply to all areas of language. More research is needed to assess whether an explicit focus on radial categories in the classroom and in language teaching materials will facilitate second language learning.

4
More about Spinsters and their Cats: Encyclopaedic Knowledge and Second Language Learning

4.1 Introductory comments

We saw in Chapter 1 that the words *bachelor* and *spinster* mean much more than 'unmarried man' and 'unmarried woman'. The word *bachelor* connotes ideas of freedom and licentious behaviour, whereas the word *spinster* for many people connotes ideas of old age, loneliness, lack of desirability (and possibly the possession of lots of cats). These connotations are arguably as much part of the 'meaning' that these words have for a given individual as the state of celibacy, and thus reflect a person's **encyclopaedic knowledge**. Encyclopaedic knowledge refers to all the information we store in our minds, which, according to Evans and Green (2006: 206) constitutes 'a large inventory of structured knowledge'. Different areas of this inventory are triggered by the use of different words and phrases. The content of this inventory extends well beyond denotative information, and includes all the connotations that have come to be associated with those words and expressions, over the period during which we have been exposed to them. Thus 'linguistic knowledge' cannot be seen as being separate from 'world' knowledge, and 'semantic' knowledge cannot be seen as being separate from 'pragmatic' knowledge' (*ibid.*). Encyclopaedic knowledge is made up of a complex network of links between ideas.

One of the main contributions that a focus on encyclopaedic knowledge can make to second language learning is in vocabulary teaching. Traditionally, knowledge of L2 vocabulary has been divided into two types: vocabulary *breadth* (how many words a learner knows) and vocabulary *depth* (how much a learner knows about individual words); see, for example, Schmitt (2000). However, more recently, researchers such as Meara and Wolter (2004) and Read (2004) have argued that 'vocabulary depth' is too broad a construct and that it is too often measured by looking only at what the learner knows about a small number of words presented out of context. They argue that a much more useful construct for teachers and researchers to study is how the L2 words are related to one another in the learner's mind. They call this construct **network knowledge**, and use the term **network building** to describe the process through which learners continually restructure their semantic network in order to accommodate new words.

Viewing and studying L2 vocabulary knowledge as an integrated network is much more realistic than viewing and studying it as a list of unrelated words, which learners know more or less about (Haastrup and Henrikson, 2000). A strong argument in support of this claim is that tests of 'deep' vocabulary knowledge always require learners to describe the words using other words in the target language, and therefore involve word association. Meara and Wolter (2004) thus talk in terms of **word association networks**. They argue that two things distinguish L1 word association networks from such networks in the L2. These are the size of the network, and the number of links that exist between the words in the network. To put it simply, L1 speakers know more words and are aware of more links between them, thus making their word association networks both broader and denser than those of language learners. Several studies involving word association tests have provided evidence in support of this view (Wilks and Meara, 2002; Meara, 2007). Thus the process of vocabulary learning in a second language not only requires learners to learn more words, but to learn how these words link to other words in the lexicon. Indeed, for both Meara and Read, 'learning' itself is equated with the building of links in the 'giant multidimensional cobweb' that is the mental lexicon. In other words, vocabulary growth 'entails the building of more extensive linkages between items in the mental lexicon' (Read, 2004: 221). These links can be **paradigmatic** or **syntagmatic** . Paradigmatic links involve words that are from the same semantic field, so a stimulus item *chair* might produce paradigmatic responses, such as *furniture* or *table*. Syntagmatic links involve sequential or collocational relationships to the prompt word. For example, syntagmatic responses to the word *chair* might include a sequential response, such as *sit*, or a collocational response, such as *a meeting*. We return to these later in this chapter.

Clear parallels can be drawn between word association networks and encyclopaedic knowledge. Language knowledge cannot be divorced from world knowledge, so 'encyclopaedic knowledge' and 'the mental lexicon' are to some extent two sides of the same coin. In native speakers, the relationship between them is fairly straightforward, but for language learners the picture becomes a little more complicated. Unless they are very young children, second language learners will already have built up a complex network of encyclopaedic knowledge, which is reflected in their L1 mental lexicon; when they learn a second language, they clearly do not need to build up their encyclopaedic knowledge from scratch. What they are more likely to try and do, at least in the early stages of L2 acquisition, is to map their L2 mental lexicon onto the existing structure, thus creating links that resemble those used in their L1. What successful L2 acquisition requires them to do is to reconfigure their mental lexicon to incorporate L2-style links, thus bringing it closer to that of an actual L2 speaker. This means that as they become more proficient in the target language, there will be changes in how their encyclopaedic knowledge is structured and variations in the types of links in the mental lexicon begin to appear. For many words, the links will be very similar to those in their L1. For example, the words *table* and *chair* in English are likely to relate to one another in the same way as the words *table* and *chaise* in French. However, in other cases, the links will vary, either in terms of direction or in terms of strength.

For example, in an unpublished piece of research, Littlemore and Boers gave a set of ten English words to a group of 15 English speakers and a group of 15 Dutch-speakers, and asked each person to come up with ten associations. Various associations were present in the English-speakers' data but not in the Dutch-speakers' data, and vice versa. These included *ceiling* (triggered by the word *glass* for the English-speakers but not the Dutch speakers) and *race* (triggered by the word *boat* for the English speakers but not the Dutch speakers). These probably reflect encyclopaedic knowledge of '*glass ceilings*' (a common collocation in English, referring to the fact that women often find it difficult to progress beyond a certain level in organizations), and of the annual Oxford versus Cambridge university boat race. These examples show how encyclopaedic knowledge affects the structure of our word association networks. They also hint at the relationship between language and culture.

Cognitive linguistic studies of encyclopaedic knowledge tell us about how such knowledge is structured and about the processes that help it to develop. If encyclopaedic knowledge and the mental lexicon are two sides of the same coin, then cognitive linguistic work on encyclopaedic knowledge may help us to understand how the mental lexicons of second language learners are structured and how they develop.

In the rest of this chapter I outline the cognitive linguistic view of encyclopaedic knowledge and reflect on how it might help us to understand the L2 mental lexicon. I begin by looking at work on 'frames' and 'idealized cognitive models'. I then discuss the various clines of encyclopaedic knowledge that have been identified. I consider how each of these areas contributes to existing findings in word association studies, and make suggestions as to how language teachers might help their students build up their encyclopaedic knowledge in their target language.

4.2 What is meant by 'encyclopaedic knowledge'?

Rather than thinking of words as expressing separate 'concepts', it is, according to cognitive linguists, more appropriate to think of them as tools that cause listeners to 'activate' certain areas of their knowledge network, with different areas activated to different degrees in different contexts of use. Cognitive linguists thus see words and phrases as 'ways into' a complex knowledge network. They are therefore referred to as 'access nodes' (Langacker, 1987: 163). Words and phrases simply act as 'prompts for meaning construction' (Evans and Green, 2006) and do not contain any full meanings in themselves. Lee (2001: 206–7) refers to this as **underspecification**:

> The general point is that any utterance grossly underspecifies the situation on which it reports. Such underspecification is essential, since the task of encoding all the features of a given situation is simply not feasible, nor is it one in which either the speaker or the addressee has any interest. Underspecification is effective because of the fact that the addressee's knowledge base forms a major part of the task of meaning construction. An inevitable corollary of this process is that meaning escapes the control of speaker intention.

Encyclopaedic knowledge is one of the resources that we use to help us infer what a speaker means from the hugely underspecified linguistic content of any typical linguistic exchange. It is thus involved in both the production and comprehension of language, and a mismatch between the encyclopaedic knowledge networks possessed by the speaker and the hearer can result in communication failure. This can (and does) happen between native speakers of a language, but it is more likely to happen between speakers of different languages. This suggests that one aim of language teaching is to help learners extend and reshape their encyclopaedic knowledge networks (and thus their corresponding word association networks) so that they resemble those of L2 speakers. In order to do this, it is useful to be aware of those areas of encyclopaedic knowledge that are most susceptible to variation across languages. In order to identify these areas, it is useful to have some idea of the way in which encyclopaedic knowledge tends to be organized in the mind.

4.3 Encyclopaedic knowledge and frame semantics

Encyclopaedic knowledge networks are large and complex, but they are not randomly organized. According to cognitive linguists, encyclopaedic knowledge networks are structured around certain **frames**. The idea of **frame semantics**, which was first proposed by Charles Fillmore (1975), is best illustrated with an example. If someone asked us to explain what is meant by *a goal* (in its literal sense), we could tell them that it is a structure with two poles, a bar across the top, and a net at the back. However, this would not give them a good idea of what a goal actually is unless they were familiar with games such as football, or hockey or handball. In order to really understand what is meant by the word *goal* we need to have a significant amount of background knowledge about what these games are, and how and where they are played. 'Football', 'hockey' and 'handball' therefore constitute possible frames against which the word *goal* can be understood. Other examples that are often given in the literature to illustrate frame semantics are *wicket*, which needs to be understood against the frame of 'cricket'; *uncle* which needs to be understood against the frame of 'relations'; and *hypotenuse* which needs to be understood against the frame of 'right angled triangle' (Lee, 2001). Many words can be understood against more than one frame. The example that is often used by cognitive linguists to illustrate this fact is the word *mother*, as it appears in sentences such as (19), taken from Lakoff (1987: 74):

> (19) Although both tragedies were immeasurably traumatic, finding out that my **mother** wasn't my real **mother** was the more devastating.

Here, Lakoff points out that the two instances of the word *mother* draw on different aspects of the encyclopaedic knowledge that we might typically possess for the word *mother*, or in Fillmore's words, they draw on our ability to use the word *mother* to tap into at least two different frames. The first instance of the word taps into the frame of 'mother as carer', or provider of love and warmth, whereas the second instance taps into the frame of 'biological parenthood'. Thus different frames can be activated by the same word, and the context serves a disambiguating function.

Thus frames provide a way of understanding how a word's connotations are structured. In language teaching they might be a useful device for explaining the rationale behind the different connotations that words have. The example above shows that for speakers of English, a full understanding of the word *mother* involves an appreciation of the fact that it taps into the frames of parenthood and caring. Although this is probably true of the equivalent word for 'mother' in most, if not all languages, other words will tap into different areas of encyclopaedic knowledge in different languages. For example, the word *weekend*, for most people in Western Europe and the US, refers to Saturday and Sunday, two days when they do not have to go to work. In Islamic countries, the weekend is more likely to mean Friday and Saturday, and for many individuals in those countries it will have strong religious connotations that it no longer has for the majority of people living in the West. Even within a group of people who speak the same language, the encyclopaedic knowledge frames that are triggered by the word *weekend* will vary. For someone who works part-time, the weekend might start on a Wednesday. For someone who spends their weekends walking in the countryside, the encyclopaedic knowledge that is potentially activated by the word *weekend* will incorporate this fact, whereas for someone who spends their weekends lying in bed and doing crossword puzzles, a different area of encyclopaedic knowledge has the potential to be activated. Note here, I use the expression 'potential to be activated'. This is because the area of encyclopaedic knowledge that is actually activated also depends on the context in which the word is used, as we can see in the following examples (20)–(24) of the word *television*, which are taken from the British National Corpus:

(20) **Television** goes along with this.
(21) His Mum had gone to **switch the television on.**
(22) ... sharing their lives the way they always had, **before television shrunk the world** ...
(23) The Super Nintendo Scope light guns –; which enables you to **shoot at the television set** ...
(24) ... the average individual **watches around three and a half hours of television per day.**

In these examples, the word *television* refers to different things and can be understood against different frames. In some of the examples, it refers to the actual piece of equipment; the television 'set', whereas in others it refers more vaguely to the people who work in television, the process of 'televising', or the services offered by 'television'. We combine our encyclopaedic knowledge of the word *television* with our ability to use contextual cues, to help us identify the intended sense. Context can take different forms, including the words immediately surrounding the target item (i.e. the 'co-text'), the relationship between the speakers, the medium of communication, and the intonation patterns being employed.

As a final example, it is because of our encyclopaedic knowledge and our ability to adjust to the relevant context that we are able to understand the different meanings of *university* in the following three sentences (25)–(27):

(25) I'm walking across the **university**
(26) The **university** has a new staffing policy
(27) We're playing the **university** next week

Each of these sentences involves isolating different parts of the word's encyclopaedic meaning. The university is first construed as a physical place, then as an organization, then (metonymically) as a sports team.

Frames are thus important as they account both for the connotations of words, as we saw in the *mother* example, and the semi-polysemous uses that we saw in the *television* and *university* examples. Frames allow us to use language flexibly, and to convey different information with the same words.

Much of the work on the second language lexicon starts out with an assumption that words correspond to certain 'concepts' in the mind, and then looks, for example, at the influence of 'L1 concepts' on the formation of 'L2 concepts' (e.g. Jiang, 2004; Wolter, 2006). As we saw above however, what frame theory tells us is that, rather than corresponding to individual concepts, words and phrases are tools that cause listeners to 'activate' certain areas of their knowledge network, with different areas activated to different degrees, in different contexts of use. If we take this as our starting point then we might be better placed to understand, for example, why deep vocabulary learning appears to take place at such a slow rate (Jiang, 2004; Schmitt, 1998). Learners need to be exposed to words in different contexts so that they become aware of the full range of frames that those words tap into. This knowledge, which is very subtle, is likely to be acquired implicitly and will stay below the level of consciousness unless it is explicitly teased out by the teacher. Frames are also likely to underlie student behaviour on word association tests. In recent years, a great deal of work has been carried out on the use of word association tests. Paul Meara and his colleagues have devised an ingenious set of tests that are designed to assess both the number of links between words that language learners have, and the strength of these links. One finding from this area of research is that L1 vocabulary networks interfere with the acquisition of L2 encyclopaedic knowledge, even in relatively high-level learners. For example, Verspoor (2008) looked at the word associations provided by upper-intermediate Dutch and English speakers for the English word *abandon*. Her findings showed that the Dutch informants had a non native-like association of the word *abandon* with 'banishment', while they did not have the native-like association of 'giving up' that was present in the native-speaker data. In cognitive linguistic terminology, the Dutch equivalent of the word *abandon* tends to evoke a slightly different set of frames from its English equivalent. Vocabulary classes could usefully explore these different frames, making them more explicit to learners.

In a similar vein, Verspoor *et al.* (2008) conducted a study in which they compared the amount of time taken by native speakers of English to recognize English and Dutch word associations to the amount of time taken by native speakers of Dutch. All of the tests were conducted in English. Unsurprisingly, they found that the native speakers of English were faster at recognizing the English word associations, and that the Dutch participants were faster at recognizing the typical Dutch associations. However, these relationships were only statistically significant for *frequent* lexical items. This finding implies that sensitivity to L1 word association patterns is dependent upon the number of times a learner has been exposed to the lexical item in question. They also found that the relationships were much stronger for nouns than for verbs, which implies that L1 encyclopaedic knowledge networks for nouns are perhaps more entrenched and more likely to interfere with L2 systems than they are for verbs. In their article, they also emphasize the fact that the development of L2 encyclopaedic knowledge is likely to operate as a complex system with different types of knowledge being gathered at different rates, with frequent periods of knowledge loss as well as knowledge gain. The development of L2-specific encyclopaedic knowledge networks should not be seen as a linear phenomenon, but as something that is in permanent flux: links between words can be lost as well as formed.

Frame theory could usefully be introduced into language teaching settings. For example, when new words are introduced, students could be encouraged to reflect on the different frames against which they can be understood. Because languages vary in terms of the frames which words conventionally tap into, an explicit discussion of frame theory might highlight differences between the L1 and the L2 and help learners grasp the connotations and semi-polysemous nature of L2 items in a more structured manner. These ideas are discussed in more depth in Section 4.7.

4.4 Idealized cognitive models

Lakoff (1987) extended and developed the theory of frames to create his, arguably more inclusive, theory of idealized cognitive models (or 'ICMs'). ICMs are relatively stable mental representations of what we know about the world. Although they can be very rich in detail, they need to be sufficiently abstract and vague, or in cognitive linguistic terminology, **schematic**, to allow us to generalize across a series of examples. ICMs are categories in their own right, and they thus have a radial structure (see Chapter 3). For example, the *university* example above suggests that we have an ICM for universities in which we know that they are generally places where people go to obtain degrees; they often have campuses; they have large administrative structures; and they have extra-curricular activities. Some of this knowledge (such as the fact that people go there to obtain degrees) is more prototypical than others (such as the fact that universities generally have extra-curricular activities) but it all contributes to our ability to understand things that people might say about universities. The reasons why Lakoff chooses to use the term 'ICM' for this concept are that ICMs are thought to be abstract and applicable across a range of contexts (hence they are 'idealized'), that they are in the mind (hence 'cognitive'), and that they are only representations (hence 'models').

According to Lakoff, there are five main types of ICM: propositional ICMs, image schema ICMs, metaphoric ICMs, metonymic ICMs, and symbolic ICMs. Each type of ICM works in its own way to contribute to the meaning that is underspecified in language itself. Four of these ICMs are discussed in depth in subsequent chapters so they will not be explored in detail here. In this section, the focus is on the first type of ICM, the **propositional ICM**, as this gives us an insight into the essence of encyclopaedic knowledge, and underlies many of the features of the bilingual mental lexicon.

The *bachelor, mother, television* and *university* examples cited above all involve propositional ICMs, in that they depend on stereotypical scenes of what the world is like, or of what usually tends to happen in a particular situation. Propositional ICMs have much in common with 'scene schemas' and 'event schemas' (G. Cook, 1997) as well as with 'cultural models' (Shore, 1996). They encode the conventional knowledge that we have about the world, and we use them to understand language. For example, if a friend tells us that they 'went out last night' we might use a propositional ICM for *going out*, along with contextual information and what we know about our friend to infer that they probably went to a pub or a restaurant, or maybe the cinema, that they may have had a drink (possibly an alcoholic one), met up with some friends and so on. Although none of this information is actually contained in the verbal utterance 'I went out last night', our friend is assuming that we have sufficient propositional ICM knowledge to understand them.

Problems may occur for language learners when the content of propositional ICMs varies from culture to culture. For example, the ICM for 'going to the beach' in South Korea does not generally include sunbathing and the wearing of swimsuits or bikinis by women, as pale skin on women is more highly regarded than tanned skin. Moreover, Koreans over the age of thirty often feel uncomfortable exposing bare skin in public because Korean traditional education banned such physical exposure. So if an older South Korean woman tells a westerner that she is going to the beach, the image created in that listener's mind may be very different from that intended by the speaker (Yeongsil Ko and Grace Wang, personal communication). The westerner may therefore not have 'understood' her in quite the same way as a Korean native speaker would have.

If the development of the L2 mental lexicon involves the creation of links between words that resemble those of the native speaker, then we can see how different propositional ICMs may make us structure the lexicon in different ways. As we have seen, one of the main associations that the word *beach* has for many English speakers is 'sunbathing'. Some Korean learners of English may be less likely to make this association. Part of learning a second language involves the ability to use the available input to infer what propositional ICMs speakers of that language possess, and to use these to develop target-language-style links in the lexicon. In many cases, such learning will probably be implicit, as propositional ICMs are rarely covered in textbooks or language classes. An additional burden is that knowledge of propositional ICMs needs to be inferred from context, which makes it much more difficult to acquire than more surface linguistic features, such as, say, the plural -*s* ending in English.

Propositional ICMs thus provide a cognitive explanation for the way in which the mental lexicon is organised, and go some way towards predicting how the relative lexicons of L1 and L2 speakers might be structured. They are particularly likely to underlie paradigmatic relationships between words. For example, the propositional ICM that a British person has for *dog* is likely to include things such as the fact that dogs have four legs and a tail, that they are often kept as pets, that they are usually given names, and so on. To illustrate, let us look at the following list of word associations that native speakers produce for the word *dog* in the Edinburgh Word Association Thesaurus (http://www.eat.rl.ac.uk/). This thesaurus contains word associations for 8,400 words, given by 100 native speakers of English. We can see from this list that many of the associations draw on this propositional ICM:

CAT	JASPER
COLLAR	LABRADOR
BARK	LEAD
LEG	LEASH
ALSATIAN	LEGS
ANIMAL	MAN
BERRY	MOUSE
BITE	MUCK
BLACK	OURS
BOW	PAW
CARNIVORE	PET
CHEESE	RACING
COUNTRY	RUN
DARK	SHAME
DINNER	TAIL
FIGHT	TONGUE
GUN	WHISTLE
HOT	

It has been found that L2 learners tend to produce fewer paradigmatic responses to word association tests than native speakers and that the tendency to produce paradigmatic responses increases with proficiency (Soderman, 1993). Moreover, in both native and non-native speakers, the tendency to produce paradigmatic responses for a given word is directly related to how well the participants feel that they 'know' that word (Wolter, 2001). This finding can be explained by the fact that paradigmatic knowledge is strongly linked to the acquisition of target-language-type propositional ICMs. For example, for many speakers of English, the propositional ICM for *Christmas* includes 'a focus on family', whereas in South Korea it does not. Instead, Christmas in South Korea is a day that is primarily celebrated by young couples, a bit like Valentine's Day in the UK. Therefore the paradigmatic link to *family* would not typically be present for monolingual and monocultural Koreans. Korean learners of English would need to learn this link through contact with Western culture. In the same way, Koreans have very different conceptions of *salad*. 'Salad' in Korea usually refers to mayonnaise-laden shredded cabbage, so a Korean learner of English would need to develop paradigmatic links between the word *salad* and, for example, *lettuce* and *tomatoes*, whereas an English-speaking learner of Korean would need to strengthen the links to the Korean word for 'shredded cabbage'. Both of these examples (for which I thank Yeongsil Ko and Sung Ho Lee) show the extent to which links within the mental lexicon can be determined by culturally based propositional ICMs. There are therefore clear links between propositional ICMs and paradigmatic knowledge, but what about syntagmatic knowledge?

At first sight, syntagmatic knowledge appears to be more of a surface-level feature of language than paradigmatic knowledge, and perhaps lends itself more easily to perceptual learning. Learners pick up collocations by hearing them, whereas paradigmatic relationships that rely on propositional ICMs require a deeper analysis of the target-language culture. But is this really the whole story? Are syntagmatic relationships or collocations always a surface feature of language, or do they too sometimes reflect underlying ICMs? Traditionally, collocation is seen as a somewhat superficial, surface-level phenomenon that simply has to be learned by language learners, but recent research is beginning to show that in many cases collocations often reflect underlying word meanings, albeit in an indirect way (Walker, 2008a,b). In cognitive linguistic terms, collocation is thus 'motivated' to a certain extent by other factors; and is not always arbitrary. To illustrate, let us look at the strongest collocates for *dog* in the Bank of English:

a	his
eda (sic.)	like
dog	cat
your	walking
s	my

hot	owners
the	owner
eat	walk
her	pet
mad	barking
food	eared
man	

It is easy to see how the majority of the words in this list relate to propositional ICMs that we might have for the word *dog*. The propositional ICM that many speakers of English in the UK and the US have for the word *dog* will include things like the fact that dogs are *pets*, that they are *owned* by humans *(*hence *my, yours* and *his)* who give them *food*, that they like being taken for *walks*, when they wear a *collar*, that they tend to *bark*, and chase after *cats*; so we can see how it influences word association patterns. As we will see in subsequent chapters, the other items in this list *(mad, hot* and *eared)* are related to metaphorical and metonymic ICMs. Thus the in-depth knowledge of the ICMs that native speakers and advanced learners have for words and concepts may account in part for their use of authentic-sounding collocation patterns. It may therefore be worth studying ICMs with language learners in order to give them a better idea of the paradigmatic and syntagmatic relations that words have in the target language, and by extension, to improve their depth of vocabulary knowledge and their collocational competence.

The other four types of ICM that Lakoff proposes and that will be discussed in subsequent chapters are: image schema ICMs, metaphorical ICMs and metonymic ICMs, and symbolic ICMs. **Image schema ICMs** are abstract conceptual representations that arise directly from our day-to-day interaction with the world. They derive from sensory and perceptual experience and are thus thought to be 'embodied' (Evans, 2007). For example, as infants we learn that we can put things in and out of containers, that things go up and down, or that things can be hot or cold. When a child has abstracted these general experiences away from their immediate causes, and is able to see them as more general human experiences, then they are said to have developed image schemata. Other image schemata include movement, balance and force, all of which are bodily-based in the first instance. In Chapter 7, I explore embodiment in more depth and look at how these basic physical experiences are used to talk about more abstract concepts. This has important implications for language learning and teaching: although the metaphorical extensions of these embodied experiences vary from language to language, the basic physical experiences themselves are universal. Various language teaching techniques have been proposed that exploit this phenomenon, and in Chapter 7 I discuss the relative effectiveness of these techniques. For now, I will simply say that image schemata ICMs influence links between words in the mental lexicon in the same way as propositional ICMs do. These links can be completely literal (e.g. 'up' is lexically linked to 'down') or more metaphorical (e.g. 'heat' is linked to 'passion'). Variation in the ways in which languages metaphorically extend image-schema ICMs will lead to different types of links in the mental lexicon.

Lakoff also postulates **metaphoric and metonymic ICMs**, which will be discussed in depth in Chapters 5 and 6. Although Lakoff (1987) sees metaphor and metonymy largely as static ICMs, other researchers (e.g. Ruiz de Mendoza and Mairal Uson, 2007) have shown how they also operate as *dynamic* cognitive processes that operate *within and between existing* ICMs. There are a number of conceptual metaphors and metonymies that have arisen out of our need to understand abstract ideas in terms of concrete experience. Several studies have explored cross-linguistic variation in conceptual metaphors, the language teaching potential of conceptual metaphors (but not metonymies), and the relationship between conceptual metaphor and collocation. These studies, which have important implications for vocabulary learning, are discussed in depth in Littlemore and Low (2006a) and in Chapters 6 and 7 of this book. Let us just say for now that many of the word associations and collocations that appeared in the above lists for the word *dog* involve conventional metaphorical and metonymic extensions. For example, *cheese* may be related to hotdogs, *dinner* may be related to the idiom 'a dog's dinner' and *shame* may be relate to the idiom 'to be in the doghouse', which means to be in disgrace. The word *leg* in this list may reflect the metaphoric expression 'dog leg', which refers to a sudden bend in the road or path. In the collocations, *mad* may refer to the song 'mad dogs and Englishmen go out in the midday sun' and/or to nicknames of violent or powerful men, and *eared* probably reflects the expression 'dog-eared' which means tatty and torn.

Finally, in his **symbolic ICMs**, Lakoff argues that language is inherently symbolic and that form–meaning relationships extend beyond the level of the word. He argues that grammatical constructions have a real cognitive status and are not mere epiphenomena arising from more general grammatical rules. In doing so, he provides the foundation for the construction grammar approach to language, whose applications to language teaching are discussed in Chapter 9.

In this section we have seen that Lakoff proposes five types of 'idealized cognitive model'. The first (propositional ICMs) may underlie many paradigmatic and syntagmatic relationships between words in the mental lexicon. Differences between first-language and target-language ICMs may explain why L2 learners provide different responses from native speakers on word association tasks. It takes a long time for learners to acquire target-language ICMs and this may explain why vocabulary networks build up so slowly in the L2, particularly those that involve paradigmatic links. It remains to be seen whether the explicit teaching of target-language ICMs will help learners to increase the density of their L2 vocabulary networks, and thus deepen their L2 vocabulary knowledge. In the next section we turn to another way in which the concept of encyclopaedic knowledge may deepen our understanding of how the mental lexicon is structured; this is the idea that encyclopaedic knowledge is positioned along **clines**.

4.5 Clines of encyclopaedic knowledge

We have seen so far that although encyclopaedic knowledge networks are vast and complex, a certain amount of structure can be identified within them. In addition to this, it has been argued that most types of encyclopaedic knowledge sit somewhere along one of a finite number of clines. Evans and Green (2006) outline four such clines: the generic to specific; the intrinsic to extrinsic; the conventional to non-conventional; and the characteristic to non-characteristic. In order to show how these clines relate to vocabulary networks, I will discuss each of them in relation to the word associations that were triggered by the prompt *dog* in the Edinburgh Word Association Thesaurus, and to the collocations for *dog* that we saw above.

The **generic to specific** cline refers to the extent to which the knowledge can be applied to different members of a category. For example, a person's knowledge of the fact that a particular dog they happen to know is white with brown spots constitutes what Evans and Green would describe as 'specific' knowledge, whereas knowledge of the fact that dogs are often furry sits more towards the 'generic' end of the cline. In the list on page 81, words such as *tail*, *tongue* and *legs* reflect generic knowledge, whereas words such as *dark*, *black* and *Jasper* reflect more specific knowledge.

The **intrinsic to extrinsic** cline refers to the extent to which knowledge relates to the internal properties of the entity in question. So our intrinsic encyclopaedic knowledge of a dog includes the fact that dogs generally have four legs, fur, and a tail. Extrinsic knowledge includes things like the fact that they are taken for walks by humans and that some appear in dog shows. Extrinsic knowledge is likely to be heavily influenced by culture, and may thus present the most significant challenge to language learners. The characteristics of dogs are fairly universal, but what you do with a dog (i.e. whether you are more likely to take it for a walk, put it in a show, or eat it) depends very much on the culture into which you are born. Towards the extrinsic end of this cline, we have the so-called 'characteristics' of dogs that might be said to be culturally imposed upon them, such as the fact that, in some Western cultures, they are supposed to be loyal, friendly, 'man's best friend', and so on. In the list of word associations given in the Edinburgh Word Association Thesaurus for the word *dog* on page 81, words such as *paw*, *bark* and *legs* reflect intrinsic knowledge, whereas words such as *collar*, *fight*, *pet*, *whistle*, and *racing* all reflect extrinsic knowledge as they refer to things that dogs have imposed on them by humans in some societies. Extrinsic knowledge is likely to present the most significant challenge to language learners as it will not always be based on their practical experience with the entity under discussion, and needs to be inferred from what they read and hear in the target language. It also explains why some vocabulary links that are strong in the word association networks of native speakers, are weaker, or even non-existent, in those of language learners.

The **conventional to non-conventional** cline refers to the extent to which the knowledge is known by, and shared between, different members of a speech community. Non-conventional encyclopaedic knowledge is the idiosyncratic knowledge that individuals may have about dogs. In the list of word associations in the Edinburgh Word Association Thesaurus on page 81, words such as *tail*, *bark* and *paw* reflect conventional encyclopaedic knowledge about dogs. The non-conventional knowledge that a person might have about dogs might include, for example, the fact that their dog tripped them up when they were walking down the stairs that morning. This sort of knowledge is unlikely to appear in high- frequency word-association counts as it varies considerably across individuals. It is important however to bear in mind that learners will all have this sort of knowledge, and that it contributes to the fact that individual students respond differently to the same tasks and language input, and to why the learning outcomes of any language lesson are never fully predictable.

The **characteristic to non-characteristic** cline refers to the extent to which the knowledge is unique to a particular entity. Characteristic knowledge is what sets the entity apart from similar entities. For example, in the above list, some of the words, such as *bark, Alsatian* and *Labrador,* are particularly applicable to dogs, whereas others, such as *legs, paw* and *run* could be applied to any animal.

These clines could provide a useful framework on which to base in-depth vocabulary learning sessions, in which learners are helped to strengthen their word association networks and to consider the cultural content of word meaning. The characteristic to non-characteristic cline may be useful for defining specialist vocabulary and technical terms. I look at how this might be done in Sections 4.6 and 4.7.

To sum up this section, syntagmatic and paradigmatic relationships between words are best seen as epiphenomena reflecting underlying frames, ICMs and clines of encyclopaedic knowledge. Encyclopaedic knowledge and its corresponding word association networks are usage-based and dynamic. That is to say, they build up through our daily interaction with the world, and will grow or contract in a non-linear way, depending on the nature and extent of our interactions with different phenomena. During the early stages of learning, the L2 encyclopaedic knowledge network is likely to have a parasitical relationship with the L1 network, but it will gradually acquire its own identity as proficiency increases and new links are formed within it. However, it has been observed that network-building in the L2 is extremely slow; almost 'tortoise-like' (Aitchison, 1994: 179). In order for the links to form and become entrenched, words need to be encountered in a variety of different contexts and in the company of different types of words. Verspoor *et al.* (2008) argue that over time, language learners develop links that are characteristic of the target language, but that they retain the links that are present in their native language. Thus the bilingual lexicon is much richer and denser than the monolingual lexicon, and develops at a very slow rate. In order to increase the speed at which links are formed within the bilingual lexicon, there should perhaps be an explicit focus on frames and ICMs in the language classroom.

4.6 What aspects of encyclopaedic knowledge should be taught?

We saw in the previous section that encyclopaedic knowledge is an important component of second language learning because it relates to deeper L2 vocabulary knowledge. When vocabulary is learned, it is not only the denotative meaning that needs to be considered, but also the connotative meaning and relevant frames and ICMs. Students should be discouraged from looking for direct one-to-one correspondences between words and 'concepts'. Instead, they need to be made aware of the various frames and ICMs that the vocabulary items habitually provide access to, as well as encouraging them to be prepared for fuzzy categories of meaning that can adapt themselves easily to different contexts. This sort of approach is necessary if learners are to be able to use the language they are learning with any degree of flexibility and creativity. The question is, what aspects of encyclopaedic knowledge can be taught, and *how* can they be taught?

Teaching encyclopedic knowledge in any kind of explicit way inevitably involves in-depth discussions of the meanings and connotations of words. This is what Nation (2001) refers to as **rich instruction**. As Nation points out, it is unfeasible to use rich instruction when teaching every word that the learner encounters, as this would overwhelm the learner. Teachers need to identify, for their own learners, which vocabulary items need to be studied in detail, and which can be glossed. Although this will vary according to context, there are at least two principles upon which teachers might base their decision. Firstly, Nation argues that 'rich instruction' should be mainly directed towards the high-frequency words in the language. I would add that what teachers need to consider is the frequency of those words within the particular discourse community that the students are being trained to enter. A second set of words that are good candidates for this sort of instruction are what Wierzbicka (1997, 2006) refers to as **cultural keywords**. She argues that cultural keywords act as 'focal points' for entire sets of cultural values and they thus provide access to different world views that are expressed in different languages. They distil sets of culturally specific values into a single word or expression and are very hard, if not impossible, to translate without a great deal of paraphrasing. There are thus concepts that can be expressed succinctly in some languages but not in others. The Japanese word *monoganashii* is a good example of this. Basically it means something along the lines of 'I'm sad because everything is so fleeting and nothing is permanent' but it is difficult to explain its exact meaning in English. Another example is the French expression 'Il n'est pas bien dans sa peau' ('he is not good in his skin'), which means that he is feeling somewhat uneasy or uncomfortable with his current state of affairs.

The concept of cultural keywords also works at a morphological level. The Spanish diminutives *ita* and *illa* are good candidates for the title of 'cultural keyword'. Ruiz de Mendoza (2008) shows how these diminutives have separate, but overlapping, senses that are highly culturally specific. These senses refer not only to smallness, but also to notions of cuteness, desirability, contempt, irony, and vagueness, which, according to Ruiz de Mendoza, operate within overlapping radial categories. The ability to use these senses appropriately will make a learner's Spanish sound much more authentic and idiomatic. Studying the different senses and areas of encyclopaedic knowledge that are accessed by cultural keywords is likely to be useful in the language classroom as it provides learners with a 'way into' the target language and culture that is at once cognitive and sociolinguistic.

In her (1997) work, Wierzbicka relates the concept of cultural keywords to that of **cultural scripts**. These are sets of cultural values and ideas that are often historical, or related to a country's politics or religion. Because they are so strongly embedded in the culture, they start to appear in the language. For example, she suggests that in English there is a strong cultural script associated with freedom and autonomy and consideration for the other person's feelings and points of view, which she argues is expressed through politeness and distancing devices. In contrast, in Russian there is a cultural script related to the importance of the soul and fate, which gives these concepts a particular poignancy that they do not have in English. It has been argued (Goddard, 2004) that cultural scripts provide a useful tool for language teaching as they lead to a deeper understanding of politeness phenomena in the target language. However, if cultural keywords and scripts are used in the language classroom they will need to be used with caution as they can easily lead to generalizations and stereotyping. A good approach might be to make use of extracts from literature in the target language, or even relevant art and music, as this would provide students with authentic input that they could then use to draw their own conclusions. The 'cultural scripts' would thus be presented in the original voices of L2 speakers, without being mediated by a language teacher.

4.7 How can encyclopaedic knowledge be taught?

Having looked briefly at *what* aspects of encyclopedic knowledge should be taught, we now turn to the trickier question of *how* they can be taught. We saw above that much of the encyclopedic knowledge that language learners acquire will be obtained very slowly through implicit learning. This is because it builds up through repeated exposure to words in different contexts. However, teachers do have a role to play in making their students aware of the more culturally specific areas of encyclopedic knowledge, and therefore at times a more explicit approach may be appropriate. One possible way to build up encyclopedic knowledge is to engage in explicit discussions of the encyclopaedic knowledge clines that were mentioned above. This would highlight the relationship between encyclopaedic knowledge, cultural connotations, word association networks, and collocation, thus introducing a degree of metalinguistic awareness into the classroom (Svalberg, 2007). Work in the area of encyclopaedic knowledge also implies that it may not be such a bad idea to resurrect the use of contrastive analysis and translation in the language classroom. Indeed, recent research has shown that by engaging in explicit classroom-based discussions of cross-linguistic differences concerning the areas of the encyclopaedic knowledge network that different words tap into, teachers can significantly enhance vocabulary learning in terms of both depth of knowledge and collocational awareness (Laufer and Girsai, 2008).

Another way to help learners to develop their encyclopedic knowledge of the target language is through the use of **enhanced input**. Enhanced input refers to a range of techniques that are designed to draw a learner's attention to particular (usually grammatical) forms in the target language (Sharwood-Smith, 1993). Enhanced input techniques range from simply underlining or highlighting a target-language structure to explicitly explaining a grammar rule, or providing error correction in class. Research in general has shown that enhanced input does lead to gains in acquisition, but that these gains are not equal across all areas of language (Han *et al.*, 2008). The question is, could enhanced input work for the teaching of encyclopedic knowledge, and if so, what form could it take?

One rather creative response to this question, which ties in with what we said above about cultural scripts, is suggested by Picken (2007). He makes a very strong case for the use of literature in the second language classroom. A central pillar of his argument is that literary language often involves using words in unusual ways and thus foregrounds the linguistic features of a text, causing readers to slow down as they pay attention to particular words and phrases. This, argues Picken, has a 'schema refreshing' effect which encourages interpretative reflection on the language, which in turn leads to language learning. Picken's ideas could very easily be applied to the teaching of encyclopaedic knowledge. For example, in this short extract from the poem, 'Tonight at Noon', by Adrian Henri, we can see that by saying the opposite of what we would expect, he makes us acutely aware of a series of existing ICMs, and helps us to identify several cultural scripts that are at work in (British) English:

Tonight at noon
Supermarkets will advertise 3p extra on everything
Tonight at noon
Children from happy families will be sent to live in a home
Elephants will tell each other human jokes
America will declare peace on Russia
...
And you will tell me you love me
Tonight at noon.

The encyclopaedic knowledge that is being presented in this poem includes the facts that: supermarkets usually advertize reductions in price, not increases; children from unhappy or 'problem' families are sometimes sent into care homes; there are lots of well-known jokes about elephants; and America and Russia have a somewhat antagonistic relationship. Although some of this encyclopaedic knowledge may be slightly out-of-date, the poem could still be used to trigger discussions about which of these areas of encyclopaedic knowledge are universal and which are more culture-specific. Students could then be encouraged to think of other candidates for the poem and perhaps write their own poem along the same lines as this one. Indeed, the relationship between encyclopaedic knowledge and semantic-network building provides a strong justification for the use of literature, art and music in the language classroom, as they provide the best way of exposing learners to 'foreign' conceptualizations of words and to the target language culture (Lantolf, 1999; Niemeier, 2004).

Another way to introduce encyclopaedic knowledge into the language classroom would be to have learners carry out some of the word association tasks that have been used by Paul Meara and his colleagues. They could then be asked to discuss the reasons behind their choices, and afterwards they could be encouraged to look at the aforementioned Edinburgh Word Association Thesaurus to see what associations native speakers produce for the same words, discussing possible reasons for these associations with their teachers. Such discussions would reveal areas of overlap and discrepancy in their ICMs which could usefully be explored.

Something that this chapter has been somewhat guilty of thus far is setting up native-speaker encyclopaedic knowledge as some sort of 'norm' to which language learners should aspire. In recent applied linguistic research, this idea has rightly received substantial criticism, as many language learners in fact have no intention of ever sounding like a native speaker, or of ever interacting with one. Indeed, most interactions in English take place between non-native speakers of English, and the most common role of English worldwide is to serve as a means of contact between people who share neither a native language nor a common (national) culture (Seidlhofer, 2005). To such learners, activities that involve comparing their word association networks with those of native speakers might seem at best irrelevant, and at worst, insulting. According to Seidlhofer (2004), this means that we should view speakers of English as a lingua franca (ELF) as 'language users in their own right' and acknowledge 'the legitimacy of, and indeed the need for, a description of salient features of English as a lingua franca, alongside English as a native language' (*ibid.*: 209).

The question is, if encyclopaedic knowledge is so important in building network knowledge, then how will speakers of English as a lingua franca build up sufficiently similar networks of knowledge to understand one another? The answer probably lies in their reason for communicating with each other in the first place. As global communication increases, and new discourse communities develop across national boundaries, one's encyclopaedic knowledge will be less and less defined by the country where one lives, and will increasingly be shaped by that of friends and colleagues who live abroad but who share the same interests or profession. Speakers of ELF will develop their own frames and ICMs that cross national boundaries and vary according to different discourse communities. The challenge for ELF investigators who are interested in producing language descriptors for ELF, is to identify these new frames and ICMs as they emerge, and to investigate how they impact on the vocabulary networks that different ELF communities develop.

4.8   Concluding comments

In this chapter we have seen that encyclopaedic knowledge provides a useful way of looking at vocabulary networks. We have also seen how frames and ICMs are involved in the creation of paradigmatic and syntagmatic relations within these networks. Clines of encyclopaedic knowledge may help us to identify potential areas of difficulty that language learners might encounter when building up their word association networks in the L2. We have seen that cultural keywords and cultural scripts provide a way into target-language encyclopaedic knowledge networks, and that these are perhaps best introduced through target-language literature, art and music, or through the use of word association tasks. In the next two chapters we turn to two concepts that are closely related to the idea of encyclopaedic knowledge: metaphor and metonymy.

5
'Eyebrow heads' and 'yummy mummies': Metaphor and Second Language Learning

5.1 Introductory comments

Metaphor and metonymy constitute two cognitive processes which lie at the heart of much human thought and communication. In very basic terms, metaphor draws on relations of substitution and similarity, whereas metonymy draws on relations of contiguity. In metaphor, one thing is seen in terms of another and the role of the interpreter is to identify points of similarity, allowing, for example, a football commentator to describe a particularly easy victory as being *'a walk in the park for The Reds'*. In metonymy, an entity is used to refer to something that it is actually related to, For example, 'Hollywood' refers to the American film industry and 'Wall Street' refers to America's financial services sector. Jakobson (1971) famously argued that metaphor and metonymy constitute two fundamental poles of human thought, a fact which can be witnessed through their prevalence in all symbolic systems, including art, language, music and sculpture. More often than not, metaphor and metonymy work together and are so deeply embedded in the language we use that we do not always notice them. However, languages vary both in the extent to which, and the ways in which, they employ metaphor and metonymy, and this can have important ramifications for those endeavouring to acquire a second language.

We saw in Chapter 3 that even advanced language learners tend to avoid using metaphorical senses of words, preferring to stick to more literal uses. This is the case even when the language to which they have been exposed contains a great deal of metaphor. There are two possible explanations for this. The first is that for some reason they have not noticed the metaphorical uses of language that are present in the input to which they are exposed. Metaphorical word meanings may not be salient to them, or they have not learned to pay attention to them. A second explanation could be that the metaphorical meanings do exist in their passive vocabulary but have not yet crossed into their active vocabulary, possibly because they lack the confidence to use them correctly. Either way, these findings suggest that language learners need to be helped to use metaphor appropriately in the target language.

They may also need help in understanding metaphor. Picken (2007) reports that when his Japanese learners of English encounter conventional metaphoric language in English, they tend to find it highly novel and creative. They focus on the basic senses and try to use these to understand the meanings in context. This finding is in keeping with other recent work in the area (e.g. Kecskes, 2006), which shows that the basic senses of metaphoric expressions tend to be more salient for language learners than for native speakers, and that language learners are thus more likely than native speakers to attempt to decompose metaphoric expressions. This work has important implications for language learning and teaching, as it suggests that the metaphor/idiom comprehension strategies used by language learners do not necessarily resemble those used by native speakers, and that theories that are based on first language processing cannot automatically be transferred to the second language classroom. If learners are processing metaphor in a much more mechanical way than native speakers, then this could be exploited for language learning purposes.

There is a great deal to be said about the teaching and learning of metaphor in SLA and a book-length treatment of the subject can be found in Littlemore and Low (2006a). My aim here is not to repeat the ideas that were presented in that book; rather, it is to evaluate the *cognitive linguistic* view of metaphor, and recent developments in that area, in terms of their applications to language learning, and to report on developments that have taken place since the publication of that book. I begin by outlining conceptual metaphor theory (CMT), and then discuss some challenges that have led to the theory itself being developed and refined. Throughout the chapter, I focus on how these developments relate to second language learning and teaching.

5.2 Conceptual metaphor theory

According to conceptual metaphor theory, our ability to engage in higher-order reasoning and deal with abstract concepts is related to our more direct physical interactions with the world by means of a number of conceptual metaphors. For instance, we relate the abstract concept of moving forward through time to the physical experience of moving forward through space by means of the conceptual metaphor MOVEMENT THROUGH TIME IS MOVEMENT THROUGH PHYSICAL SPACE. This conceptual metaphor gives rise to expressions such as 'looking back', 'let's take this forward', 'moving on', and so on. Through the process of embodiment (which will be discussed later in the book), 'understanding' and 'thinking' are often expressed in terms of 'seeing', as in expressions such as 'I see what you mean'.

Thus, according to CMT, conceptual metaphors are metaphors that we have in our minds, which allow us to produce and understand abstract concepts. The theory was first expounded by Lakoff and Johnson (1980), who argued that conceptual metaphors structure how people perceive, how they think and what they do. According to Lakoff (1993), conceptual metaphors represent habitual ways of thinking, in which people metaphorically construe abstract concepts such as time, emotions, and feelings, in terms of more concrete entities.

Conceptual metaphors are usually expressed in an A IS B format, using capital letters. For example, in the conceptual metaphor, PROGRESS THROUGH TIME IS FORWARD MOTION, progress through time (an abstract concept) is viewed metaphorically as forward motion (a more concrete entity). 'Forward motion' constitutes the **source domain** and 'progress through time' constitutes the **target domain**. This conceptual metaphor might be seen to underlie expressions from the Bank of English such as (28)–(32):

(28) We need to *plan ahead*
(29) *Back in the spring* of 1754
(30) Now it's time to *move on*
(31) He was the right man *to take it forward*
(32) We can *look back to* Greek and Roman civilization

Lakoff (1993) describes the relationship between the two domains of a conceptual metaphor as a 'function', where specific properties of the source domain are 'mapped onto' the target domain. So in the conceptual metaphor PROGRESS THROUGH TIME IS FORWARD MOTION THROUGH A LANDSCAPE, properties of the source domain, FORWARD MOTION, such as the fact that it can be fast or slow, difficult or easy, straight or winding, are mapped onto the target domain of 'progress through time', allowing us to talk about 'time passing very quickly', 'having a supremely difficult time', or a 'time horizon' (Bank of English examples). The relationship is one way: progress through time is treated as forward motion, but forward motion is not treated as progress through time. Source domains are thus broad, often complex, cluster-like categories that can provide a rich source of mappings (Littlemore and Low 2006a). As we saw in Chapter 4, they are sometimes described as **image schema ICMs** as they constitute one of the main ways in which encyclopaedic knowledge is stored and accessed. Conceptual metaphors are thought to be acquired through our physical interaction with the world, through the way in which we perceive the environment, move our bodies, and exert and experience force. Other people's habitual ways of selecting and using image schemas will also be influential.

One of the most productive conceptual metaphors is the conduit metaphor in which communication is seen as transfer from one person to another, allowing us to talk, for example, about 'conveying information', and 'getting the message across'. In the same way, 'argument' is often thought of in terms of 'warfare'; 'understanding' is often expressed in terms of 'seeing'; 'love' is often thought of in terms of a 'physical force'; and 'ideas' are often thought of in terms of 'objects'. Conceptual metaphors are thought to exist for every abstract concept that we have, although there is no one-to-one mapping; a single abstract concept can be understood through several conceptual metaphors, and a single conceptual metaphor can be used to explain several abstract concepts.

5.3 Conceptual and linguistic metaphor: cross-linguistic variation and implications for language learning

It is useful to distinguish between conceptual metaphor and linguistic metaphor. Conceptual metaphors are cognitive structures that are deeply embedded in our subconscious minds, whereas linguistic metaphors are surface-level linguistic phenomena. It is important to note that the precise words used to describe the two domains in a conceptual metaphor (like TIME and MONEY) are not important, or at least not crucial. This is very different from the situation with linguistic metaphors, where it is the exact words that constitute the metaphor (Littlemore and Low 2006a). Indeed, the whole point of a conceptual metaphor is that it stands apart from actual exemplars. Table 5.1 shows the main differences between conceptual metaphors and linguistic metaphors.

At times, our ability to understand linguistic metaphors (when they are first encountered) may rely on the successful identification of a relevant conceptual metaphor, at other times it may not. However, the

Table 5.1   The main differences between conceptual and linguistic metaphors

Conceptual metaphors e.g. ARGUMENT IS WARFARE	Linguistic metaphors e.g. **Mr Marshall had the knives out for Mr Manning**
They involve the drawing together of incongruous domains.	They involve the drawing together of incongruous words.
They are structures that are deeply embedded in the collective subconscious of a speech community.	They are surface level linguistic features.
They are thought to constitute a structured system upon which much abstract thought is based.	They are usually used to get a particular point across, or to perform a particular function.

ability to identify an appropriate conceptual metaphor in itself is rarely sufficient to allow a complete understanding of a linguistic metaphor. Additional metaphoric thinking is usually required, which takes into account the context in which the metaphor appears and the function that it is intended to perform. For example, in order to understand the metaphor *slavery was well on the road to extinction* it may be helpful (but not necessary) to think in terms of the conceptual metaphor PROGRESS THROUGH TIME IS FORWARD MOTION. However, further metaphoric thinking is required to understand that considerable progress has already been made and that there is likely to be no turning back. Thus conceptual metaphors sometimes help us to understand linguistic metaphors, but they are not always a necessary prerequisite, nor a sufficient condition.

Conceptual and linguistic metaphor present both a challenge and an opportunity to second language educators. Many conceptual metaphors are universal, whereas others vary from language to language. Even when the same conceptual metaphors exist across different languages, they are usually exploited in different ways (Deignan *et al.*, 1997; Kövecses, 2002). For example, Wu (2008) notes that the following metaphorical extensions of body parts are possible in Chinese, but not in English:

Car head (nose of car)
Boat head (nose of boat)
Brush head (tip of brush)
Eyebrow head (tip of eyebrow)

Road mouth (intersection)
Sleeve mouth (cuff)
Door mouth (doorway)
Carry heart (worry)
Put down heart (don't worry)
Open heart (happy)
Small heart (careful)
Hot heart (enthusiasm)
Concentrate heart (concentrate one's mind)

These expressions all appear to be based on conceptual metaphors that we have in English: THE HEAD IS THE FRONT OR THE TOP OF SOMETHING; A MOUTH IS AN OPENING; THE HEART IS THE SEAT OF THE EMOTIONS; but they exploit these conceptual metaphors in different ways.

A substantial body of research has investigated the benefits of using conceptual metaphors to structure vocabulary teaching, particularly with respect to phrasal verbs. An in-depth review of this research can be found in Littlemore and Low (2006a: chapter 2) so I will not repeat the discussion here. The main conclusion from our review was that, on balance, using conceptual metaphor in the language classroom is significantly more effective than less systematic approaches to vocabulary teaching, and that those learners who have been subjected to such an approach are able to extrapolate from what they have learned to help them understand new vocabulary. However, more systematic research is needed into the long-term benefits of the approach in terms of both retention and production.

5.4 Recent developments in CMT and their implications for language learning and teaching

Although conceptual metaphor theory has been hugely influential in cognitive linguistics and beyond, it has come in for a certain amount of criticism in recent years, which has led to the theory itself being developed and refined. Some of the main criticisms of conceptual metaphor theory have been that: the number of conceptual metaphors has had a tendency to proliferate; that they vary significantly in the extent to which they are employed and elaborated; and that there is a huge amount of overlap between them. Moreover, as Low (1999a,b, 2003) points out, although it may be tempting, for example, to identify the conceptual metaphor ARGUMENT IS WARFARE in a text containing the sentence 'Mr Marshall had the knives out for Mr Manning' the analyst has no proof that warfare was ever present in the writer's mind when he or she wrote this sentence. If the conceptual metaphor isn't in the writer's mind, then where is it? Could it be that it exists only in the analyst's mind?

5.4.1   Primary metaphor

In a partial response to criticisms such as these, Grady (1997) suggests that conceptual metaphors do not in fact constitute the most basic level of mapping. Instead, he proposes the idea of 'primary metaphors', which constitute a more fundamental type of metaphor (Grady and Johnson, 2002). Primary metaphors arise out of our embodied functioning in the world (Gibbs, 2006) and as such are more basic than conceptual metaphors. They include very basic concepts, such as CHANGE IS MOTION, HELP IS SUPPORT, and CAUSES ARE PHYSICAL SOURCES. One primary metaphor can often underlie several conceptual metaphors. For example, the primary metaphor EXPERIENCE IS A VALUED POSSESSION is held to underlie the conceptual metaphors DEATH IS A THIEF, A LOVED ONE IS A POSSESSION and OPPORTUNITIES ARE VALUABLE OBJECTS.

Primary metaphors are experiential, in that they result from a projection of basic bodily experiences onto abstract domains. As such, they are representative of a wider view of human cognition that gives a central role to embodiment. Proponents of embodied cognition argue that we understand abstract concepts in terms of our physical experiences with the world, and that the two are impossible to separate. Primary metaphors thus constitute a more clearly delimited, cognitive, embodied phenomenon, and lend themselves much more readily to rigorous empirical testing than conceptual metaphor. A discussion of the potential applications of embodiment theory to language teaching and learning can be found in Chapter 7.

5.4.2   Creative metaphor

Another criticism of conceptual metaphors is that they often give only a partial explanation of more creative linguistic metaphors, and the relationship between the two is unclear. In order to address this criticism, Goatly (1997) has extended conceptual metaphor theory to take account of the more creative extensions of conceptual metaphors. Instead of conceptual metaphors, he refers to 'root analogies'. He uses this term to reflect the fact that the original analogy often remains hidden and its relationship to the creative expression is not always clear, in much the same way as the link between a flower and the root of the plant that produced the flower is alive, yet unobtrusive. To illustrate his point, Goatly cites the expression 'the algebra was the glue they were stuck in'. This novel metaphorical expression is a creative extension of the root analogy DEVELOPMENT IS FORWARD MOVEMENT but the relationship is complex and not immediately apparent. The root is there, but it cannot actually be seen. Thus although creative metaphors are related at some level to conceptual metaphor, the link is often less than apparent. For language teaching purposes, it may therefore be appropriate to work at a linguistic, rather than a conceptual level, when dealing with creative metaphor.

The introduction to this chapter suggested that even advanced learners tend to avoid using metaphor in the target language, and that they tend to see even conventional metaphor as being somehow 'creative'. This suggests that it may be worth trying to help learners to develop their ability to understand and produce what they perceive as 'creative' metaphor. In an attempt to do this, Littlemore and Azuma (forthcoming) conducted a small exploratory study into the relative effects of attribute-matching and *gestalt* training (see below) on the ability of Japanese university-level learners of English to understand and produce metaphoric expressions in English. We were particularly interested in helping these students to think of possible metaphoric extensions of word meaning in English. We gave the students pre- and post-tests in which they had to: (a) come up with possible meanings for metaphoric expressions in English that they had not encountered before, and (b) create their own metaphoric extensions of everyday English words. The students were divided into two groups and both groups were given pre- and post-tests to measure these skills. In the next part of the study, the training session, the participants were divided into two groups. The first group was given the attribute-matching training, and the second group was given the *gestalt* training.

In the attribute-matching sessions, the students were given a brief introduction to the idea of attributes, and of their role in metaphor. After this, they were asked to think of all the attributes that might be activated by the linguistic metaphor, 'my teacher is a witch' (for example, they might identify relevant attributes as being the fact that she is female, unkind, and maybe ugly). Next, they were asked to match three famous people with a series of shapes, and to list the reasons for their choices. The instruction to list the reasons for their choices was designed to activate detailed consideration of their relevant attributes. In the final exercise, the students were asked to think about the three famous people and to decide for each, what colour, animal and food they would be, and to give reasons for their choices. The students in the *gestalt*-training group were first asked to match a series of emotions with a series of shapes. They were not asked to think about the reasons for their choices, but simply to use their 'gut feeling'. They were then asked to sketch shapes that corresponded to a further set of emotions and sounds, again without any form of analysis. Then, like the attribute-matching group, they were given the 'famous people' exercises, but they were not asked to explain any of their choices. We found that the students who had received the attribute-matching training made significant progress in their ability to metaphorically extend word meanings, but that the students who had received the *gestalt* training made no progress. We thus concluded from this tentative study that attribute-matching training may facilitate this aspect of metaphoric competence in second language learners. This finding supports the idea introduced at the beginning of this chapter that language learners deal with metaphor in a much more mechanical, analytic way than native speakers. Teaching activities that are designed to help learners deal with creative metaphor should take account of this fact.

5.4.3 Metaphor and phraseology

Another criticism of conceptual metaphor theory has been that the examples used to illustrate the conceptual metaphors are not taken from real data. Significant efforts are now being made to address this issue, many of which are reported in Stefanowitsch and Gries (2006). The studies reported in this volume use language corpora, not only to identify examples of conceptual metaphors, but also to refine and develop conceptual metaphor theory itself. This approach allows for a more systematic assessment of the types of source domains that feature in different genres, and of the complex interplay between conceptual and linguistic metaphor. In the same vein, Deignan (2005) has observed that the phraseological patterns surrounding the metaphorical senses of a word often differ from those surrounding its more literal senses. Phraseological patterning is thus likely to make an important contribution to the creation of meaning. The fact that phraseology has been shown to be such an important carrier of meaning indicates that it must be taken into account when working with metaphor in the second language classroom. Any approaches that involve a focus on conceptual metaphor will need to be supplemented by other approaches that help students to use metaphor in phraseologically appropriate ways.

5.4.4 Metaphor as a dynamic process

Although classic conceptual metaphor theory tends to see metaphor in a rather static sense, it is increasingly being viewed as a dynamic cognitive process (e.g. Ruiz de Mendoza and Mairal Uson, 2007). In other words, identifying metaphoric links between concepts is something that we do on a regular basis, and it contributes to our ability to understand and extract meaning from our environment. In a similar vein, Cameron and Deignan (2006) focus on the way in which metaphor emerges in discourse. For them, metaphor understanding has as much to do with one's previous exposure to language as with any preexistent 'conceptual metaphors'. They see metaphor as something that emerges from the complex interplay between various social and psychological factors. By viewing human interaction as a complex system in which individual, small events can produce changes that are way out of proportion with their original significance, Cameron and Deignan are able to show how metaphors emerge in an apparently random manner, with specific, often very narrow, pragmatic meanings and fixed phraseologies, neither of which are directly translatable between languages.

According to Cameron and Deignan (*ibid.*), successful metaphor acquisition by a second language learner would require them to encode three types of information. Firstly, they would need to acquire the relevant *linguistic* information, and be aware of the kinds of lexico-grammatical patterns that typically accompany the metaphor. Secondly, they would need to acquire the relevant *conceptual* information, and be aware of what conceptual metaphor it relates to. Thirdly they would need to acquire the relevant *pragmatic* information, and know what kind of evaluative slant the metaphor typically conveys and what kinds of contexts and genres it is usually found in. Conceptual metaphor theory could help them with the second of these aims, but in terms of effective communication, this is arguably the least important of the three.

The situation is further complicated by the fact that different metaphorical meanings emerge in different discourse settings. Not every discourse community uses metaphor in the same way, and many communities have their own metaphors (with corresponding phraseologies) that are related to, but different from, more mainstream usage. This presents a challenge to language learners, as they need to develop sufficient cognitive flexibility to understand and make use of these subtly different meanings. Metaphoric utterances do not carry fully specified, pre-packaged meanings; their meaning needs to be 'soft assembled' in real time by the hearer or reader (Gibbs, 2006) using contextual cues and drawing on their own encyclopaedic knowledge. Activities that are designed to promote metaphoric competence thus need to help learners to deal with the dynamic nature of metaphor.

5.4.5   Conceptual metaphor and blending theory

Another important cognitive linguistic theory which has huge implications for conceptual metaphor theory is **blending theory** (Fauconnier and Turner, 1998, 2002). According to blending theory, the two parts of a metaphor come together in a separate domain or 'blended space' and the result is a meaning that is not clearly related to either the target or the source domain. This meaning is sometimes referred to as *emergent structure*. Under blending theory, the source and target domains of a conceptual metaphor are not fixed, rigid entities where senses are mapped from one to the other. Rather they are dynamic and temporary 'mental spaces' that are constructed as and when they are needed, to communicate meaning, according to the context. Blending theory therefore sees metaphor as a much more dynamic, 'on-line' process than does conceptual metaphor theory. Blending theory has a wide variety of applications and extends well beyond the field of metaphor, but here we will stick to metaphor. To illustrate both blending theory and the dynamic systems accounts of metaphor, let us look at the use of the expression 'yummy mummies' in the following extract, which is taken from *The Times* newspaper in the Bank of English:

> [This] will mean a small blip in Jenner's profits ... as the *yummy mummies* who gather at the school gates of Edinburgh's public schools cut back on their dress allowances to ensure little Mungo and Caledonia get the education they deserve.

A conceptual metaphor account of this expression would appeal to the metaphor DESIRE IS HUNGER but there is far more to the expression 'yummy mummies' than this. It is clear from this extract that the expression is meant to arouse a certain amount of contempt in the reader. Yummy mummies are not something that one would aspire to be. Although they are considered attractive, they are also portrayed as being shallow, competitive, and obsessed with their children's education and their own appearance. Under a blending theory account, these extra connotations emerge from the blend of a number of mental spaces including desire and hunger, but also parenting, stereotypical views of women, wealth, and so on. What a dynamic systems account adds to this analysis is a consideration of the point in time that the expression became popular. The expression arose from a complex inter-action of factors including current issues, events and attitudes, as well as the fact that it contains assonance and alliteration (see Chapter 8). Whether or not the expression remains in the language will depend on the way in which these factors continue to interact. It summed up a particular attitude towards a particular group of people at a particular moment in British history. The challenges that these cultural compo-nents of metaphor present to second language learners are discussed in the following section.

Thus we can see that metaphor comprehension does not always involve a straightforward transfer from the source to the target domain. New meanings emerge that cannot be attributed to either domain. This presents a challenge to language learners, as the meanings can-not always be worked out analytically. In such cases, learners need to be provided with sufficient contextual cues to allow them to infer the additional semantic or pragmatic content of the metaphor.

Blending theory can also account for findings with regard to the pro-duction of metaphors by language learners. In a study of the use of metaphor by intermediate Polish students of English in their academic writing, Koltun (2006) found considerable evidence of the transfer of Polish linguistic and conceptual metaphors into English. He also found a number of other metaphors that do not exist either in Polish or in English and that had apparently emerged from the learning context. This finding could also be attributable to the over-extension of concep-tual metaphors that learners have identified in their own language and in the target language.

5.5 Concluding comments

In this chapter, I have outlined the theory of conceptual metaphor and mentioned several recent developments in the field. I have argued that a focus on conceptual metaphors may take language learners some way towards the development of metaphoric competence in the target lan-guage, but that it is equally important for them to develop an awareness of discourse constraints and the relevant lexico-grammatical patterns that signal metaphorical uses of words in the target language. Learn-ers also need to be equipped with appropriate skills that will allow them to deal with metaphor as it emerges in discourse, and understand new metaphorical meanings with which words are imbued by different discourse communities. Although language learners have a natural tendency to process metaphor analytically, drawing on their knowledge of the basic sense of the word, at times they need to be encouraged to focus more on contextual cues, as entirely new meanings can emerge from the blend. In the next chapter, we turn to a very close relation of metaphor: metonymy.

6
'You'll find Jane Austen in the basement'... or will you? Metonymy and Second Language Learning

6.1 Introductory comments

Recently, I had a conversation with a postgraduate student from Singapore who had a part-time job at the university nursery. She told me that when she first began working at the nursery she had been puzzled by the expression 's/he's got a loose nappy', which was used frequently by the nursery staff to talk about one of the babies. Whenever she heard this, she duly checked that the baby's nappy was fitted correctly. It was only after a few days in the nursery that she realised the expression did not actually mean that the nappy was literally loose, but meant, in fact, that the nappy needed changing. It was not the nappy itself that was loose, but the bowels of the baby in question (Tang, 2007). What she had not understood was that the expression 'loose nappy' was not being used literally, but *metonymically*.

Metonymy is the mental and linguistic process where one thing is used to refer to something that it is related to, or, more often, to something that it forms only a part of. Indeed, like metaphor, it is thought by cognitive linguists to be a fundamental component of human cognition, as it allows us to use what we know to infer information about what we do not know. It allows us to extrapolate from our limited experience of the world to draw hypotheses about things that we cannot actually see or experience first-hand. Like metaphor, metonymy is as much a cognitive process as a linguistic one. To illustrate this, I would like to mention a brief anecdote from my school days. At my school there was a 'quiet study room' where pupils would go to study at lunchtime and break time. This study room was often 'supervised' by a very strict teacher who sat at the front desk watching the pupils very carefully and pouncing on them if they talked to one another. Whenever he took a short break and left the room, he would leave his glasses on the desk looking at all the pupils. Such was the strength of the personality of this teacher that we pupils would continue to remain silent, even when only his glasses remained in the room 'looking' at us. This demonstrates the power of metonymic thinking (where the glasses stood for the actual presence of the teacher) and illustrates that metonymy is not always simply a linguistic phenomenon. We regularly engage in metonymic thinking such as this, which means that the language we use is littered with both novel and conventional metonymic expressions. As Gibbs (1994: 320) argues, metonymy is ubiquitous in language because it is a property of our conceptual system. Despite its ubiquity, metonymy has received relatively little treatment in the language teaching literature, but as we will see in this chapter, it is something that language learners need to be able to recognize and use. The two main reasons for this are that metonymy serves a variety of important functions in language, and that the way in which it is used varies significantly across languages.

I begin this chapter by looking at what is meant by metonymy, and exploring the interactions between conceptual and linguistic metonymy and between metonymy and metaphor. I then go on to describe the functions performed by metonymy and look at the challenges that these present to language learners. I close with a few proposals as to how language learners might be helped to deal with metonymy in the target language.

6.2   Conceptual and linguistic metonymy

Metonymy is the mental and linguistic process where one thing is used to stand for something that it is related to. Linguistic metonymy is used all the time in all types of discourse. One example of linguistic metonymy is the use of a place name to refer to the people in that place. For example, 'the White House' and 'Number 10' are used respectively to refer to the US and British Governments. By extension, metonymy is also present in terms such as 'Iraq has invaded Kuwait', where 'Iraq' refers to the Iraqi army, not the whole of Iraq. We can see from these examples that metonymy is necessary, as it provides us with a ready-made shorthand that we can use to make ourselves understood without having to spell everything out. As we can see in the 'Iraq invaded Kuwait' example, it can also be used for political purposes, to avoid placement of blame and so on. We will return to the functions performed by metonymy below. For now, I would like to look a bit more at the characteristics of metonymy itself, and introduce some of the terminology that is used to describe it.

As with metaphor, the terms **topic** and **vehicle** are sometimes used. In the White House example above, the White House is the vehicle of the metonymy, and the United States government is the topic. Like metaphor, metonymy can be **conceptual** (conceptual metonymies expressed in small capitals in the discussion which follows), or **linguistic** (expressed in lower-case). As with metaphor, in cognitive linguistic theory, a small number of higher-order *conceptual* metonymies give rise to a wide range of metonymic expressions. For example, the conceptual metonymy, PRODUCER FOR PRODUCT underlies linguistic metonymies, such as: 'you'll find Jane Austen in the basement' (heard in a bookshop) or 'Is that a Picasso?' In these examples, what people are referring to are of course 'books that have been written by Jane Austen' and 'a painting by Picasso'. The conceptual PART FOR WHOLE metonymy lies behind linguistic metonymies, such as 'nice set of wheels' or 'he fell asleep at the wheel'. Here different parts of a car are used to refer to the car as a whole, but they focus the reader's attention on different things. ACTION FOR COMPLEX EVENT metonymies are used when we refer to a whole chain of events by simply mentioning the action that triggers them. For example, to refer to the process of making a cup of tea, we might just say 'I'll put the kettle on', or to refer to our intention to leave a party, we might say 'I'm getting my coat'. It would be pedantic and strange to list the whole series of events in each of these cases; they are simply inferred by the listener, based on their familiarity with the 'script'. MEMBER FOR CATEGORY metonymies involve mentioning just one member of a category to refer to the whole category. For example, we might use the word 'aspirin' to refer to any painkilling tablet. In DEFINING PROPERTY FOR CATEGORY metonymies, we refer to the most interesting or salient property of something and use it to stand for the whole thing. These are often used about people; for example, we might talk about the 'love interest' in a film to refer to an attractive actor. In POSSESSED FOR POSSESSOR metonymies we refer to the thing that someone owns when what we are actually talking about is the person themselves; for example, we might say 'he married money' to mean that he married a rich woman. We can see from this example that there is some overlap here with the DEFINING PROPERTY FOR CATEGORY metonymy. Finally, in CONTAINER FOR CONTAINED metonymies, we use the container to refer to its contents, so for example, when pouring out orange juice, we might ask someone if they would 'like a glass'. As with metaphor, there are limitations on the extent to which conceptual metonymy can help us to understand and explain the wide variety of linguistic metonymies that occur in everyday discourse, although conceptual metonymy does give a rough indication of the more common types of linguistic metonymy that we may expect to find.

Whether or not conceptual metonymies exist in the mind in any kind of 'rigid' format is unknown, but there is certainly plenty of evidence of metonymy in everyday language, where it acts as a kind of quick reference, particularly amongst speakers who are very familiar with one another. According to some cognitive linguists (e.g. Ruiz de Mendoza and Mairal Uson, 2007), metonymy is a generic 'on-line' cognitive process in which the most salient or accessible aspect of a phenomenon is used to refer to, or in cognitive linguistic terminology, to 'gain mental access to', the phenomenon itself. A further interesting fact about metonymy is the way it appears to underlie the verbalization of nouns. Often, when nouns are transformed into verbs, there is a metonymic focus on one feature of those nouns which allows the transformation to take place. For example, we might talk about 'pencilling it in', 'legging it' or 'elbowing someone out of the way'. As we can see in these examples, as linguistic metonymies become conventional, they often acquire semi-fixed phraseologies in the same way that metaphors do.

6.3   The relationship between metonymy and metaphor

There are several overlaps between metaphor and metonymy, which means that it is often difficult to tease them apart. The main differences between them are that whereas metaphor tends to draw comparisons between apparently unrelated entities, metonymy uses one entity to refer to another entity to which it is already related, or even to refer to an entity that it already forms part of (a relationship that is sometimes referred to as *synecdoche*. It is therefore often said that metaphor performs an evaluative function whereas metonymy tends to serve more of a referential function; however, this is not always the case, and it is often very difficult to work out whether an expression is metaphor, metonymy, or both. An interesting idea that has been proposed by Goossens (1990) is that a great deal of metaphor actually starts life as metonymy, and that over time as the links between the source and target domains become more distant, metonymy shades into metaphor. For example, if we take the expression: 'There's no need to get so hot under the collar' (BNC data) we can see that it may have started life as a literal expression (where someone actually became hot under the collar when under pressure); but over time, 'hot under the collar' came to stand metonymically for feeling stressed or angry; and finally there was no suggestion of anyone literally feeling 'hot under the collar', so we have metaphor. Indeed, the expression, which is nearly always used about someone else, rather than oneself, has acquired a slight distancing feel to it; people who are described as 'getting hot under the collar' are often (though not always) being gently scorned, as in the following Bank of English citation: '*The Mail* got itself all hot under the collar at the news'. This process is described by Goossens as 'metaphor from metonymy' or 'metaphtonomy'. When working with metaphor and metonymy in the language classroom, it may be counter-productive to focus on the differences between them, as this can be very confusing for learners, and much of the time they operate in conjunction anyway. Bearing this caveat in mind, let us now turn to the functions of metonymy. We will see below that metonymy is used to perform a wide variety of functions, which means that it is well worth making language learners aware of its existence.

6.4   The functions of metonymy

Although the functions of metaphor have been widely studied, this is less true for metonymy. It is important to be aware of the different things that metonymy does as these are what make it important for language learners. The most widely cited purpose of metonymy is to serve a **referential function** where it acts as a kind of communicative shorthand, allowing us to refer to things without going through a lengthy descriptive process each time we do so. The oft-cited example (from Lakoff and Johnson, 1980: 35) of the waitress, who is talking to one of the other waitresses in a café, and who refers to one of the customers as 'the ham sandwich sitting at Table 8' is a good example of this. Both she and the other waitress know what is meant here, i.e. that she is referring to the customer, not the sandwich he ordered, but it may sound odd to an outsider if he or she interprets it more literally. The fact that metonymy provides a quick and easy way of referring to things makes it popular among discourse communities. **Discourse communities** are groups of people who work together with explicit, shared goals, and who often share a particular linguistic code (Swales, 1990). Indeed, it appears that discourse communities make frequent use of metonymy, often to build cohesion and in some cases to provide barriers to entry. It has been suggested that the use of metaphor is a key defining characteristic of discourse communities (Partington, 1998), but as we will see below, the use of metonymy can also contribute to the creation of a discourse community's identity (Littlemore, forthcoming). Many of us have been in situations where we have recently started new jobs and have simply not understood what our colleagues are talking about because they make extensive use of metonymic shorthand. For instance, at the University of Birmingham, 'The Aston Webb', 'Westmere', and 'the corridor' all refer to specific places on campus. All are used to refer to specific groups of people who work in those places, who do particular jobs (in this case, they refer respectively to the university management, postgraduate, and undergraduate teaching in the English Department). The names of the places are used to refer metonymically to the activity that is carried out in those buildings. Similarly, a colleague who attended an all-boys' school that was conveniently located next door to an all-girls' school wondered why the place where boys and girls were allowed to mix was referred to as 'Winterbourne'. Winterbourne also happens to be the name of a nearby botanical garden where girls and boys from the respective schools used to meet. When the meeting place moved, the name moved with it and although 'Winterbourne' is still the place where boys and girls from the respective schools still meet, it is nowhere near the Botanical Gardens that bear the same name. This kind of folk history can make a very powerful contribution to the creation of a discourse community, and the opacity of the resulting expressions can serve to keep outsiders out.

Metonymy can thus serve an important **relationship-building function** within discourse communities. This is present even at primary school level, as Nerlich *et al.* (1999) note. They report on a child's use of the expression 'I love being a sandwich' to mean that he liked being one of the children who are allowed to bring in a lunchbox, rather than eating a school dinner. The child's use of the expression is likely to have come from the institutional discourse of the school where defining characteristics are often used by teachers to refer to groups of children. My own children often report similar instances in their school, where the teacher will refer to groups of pupils as 'green table', 'guitars', 'dinners', and so on. As metonymy is used to build relationships within a community it can also presumably be used to keep people out of that discourse community. The deliberate use of metonymies that only an insider will understand in the presence of outsiders might thus be expected to serve a powerful **distancing** function.

Metonymy can also serve as a hedging device, or as a form of **euphemism**. For instance, the 'loose nappy' example above provides a perfect example of metonymy being used to avoid talking directly about something that may be a little bit embarrassing. In the subsequent study that she made of the nursery discourse, Tang (2007) noted several cases where metonymy was employed in the service of euphemism. For example, the word *boisterous* was used to euphemistically describe naughty and annoying children. These findings are perhaps to be expected, as one of the main functions of metonymy is to provide an indirect way of referring to things, and euphemism requires indirectness. Related to this is Chantrill and Mio's (1996) finding that metonymy is used by public speakers as a rhetorical strategy in which they personalize and simplify issues that are deemed to be too complex for their audiences.

Although it is not always stressed in the literature, metonymy is often used for **evaluative purposes**. This was also evident in Tang's (2007) nursery discourse data. She notes the frequent use by members of staff of the word *upstairs* in expressions such as 'I don't know what upstairs would think of that' or 'what is upstairs going to come up with next!'. 'Upstairs' is the location of the nursery office, where the senior management are located. The use of the word *upstairs* by ordinary members of staff was often used either as a signal of negative evaluation of the senior management, or as a distancing device reflecting something of an 'us and them' mentality. This distancing strategy appears to be a common feature of institutional discourse, as we can see in the following sequences (33)–(34), taken from the Bank of English:

> (33) the whizz kid managers 'upstairs' don't take any notice of experienced people
> (34) If the upstairs don't get you the downstairs will

Indeed, this usage is particularly evident when when *upstairs* or *downstairs* is preceded by *them*. Bank of English searches for *'them + upstairs'* and *'them + downstairs'* show that the bosses are nearly always 'upstairs' and the workers are nearly always 'downstairs':

> (35) It still shocked them upstairs a bit
> (36) Bribed them upstairs with unsuitable videos
> (37) Tell them downstairs that I have specifically requested you to...
> (38) tell them downstairs that I insist.

The use of metonymy for evaluative purposes appears to be common in everyday English. For example, it appears in colloquial tautologies such as 'boys will be boys', where the second use of the word *boys* is a metonymic reference to their more negative characteristics. Interestingly, the majority of citations for the string 'boys will be boys' in the Bank of English are actually talking not about boys, but about *men*. So here we have another metonymic shift from 'boys' to 'men'. The citations are all evaluative in that they either condone the fact that men can behave badly, or criticize the fact that this is commonly accepted behaviour, often by using the expression ironically or in inverted commas.

Items of clothing appear to be particularly susceptible to evaluative metonymic usage. This is presumably because the habitual wearers of those clothes leave their metonymic imprint on them, and the characteristics of the wearers are metonymically transferred to the clothes themselves. For example, a search for the string *'the trousers'* in the Bank of English results in 332 citations, of which 86 contain the expression 'wearing/wears/wore the trousers'. Of these citations, the vast majority (many of which are from the tabloid press) reflect the underlying assumption that it should be the man who wears the trousers in a relationship, and express varying degrees of disapproval of types of relationships where this is not the case. In the remaining small number of citations, this prejudice is itself evaluated in some way as in: 'women have been wearing the trousers for years' or metaphorically transported into other domains: 'As far as cricket was concerned, Australia wore the trousers all day at Worcester'. This is a good example of how closely metonymy and metaphor sometimes interact.

To take another example, also in the domain of clothes, *'the suits'* appears 401 times in the Bank of English, and of these, less than half actually refer to literal suits. The remaining citations refer to either legal suits or metonymically to the people in charge of businesses. Of these, approximately 190 involve this metonymic usage, and in the vast majority of these citations, the evaluation is negative, focusing attention on (for example) the anonymity of the people in charge, their lack of imagination, or simply offering a negative evaluation of the fact that they are in charge. Examples include:

(39) The best part of working at night (is that) the suits have gone home.

(40) I don't even get a birthday card from the suits who run the company.

Interestingly, the string *'the suits* + preposition' is significantly more likely to coincide with a metonymic use of 'the suits' than any other use. Examples include: 'another turgid meeting with the suits in personnel' and 'Dunst had to confirm to the suits at Disney that she wasn't taking method acting too far'.

An interesting feature of metonymy, which is closely related to evaluation, is the fact that it can also be used **to create humour**. The humour is usually achieved by re-literalizing a fairly conventional metonymy, making both the metonymic and the literal interpretations available for processing at once. For example, the 'wears the trousers' search mentioned above revealed several humorous citations, such as 'she wears the trousers, he wears the sarong'; 'he wears the trousers – and what trousers!'; and 'there's no doubt about who wears the trousers, let alone the thongs'. Interestingly, the expression 'the suits' is never used for humorous purposes in the Bank of English, indicating that a metonymic expression perhaps needs to be reasonably fixed and conventional before it can be successfully re-literalized to create humour. Because the metonymic use of 'the suits' is less mainstream than that of 'wearing the trousers' there would perhaps be more scope for confusion if one were to try to re-literalize it for humorous effect.

The use of metonymy can also serve as a kind of deliberate **vague language** (Channell, 1994), thus serving to reduce the directness or assertiveness of an utterance, or to prevent oneself from sounding too pedantic. The expression 'loose nappy' which was referred to at the beginning of this section is an excellent example of this, where a vague euphemism is used to avoid talking directly about faeces. Interestingly, in the area of gender studies, it has been shown that women tend to make more use than men of both vague language (Channell, *ibid.*) and of metonymy (Gallop, 1987). Although these findings are somewhat tentative, it could be that there is a relationship here. The main communicative functions of both vague language and metonymy are to sound less direct and to maintain an atmosphere of friendliness and informality: all of these features have been identified as being characteristic of female discourse (Coates, 2003). Regardless of whether it is favoured by men or women, we can conclude that metonymic vague language can be used to perform interpersonal, relationship-building, and affective functions.

Finally, metonymy plays an important role in **pragmatic inferencing**, which is necessary when trying to understand indirect speech acts (Barcelona, 2006). An indirect speech act is a speech act whose actual meaning in context (or 'illocutionary force') is different from the individual meanings of the words. Meaning therefore has to be inferred. For example, someone might say 'It's very stuffy in here isn't it?' when what they actually mean is 'Please open the window'. It is well documented that the identification of a speaker's communicative intention in an indirect speech act requires some inferential work on the part of the hearer. For example, if there is a cake on the table in the dining room, and a visitor to the house utters 'Mmm, that looks good', the chances are that they are trying to convey the message 'Can I have a piece of that cake?' Traditional speech act theorists rarely discuss the nature of the inferential work involved in interpreting utterances such as these. Increasingly however, researchers in cognitive linguistics have proposed a role for metonymic thinking in this area (Gibbs, 1994; Panther and Thornburg, 1998; Perez-Hernendez and Ruiz de Mendoza, 2002). In cognitive linguistics, metonymic thinking is a means by which we are able to use a given referent to gain access to a broader script or, as we saw in Chapter 4, an ICM, which we then use to understand a speaker's intention. In the cake example above, the broader script that is evoked through the utterance 'mm.., that looks good' is one in which the host offers the guest a piece of cake and the guest accepts it. This topic is discussed in more depth below.

We have seen in this section that metonymy can be used to perform a variety of functions. As well as performing a straightforward referential function, it can be used for evaluating, hedging, relationship-building, distancing, placing and avoiding blame, and dealing sensitively with potentially face-threatening situations. In each of these cases, successful interpretation of the metonymy involves making inferences that go well beyond the words that are actually used.

6.5   What challenges might metonymy present to second language learners?

Metonymy is likely to present a significant challenge to second language learners, largely because it is often very subtle and interlocutors may not realize that it is presenting a problem. In her study of the nursery workplace discourse, Tang (2007) observed that the nursery staff appeared, at least superficially, to adjust their language in order to make it easier for her to understand. They did this by using repetition, exaggerating their intonation patterns, speaking more slowly and even (much to her annoyance) using the same sort of language that they used with the children. However, one thing that they did not do, which made them particularly difficult to understand, was to explain the instances of metonymy mentioned above. Even though she is highly proficient in English, it took Tang several days to work out exactly what was meant by 'loose nappies' and 'upstairs', and other metonymies, such as 'numbers' (to refer to the register) and 'visits' (to refer to trial periods where a child spends time with the older group), and to some extent this delayed her successful entry into the discourse community. It is probably a result of the deeply embedded nature of these metonymies, the fact that they are used so frequently, and the fact that, on the surface of it, the language used is very simple, that the native speakers did not think to adjust their metonymic language.

Much of the time, when metonymy is used to perform straightforward referential functions, it is unlikely to be problematic for language learners. However, some referential uses of metonymy rely heavily on cultural scripts, and these may prove more problematic. For instance, in Spanish, there is an expression *mas gambas*, which roughly translates as 'more large prawns'. This is a derogatory expression, used to describe the sort of people who are uninterested in issues such as politics and environment, and who are only worried about their day-to-day needs. Instead of worrying about important issues, they will simply sit in a bar and order 'more prawns'. Understanding this expression involves the activation of a great deal of cultural knowledge and conventional sets of evaluations, but the ability to use such an expression successfully would be a good indication of a high level of cultural competence. In the same way as some of the metonymic expressions used by the nursery community were characteristic of that community and were thus typical of insider language, this sort of expression performs the same function, but on a wider scale.

Another function of metonymy likely to present difficulties to language learners is euphemism. Not only do euphemistic expressions vary from language to language, but so do the subjects that people tend to be euphemistic about. Also, within the target-language culture, there will be a great deal of variation in terms of age, gender and social class as to what subjects are talked about euphemistically, and in terms of what language is conventionally used when doing so. Therefore, learning when and how to be euphemistic in a second language is likely to present a considerable challenge to the language learner. The 'how' part will often involve metonymy.

Metonymy in vague language can also present a challenge to language learners, as it is often difficult to judge the degree of metonymy intended. As an anecdotal example of this last function, a Japanese colleague was recently invited by an English family to visit them 'at Christmas'. She assumed that the invitation referred only to Christmas day and did not initially grasp the fact that 'Christmas' was being used metonymically to refer to the days surrounding Christmas.

The use of metonymy for evaluative purposes may also be difficult for language learners to grasp. For example, in Littlemore (2001) I cite an instance where an international student heard one of his lecturers talk about Margaret Thatcher's search for 'can-do' civil servants. He interpreted this expression as meaning 'able and worthy civil servants'. When asked to explain this interpretation, the student commented: 'The lecturer feels that the changes made by Thatcher could make it possible to select out a number of able and worthy Civil Servants who could perform their assigned duties properly'. This student appears to have missed the implication that 'can-do' civil servants are motivated, 'positive-thinking' people who are prepared to act. Misunderstanding metonymies such as these means that students are sometimes unable to assess how a situation is being evaluated.

As well as different functions, different *types* of metonymy are also likely to present different challenges to language learners. Languages vary in terms of the vehicle that is usually preferred in a given situation. The selection of an appropriate vehicle in metonymy is governed by a number of cognitive principles. Radden and Kövecses (2007) list three cognitive principles (human experience, perceptual salience, and cultural preferences); two communicative principles (the principle of clarity and the principle of relevance); and two overriding factors (rhetorical effects and socio-communicative effects). All of these principles and factors are likely to interact in different ways in different languages, making it very difficult for learners to select the appropriate vehicle for a metonymy if they are not already aware of it.

Typological data on the systematic differences between languages in the ways they use metonymy has revealed how different languages make use of metonymy in different ways (e.g. Panther and Thornburg, 2003). For example, in Japanese and German it is possible to use a RESULT FOR ACTION metonymy and to say 'I receive two kilos of tomatoes', which roughly translates as: 'Could you give me two kilos of tomatoes?' (Radden, 2005). In English, this construction would sound very strange, and almost presumptuous.

As with metaphor, linguistic manifestations of conceptual metonymies vary from language to language. For example, with respect to the MEMBER FOR CATEGORY metonymy, Barcelona (2004) carried out a cross-linguistic comparison of English and Spanish, using acceptability judgements of metonymic expressions where the names of famous people are used as 'paragons', standing for other people who have similar talents. Examples of these from the Bank of English include 'The Shakespeare of Welwyn Garden City' and 'the new British Picasso'. He found significant differences between the two sets of speakers, in terms of what type of person they felt was acceptable as a 'paragon', and what type of person was not.

The extent to which conceptual metonymies work across different languages has been studied in depth by Wu (2008). The results of her comparison between English and Chinese are shown in Table 6.1.

Table 6.1 Linguistic manifestations of conceptual metonymies in English and Chinese (Wu, 2008)

Conceptual metonymy	English example	Chinese example
PRODUCER FOR PRODUCT	'Hoover'	Doesn't work in Chinese
AGENT FOR ACTION	'Authoring a book'	Doesn't work in Chinese
PART FOR WHOLE	'Bums on seats'	'New hand on the road' (New hand stands for new driver)
WHOLE FOR PART	'The police turned up' 'The US invaded Iraq'	'Taipei is hot' (Taipei stands for the weather in Taipei)
ACTION FOR COMPLEX EVENT	'Let's get the kettle on'	'Stand up again' (Standing up refers to returning to a former position and restarting a new life after experiencing failure. It is comparable with the English expression 'get back on your feet'.
CATEGORY FOR MEMBER	'The pill' (To refer specifically to the contraceptive pill)	None found (possibly doesn't work in Chinese)
MEMBER FOR CATEGORY	'Aspirin' (To refer to any headache pill)	'My father is not Wong Young Chin' (Wong Young Chin was the richest man in China, therefore his name is used to stand for great wealth)
DEFINING PROPERTY FOR CATEGORY	'The love interest' 'Some muscle'	Doesn't work in Chinese
ACTION FOR OBJECT	'Can I have a bite?'	'Can I have a bite?'
CONTAINER FOR CONTAINED	'Do you want a glass?'	'Do you want another bowl?'

We can see from Table 6.1 that although many of the conceptual metonymies are productive in both English and Chinese, they are productive in different ways. Moreover, some conceptual metonymies that are productive in English do not appear to be productive in Chinese. A more in-depth study would undoubtedly reveal conceptual metonymies that are productive in Chinese, but not in English.

The different ways in which languages exploit metonymy, and the extent to which metonymic uses of language do and do not translate into other languages, is a fairly new area of study in cognitive linguistics. Researchers in this area generally work by looking at a single conceptual metonymy and comparing the ways in which it is exploited in two different languages. Findings from this research are likely to be a source of useful information for teachers of those languages, or for SLA researchers who are interested in issues such as L1 transfer and over/under-generalization. It is also important to bear in mind that metonymy does not always have to be seen as a barrier to learning. It can also serve as a device through which communication is facilitated, and which thus provides further input and opportunities for learning. As with metaphor, there are likely to be benefits in drawing the learner's attention to conceptual metonymies that exist in both the student's native language and the target language. In the following section, we address the issue of how language learners can be helped to understand and produce metonymy.

6.6   How might language learners be helped to deal with metonymy?

Finding ways in which language learners can be helped to deal with metonymy is a challenging endeavour, as metonymy is often culturally based and is to a large extent idiosyncratic. It could be argued that adult learners in particular are adequately equipped with the sorts of inferencing skills required to work out the intended meaning when speakers use metonymy, so there is no real need to deal with it in the language classroom. However, the fact that metonymic thinking is so pervasive (Gibbs, 1994), combined with the fact that second language learning will often involve noticing that the target language uses metonymy in different ways from one's own, suggests that an explicit focus on L2 metonymies may be beneficial for language learners, especially if their attention is drawn to the ways in which metonymy can be used to perform the variety of communicative functions outlined above. One approach would be to present learners with diagrams such as the one in Table 6.1, and to ask them if they can think of any correspondences in their own language. They could also be taught metonymy through the use of images and actions. Research is needed, however, to assess the potential benefits of such approaches.

One area when an explicit focus on metonymy in the second language classroom may be particularly productive is indirect speech acts. We saw above that metonymy is used to motivate indirect speech acts. By making learners explicitly aware of the metonymic relationships that are typically involved in indirect speech acts, teachers could help learners to understand and use them more easily. In task-based learning and other communicative approaches, it is usually assumed that indirect speech acts are simply 'acquired' (see, for example, Dornyei and Thurrell, 1994). The predominant view is that because they are essentially 'unanalysable' the form–meaning relationships in indirect speech acts must simply be memorized. It is rarely recommended that learners should focus explicitly on the actual words used. Unfortunately, this approach to the learning of indirect speech acts does not appear to have been particularly successful. Kasper and Roever (2005) have observed that the indirect speech acts that are produced by learners tend to remain distinctly 'non-target-like' even at high levels of proficiency and that more work is needed to help learners both notice and comprehend them.

A more in-depth analysis of the role of metonymy in indirect speech acts may help both learners and their teachers to understand how they work. Helping them to *notice* the presence of metonymy would be a good way to start. It has already been shown that deep processing of metaphor by language learners significantly enhances retention (Boers, 2001, 2004) so there is a strong possibility that deep processing, and awareness-raising of the role of metonymy, will also aid comprehension and retention. Unfortunately, this claim remains untested as there has to date been very little empirical research in this area. The only studies that I am aware of are those conducted by Bouton (1994 a,b, 1999), who found that second language learners do not readily acquire the ability to understand implicature (i.e. indirect speech acts), even when they have spent months in the target language community. He found that drawing learners' attention to implicature can aid both noticing and comprehension, but he did not encourage his learners to explicitly explore the metonymy within the implicatures, which could have been a fruitful approach. A further interesting finding by Bouton (1988) points to cross-linguistic differences in the ability to interpret implicature in English. Bouton compared the ability of several groups of learners to understand implicature in English. These groups included native speakers of German, Chinese, Spanish and Portuguese. For example, one of the items in Bouton's test was as in (41):

(41) Mai-ling: Is it very cold out today?
       Susan: It's August

 a. It'll be nice and warm today. Don't worry.
 b. Yes, even though it's August it's very cold out.
 c. It's so warm for this time of year that it seems like August.
 d. Yes, we're sure having crazy weather aren't we?

The correct implicature, according to Bouton, is answer 'a'. Of the German-speaking participants, 100% opted for answer 'a', whereas only 38% of the Chinese participants in the study chose this answer. Another item was as in (42):

(42) Brenda: I just got a new dress. How do you like it?
       Sally: Well, there certainly are a lot of women wearing it this year. When did you get it?

 a. We can't tell from what she says.
 b. She thinks Brenda has good taste in clothes because she's right in style.
 c. She likes the dress but too many people are wearing it.
 d. She doesn't like it.

The correct answer, according to Bouton, is answer 'd'. The Chinese speakers in the study tended to favour answer 'b', whereas the Spanish/ Portuguese speakers tended to favour answer 'a', and the German speakers tended to prefer answer 'c'. According to Bouton, these differences are perhaps explainable in terms of the types of metonymic inferencing that are common in these students' first languages, and suggest a degree of transfer in the area. A possible teaching application of this might be to draw out L1 inferences and to point out different patterns in the target language.

If we *were* to encourage learners to explore the metonymies contained within indirect speech acts, then it is important to consider when might be the best time to do so. In terms of production, work by Kasper and Rose (2002) suggests that learners typically follow a five-stage sequence. At the first 'pre-basic' stage, learners will produce highly context-dependent phrases with no syntax (e.g. 'me no blue'). They then proceed to a second, 'formulaic stage', where they rely on unanalysed formulas and imperatives (e.g. 'Let's eat breakfast'). After that there is a third, 'unpacking', stage where the formulas start to include productive language use (e.g. 'Can you do another one for me?'). At the fourth, 'pragmatic expansion,' stage they are able to increase their use of mitigation and employ more complex syntax (e.g. 'Can I see it so I can copy it?') and at the fifth, 'fine-tuning', stage they are able to tune their requests to accommodate to their interlocutor (e.g. 'Should I put the kettle on?'). Following this sequence, the best time to introduce metonymic analysis of indirect speech acts might be in the later stages of acquisition, between stages 4 and 5. As far as comprehension is concerned, it may be useful to get students into the habit of analysing the metonymy in indirect speech acts from the early stages of learning, perhaps even by starting with an analysis of speech acts in their L1 so that they are able to understand how they function.

Another way to initiate a discussion of metonymy in the language classroom is via the English loanwords that exist in many languages. For example, Kay (1995: 70) reports the following loanwords in Japanese:

Loanword	Derivation	Meaning
pureigaido	play + guide	ticket office
wanpisu	one piece	dress
opun ka	open + car	convertible
pepa testu	paper test	written test
oda sutoppu	order + stop	last orders
hai sensu	high + sense	good taste in fashion
chiku dansu	cheek + dance	slow dance
naton tacchi	baton + touch	passing the baton

The metonymic basis of some of these expressions is very clear. For example, in 'cheek dance', the 'cheek' stands for the touching of the cheeks, in 'open + car', one aspect of the 'car' stands for the whole thing, and in 'baton + touch', the 'touch' stands for the passing of the baton. Research has already shown that loanwords can be used to build up a learner's passive vocabulary in English (Banta, 1981). If learners were made aware of the metonymic nature of some of these loan words, they could use this to work out the basic senses of their core constituents, thus developing their target language vocabulary further.

In this section I have outlined a few ways in which metonymy might be exploited in the second language classroom. Future research could usefully explore the benefits of explicit metonymy teaching in the classroom. It would also be useful to study cross-linguistic variation in metonymy use; findings from such studies could predict areas of difficulty that might be experienced by students, particularly in the area of indirect speech acts.

6.7 Concluding comments

In this chapter we have seen that metonymy, like metaphor, works at both a conceptual and a linguistic level, and that it is ubiquitous. It is used to perform a wide variety of functions, which means that it is important for language learners to be able to understand and produce it. Some types of metonymy may be harder for learners to grasp than others; these include highly culturally specific metonymies, and metonymies that underlie humour, euphemism and vague language. Moreover, the same conceptual metonymies are exploited in different ways and to different extents by different languages, which may also present challenges. More research is needed to investigate the nature of the problems that metonymy presents to second language learners, and to assess whether or not it is useful for teachers to focus explicitly on metonymy in the language classroom.

7

What Have Bees, Macaque Monkeys and Humans Got in Common? Embodied Cognition, Gesture and Second Language Learning

7.1 Introductory comments

For many years, natural historians have been aware of the strange, highly complex 'waggle dances' that bees perform for one another in the hive. It is only very recently that researchers have discovered that the function of these 'dances' is in fact to communicate to the other bees the exact location of sources of pollen and nectar. Debbie Hadley, a natural historian who specialises in the study of insects, describes these dances as follows:

> The honey bee first walks straight ahead, vigorously shaking its abdomen and producing a buzzing sound with the beat of its wings. The distance and speed of this movement communicates the distance of the foraging site to the others. Communicating direction becomes more complex, as the dancing bee aligns her body in the direction of the food, relative to the sun. The entire dance pattern is a figure-eight, with the bee repeating the straight portion of the movement each time it circles to the center again.
>
> Honey bees also use two variations of the waggle dance to direct others to food sources closer to home. The round dance, a series of narrow circular movements, alerts colony members to the presence of food within 50 meters of the hive. This dance only communicates the direction of the supply, not the distance. The sickle dance,

a crescent-shaped pattern of moves, alerts workers to food supplies within 50–150 meters from the hive. (http://insects.about.com/od/antsbeeswasps/p/honeybeecommun.htm)

The bees who are watching this dance understand this code, presumably by picturing or feeling themselves doing the flying. It is easy to see how the 'long crescent shaped patterns' correspond to the act of flying long distances, and how the 'narrow circular movements' correspond to the act of flying towards closer sources of food. The idea that these bees may feel themselves performing the actions that are being described to them in the dance, and that this may help them to understand the information it contains, is referred to as **embodied cognition** (see Gibbs, 2006; Lakoff and Johnson, 1999; Ozcaliskan, 2007).

It is not just bees that display evidence of possible embodied cognition. Research carried out on macaque monkeys suggests that when they watch other monkeys performing motor functions, the same neurons in the ventral pre-motor cortex fire as when they are carrying out those same motor functions for themselves. Interestingly, the corresponding area in the human brain where those neurons fire is Broca's area (Gallese *et al.*, 1996; Laccoboni, in press), which suggests that the activation found in the areas of the brains of macaque monkeys is serving some sort of pre-linguistic function. According to some researchers, this constitutes evidence for a strong link between action representation and language (Rizzolatti and Arbib, 1998).

So far so good, as far as bees and macaque monkeys are concerned, but what about humans? Although this is a relatively new area of research, early findings indicate that humans too are capable of embodied cognition. On a very basic, non-linguistic level, it has been observed that when we see a person performing a particular action, such as running, gripping a pencil, laughing or crying, the neural motor circuits that are activated in our brains are the same as those that are activated when we perform those actions ourselves. Simply watching the performance of an action thus triggers corresponding motoric mental imagery. The neurons thought to be responsible for this have been referred to as 'mirror neurons' (Gallese and Goldman, 1998). Mirror neurons are thought to be partly responsible for our ability to imitate, communicate with, and empathize with others (McGlone *et al.*, 2002; Stamenov, 2002). Embodied cognition thus helps us to develop a 'theory of mind'. In other words, it helps us empathize with other people, and understand, to some extent how they might be feeling and what they might be experiencing (Gibbs, 2006: 234).

As the main form of communication in humans is language, it is unsurprising that embodied cognition is involved in understanding what people say to us and what we read. Findings from several studies indicate that when we listen to or read language, we automatically activate both perceptual and motor imagery in order to understand it (Bergen *et al.*, 2003). In other words, upon hearing a sentence such as 'Rossouw caught the ball in mid air' we mentally recreate the act of catching a ball ourselves, in order to understand it. This is interesting, given that the understanding of spoken language is often based around the identification of the verb (Rost, 2002). The implication here is that we start by using embodied cognition to work out the meaning of the verb, and that we then use this as a basis for interpreting the rest of the sentence or utterance.

Further evidence for embodied cognition in humans comes from a study by Richardson and Matlock (2007). They asked a group of participants to look at a picture of a path going across a piece of terrain. The participants were then read a description of fictive motion where the terrain was described as difficult and a description of fictive motion where it was described as relatively easy. When the participants heard the 'difficult' description, their eyes moved much more slowly than when they heard the 'easy' description, which implies that they were in some way experiencing the motion themselves, while it was being described to them.

Another part of the embodied cognition hypothesis holds that abstract thought is **experientially grounded**. In other words, as the mind and the body are not separate entities, we understand concepts (including abstract concepts) by relating them directly to our own bodily experiences. This brings us back to *metaphor*. Through metaphor, abstract concepts, such as our attitudes to our work and other people, and our understanding of political events and economic phenomena, are understood and expressed in terms of bodily experiences such as pressure, temperature, dynamic versus static positions, balance and posture, effort and fatigue. This allows us to talk, for example, about 'being under pressure from financial contributors', 'having a strained relationship with the government' and 'igniting a heated debate'. A corollary of embodiment theory is that we experience a species-specific view of the world, and our view of 'reality' is constrained to a large extent by the nature of our bodies and the way we use them to perceive our environment. In this respect, embodiment can also be considered as a special case of construal. In many ways, embodied cognition is an extension of conceptual metaphor theory, but it goes further than conceptual metaphor theory by emphasizing the role of the body, and by offering direct neurological evidence for the link between the physical and the mental worlds. Consider for example, the following extract from page 64 of the novel *English Correspondence* by Janet Davey:

> Yvette said, 'I was saying that conference facilities, even on a small scale, would give you and Paul such a boost'
> 'You think so?'
> 'I really do.'
> 'It might take more than that.'
> Yvette ignored this and said brightly, 'That's where the money is now.'
> Sylvie considered. She didn't want to talk about this sort of thing outdoors. *It made a false ceiling and took away the pleasure of being out in the open.*

In this example, the feeling of imprisonment that talk of money evokes in Sylvie contrasts sharply with the fact that she is outdoors in the open air and feeling relatively free. This piece of writing works because we are able to understand emotional or intellectual constraint in terms of actual physical constraint. This is an example of what Lakoff (1987) refers to as an 'image schema ICM' (see Chapter 4) and what Grady (1997) refers to as a 'primary metaphor' (see Chapter 6). Other examples include:

KNOWING IS SEEING
CHANGE IS MOTION
DESIRE IS HUNGER
ORGANIZATION IS PHYSICAL STRUCTURE
DIFFICULTY IS HEAVINESS
ANALYSING IS CUTTING
EMOTIONAL INTIMACY IS PROXIMITY
EMOTION IS WARMTH

It is easy to see to see how each of these primary metaphors is bodily based; they arise from our physical embodied experience and the interaction of our bodies with the world. For example, when we feel strong emotion for someone, we can sometimes physically experience warmth inside. Indeed, it has been suggested that at least some of these primary metaphors are experienced as single domains during infancy (Lakoff and Johnson, 1999). For instance, for an infant, knowing something is actually *the same as* seeing it; hunger is the only desire an infant knows, and experiencing emotional intimacy is the same as being physically close to someone. It is only in later life that the physical and more abstract senses become separated and need to be related by metaphor.

As evidence for the direct relationship between embodied experience and our understanding of the world through metaphor, Gibbs (2003) describes a study in which two groups of American university students were taken into the countryside and asked to walk across a field. While they were walking, the first group of students was told a story about a couple whose relationship was positive and 'going somewhere'. The other group of students was told a story about another couple whose relationship was not going so well, and who had encountered a number of problems. Those students who listened to the second story made substantially less progress across the field than those students who heard the first story. These findings could be due to at least two primary metaphors: it could be that their view of progress as a journey had an impact upon their own journey. Alternatively, it could be that because they were hearing about something sad they felt sad themselves, and started to slow down as a result. In addition, the findings from the study highlight the human capacity for empathy, which is also thought to be related to embodied cognition (Gallese *et al.*, 2002).

This chapter looks at the implications that the embodied cognition hypothesis has for language learning and teaching. I begin by looking at how embodied cognition has been used to facilitate the teaching of grammar and I discuss the benefits and limitations of such an approach. I then discuss one of the main ways in which embodied cognition is manifested, namely the use of gesture, assessing the role of gesture in second language learning, focusing on cross-linguistic variation in the use of gesture, the use of gesture by the teacher or interlocutor, and the use of gesture by the students themselves.

7.2   The role of embodied cognition in grammar teaching

Most research into the ways in which the embodied cognition hypothesis can be used in language teaching has concerned grammar teaching. This research has employed Talmy's (1988) **force dynamics system** and applied it to the teaching of modality and tenses. Talmy notes that many of our abstract ideas are conceptualized in terms of physical forces that we experience with our bodies. To illustrate this theory, he refers to the primary metaphor: MOVING THROUGH TIME IS MOVING TROUGH SPACE, which he uses to explain deontic modality. Sweetser (1990) extends Talmy's work to explain the relationship between deontic and epistemic modality.

Deontic modality usually denotes some kind of real-world obligation, permission, or ability, whereas epistemic modality is more to do with necessity, probability and possibility. Deontic modality is thought to be the more 'basic' of the two types of modality, and epistemic modality is considered to be a metaphorical extension of it. In support of this contention, researchers cite the finding that deontic meanings appear earlier in language than epistemic ones (Sweetser, 1990).

According to Talmy, deontic modality can be explained in terms of sociophysical forces, barriers and paths, and can be partially understood through a series of image schemas. As we saw in Chapter 4, image schemas are abstract conceptual representations that are developed during our daily interactions with the world (see Evans, 2007). They are meaningful, yet vague and flexible enough to be adjustable to a range of different contexts. Image schemas do not determine meaning in themselves, but they can contribute to our overall understanding of phrases in context, and they operate at different levels of consciousness according to the individual and the context. According to Talmy, a possible image schema for *can* involves physical movement along a trajectory with a potential – yet absent – barrier, as shown in Figure 7.1; a possible image schema for *cannot* involves the presence of a barrier, as shown in Figure 7.2; a possible image schema for *must* involves a compelling force directing the subject towards the act, as shown in Figure 7.3; and

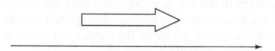

Figure 7.1 A possible image schema for *can* in Talmy's force dynamic system

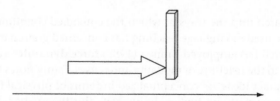

Figure 7.2 A possible image schema for *cannot* in Talmy's force dynamic system

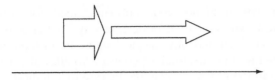

Figure 7.3   A possible image schema for *must* in Talmy's force dynamic system

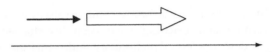

Figure 7.4   A possible image schema for *should* in Talmy's force dynamic system

a possible image schema for *should* involves a weaker force coming from behind, as shown in Figure 7.4.

Ought to, have to and *need to* also reflect obligation, but the differences are that *ought to* has strong moral overtones, *have to* has a meaning of being obliged by an extrinsically imposed authority, and *need to* is an internally imposed obligation. Talmy does not argue that every time we hear or use these words we actually form images such as those in Figures 7.1–7.4 in our minds. Nor does he argue that image schemas *determine* meaning. His argument is that image schemas such as these operate at a largely subconscious level, and that they *contribute*, along with contextual information, to our overall understanding of language.

As we saw above, it is often argued that deontic meanings appear earlier in language and are semantically more basic (Sweetser, 1990). Deontic obligation prototypically reflects social pressure external to the speaker, whilst epistemic necessity or probability reflects a reality that is internal to the speaker. Thus in deontic modality, objective, *external facts* are conceptualized in terms of external forces, and in epistemic modality, *internal states of mind* are conceptualized in terms of external forces. This move from objectivity to subjectivity also is an important theme in Langacker's (1991) theory of cognitive grammar, and is thought to lie behind a great deal of language change (Evans and Green, 2006). The two senses can be illustrated in the case of *must*, as in my examples (43) and (44):

(43) (I am telling you that) You must be home by ten.
(44) (I am concluding that) She must be home by now.

Sweetser (1990) argues that epistemic modality constitutes a metaphorical extension of deontic modality, in the sense that our internal intellectual and physiological states are metaphorically construed in terms of our external experiences. To illustrate, the epistemic use of *may* in the phrase, 'it may be the case that' indicates that there is no barrier to the speaker's process of reasoning from the available premises to reach whatever conclusion is being expressed (Sweetser, 1990: 59).

The potential applications of Talmy's and Sweetser's work to second language learning and teaching have been investigated by Tyler (2008a, b). She describes several preliminary studies that she and her colleagues have conducted to assess the effectiveness of cognitive linguistic approaches to the teaching of phrasal verbs. All the studies involved experimental and control groups of students, all of whom were international lawyers studying in the US in order to obtain Masters degrees in Jurisprudence. Students in the experimental groups were shown diagrams featuring stick men to illustrate the different types of force. She used these diagrams to trigger a discussion of the differences between the deontic senses of *can, must* and *should*. She then explained that epistemic meanings are internal mental equivalents of these external forces, and encouraged the students to use metaphorical extension techniques to work out the associated epistemic senses of these modal verbs. The students in the control groups were shown more traditional textbook explanations of the verbs. In general, Tyler and her colleagues found that the students in the experimental groups showed significantly better understanding of the verbs, better retention, and a greater ability to use them appropriately in later written work. She and her team are continuing to investigate the effectiveness of this approach with different groups of students.

A second way in which Talmy's force dynamic system can be applied to grammar teaching relates to the use of the past tense to denote psychological distancing or politeness (Tyler and Evans, 2001). The past tense in English is often used to refer to a definite event or state that is seen as distant in time, or reality, or is distant for reasons of politeness (Downing and Locke, 2002). This grammatical phenomenon relies upon the embodiment of time as physical forward motion. If events took place in the past, in terms of embodied understanding they are behind us. This embodied meaning is often apparent in academic discourse, where writers sometimes use the past and present tense to contrast work that is relatively unimportant with work that is central to the theme of their article. So for example, if they write 'Jones (1991) shows that...' they may be implying that whatever Jones shows is going to be more central to their discussion. If, on the other hand, they write that 'Jones (1991) showed that' they might in some cases be downplaying the relevance of Jones' findings to the discussion. The same rhetorical technique is used in politeness requests in English, where 'I was wondering if you could...' is deemed more polite than 'I wonder if you could...'. Again, the fact that the 'wondering' is in the past tense and is therefore behind the speaker gives the addressee plenty of space to refuse the request. Because such a refusal would not conflict with the requester's current state of mind, it would be a less face-threatening act to both parties involved. The idea that embodied experience lies behind extensions of tense usage and that this can be exploited for language teaching purposes is discussed at length by Tyler and Evans (2001). They extend the argument to look at four non-temporal uses of tense, namely: intimacy, foregrounding, epistemic stance, and mitigation. Their arguments for the role of embodied meaning in these sense extensions are powerful and convincing. Unfortunately, to the best of my knowledge, there is as yet no empirical evidence to show whether appealing to embodied cognition actually helps learners to acquire these figurative extensions of the past tense. More work is needed in the area.

Although work on the applications of embodied cognition to the teaching of grammar has produced some promising early findings, it remains somewhat limited as an approach as it relies almost exclusively on the use of static, pre-existing image schemas. Recent studies of language comprehension and acquisition have shown them to be dynamic, usage-based processes (Larsen-Freeman and Cameron, 2007). Cognitive linguists would agree with this. Rather than merely activating pre-existing abstract, conceptual representations, people use their embodied experiences to 'soft-assemble' meaning (Gibbs, 2006). In other words, the sorts of loose schematic structures proposed by Talmy and Grady and others make only a partial contribution to our understanding of contextual meaning in discourse. Image schemata, although useful, can only ever be part of the whole picture. The ability to understand what our interlocutor is trying to say to us involves the activation of several areas of knowledge, including contextual knowledge, an idea of the speaker's intentions, and relevant encyclopaedic knowledge. All of these factors are susceptible to variation and the particular meaning that a listener extracts from a given utterance will be a culmination of all these things. In addition to the types of studies conducted by Tyler and her colleagues, we also need studies that focus on the role of embodied cognition in human interaction, and on how this affects language learning.

7.3 Embodied cognition and gesture

An important external manifestation of embodied cognition in interaction is the use of **gesture**. In conversation, both speakers and listeners use gesture to communicate, co-construct and internalize meaning, as well as to establish intersubjectivity (Platt and Brooks, 2008). In recent years there has been a burgeoning of research into the role of gesture in second language learning and teaching. It is now well established that language learners produce more gestures when they speak their second language than when they speak their first language, and the use of gesture has been found to perform important functions in terms of both L2 communication and learning (Gullberg, 2008). By studying the gestures that are used by L2 learners it should therefore be possible to learn more about the connection between language and thought, and by extension, understand how languages are learned in interactive settings (Negueruela and Lantolf, 2008). The remainder of this chapter is thus devoted to a discussion of gesture and its role in second language learning and teaching.

There is, according to embodiment theorists, a 'tight synchrony of speech and gesture' (Gibbs, 2006: 169) because they are grounded in common thought processes. In other words, it is argued that both verbal and non-verbal expressions function as an integrated whole in communication; they cannot be interpreted separately because they emanate from the same semantic source in the mind (Quek *et al.*, 2002) and most likely originate in the same neural system (Corballis, 1994). Although gesture researchers differ on the exact nature of the link between language and gesture, the fact that there is a very strong link is undisputed (Gullberg, 2008).

The fact that language and gesture are so strongly linked manifests itself in a variety of ways. Firstly, gestures and speech are synchronous, thus when speakers momentarily hesitate, their gestures tend to be held motionless until speech continues, and when conveying ideas that are difficult or complex, people often employ substantial amounts of gesture (Kendon, 2004). The gestures that accompany utterances tend to have the same semantic and/or pragmatic content as the utterances, and form part of the same idea unit. Secondly, gesture appears to play an important role in conceptualizing and planning messages. PET studies have shown that people show increased activity in the pre-motor cortex (which is responsible for movement) when they are asked to retrieve the words for tools than when they are asked to retrieve words for, say animals (Grafton *et al.*, 1997, reported in Gibbs, 2006). This indicates that when we think of a tool, such as a hammer, those parts of our mind that would normally make us perform a hammering motion are activated. This is reflected in the fact that verbal accounts of movement are often accompanied by gestures showing that movement. Non-verbal visual information, such as this, is one of the most crucial variables in interpreting meaning in social interaction (DePaulo and Friedman, 1997). Thirdly, as McNeill (1992) points out, gestures and speech develop together in childhood and break down together in aphasia. Although speakers vary in terms of the amount of gesture they produce, there is remarkable uniformity within speech communities in terms of the types of gestures that they use. The fact that there is such tight synchrony between language and gesture suggests that gesture ought to play an important role in second language learning and teaching.

Gestures serve a variety of functions. Some are 'communicative', in that they facilitate communication, whereas others are more cognitive, in that they help speakers formulate expressions. Evidence for the cognitive function of gesture comes from the fact that people still use gestures, even when they are talking to themselves or to interlocutors who cannot see them (for example, when they are on the telephone). According to McNeill (1992), gestures serve a variety of different communicative functions. **Iconic gestures** bear a close resemblance to the semantic content of speech. For example, when talking about a particular house that they have stayed in, a person might gesture the shape of the roof. A second class of gesture, **metaphoric gestures**, contains those that correspond to underlying primary and conceptual metaphors. For example, when she analysed the gestures used by the speakers in a series of videotaped academic lectures, Sweetser (1998) found considerable gestural evidence for the conduit metaphor, the REASONING IS MOTION THROUGH SPACE metaphor and CONCEPTUAL STRUCTURE IS SPATIAL GEOMETRY metaphor. Interestingly, these are all primary metaphors (see Chapter 5). A third class of gestures, **beat gestures**, are used to mark important parts of the discourse. They are usually identical in form, and are used by speakers to mark those parts of the discourse that they feel to be important in pragmatic terms. Examples include marking the introduction of new characters, summarizing actions, and introducing new themes. They are used to indicate the meta-level of discourse (McNeill, 1992: 13). A fourth function of gestures is **to convey cohesiveness in discourse**. Speakers might do this by repeating a gesture that they have already used to remind the speaker that they are still talking about the same subject. A fifth function of gestures is to convey **deictics** (i.e. physical or attitudinal distance from a particular phenomenon or idea).

Finally, gestures can have a **pragmatic function** in that they can convey meanings that are only loosely implied by the dialogue itself. For example, gestures of invitation sometimes accompany straight facts or a question is implied in a gesture but not in the verbal communication (Kendon, 2004).

Another important role played by gesture, which is not mentioned by McNeill, is **to provide evidence of, and a way of unpacking, conceptual blends** (Parrill and Sweetser, 2004). We briefly mentioned blending theory in Chapter 5 under the discussion of metaphor, but it was noted at that point that blending theory extends well beyond metaphor theory. Conceptual blending is said to occur when different 'input spaces' or areas of knowledge are brought together and for one reason or another are considered as a single entity. The resulting 'blended space' has its own logic, and develops its own emergent structure (Fauconnier and Turner, 2002). For example, in English, it is perfectly natural for the question 'How far are you from the nearest shops?' to be met with the response 'About five minutes'. This involves a blending of time and space. Distance cannot be measured in minutes in real life, but it can be in the new 'logic' that is created by the blend. Another example of a blend is shown in the utterance 'I'm going to be Mrs Jones today' (which might, for example, be uttered by a supply teacher, who happens to be standing in for Mrs. Jones who is off sick). Although the replacement teacher does not actually become 'Mrs Jones', her identity is temporarily blended with Mrs Jones' role, and within the logic of this new blend it is indeed possible for her to 'be' Mrs Jones for the day. A third type of blend involves analogy, and is typified by utterances such as 'Manchester is the Venice of the North'. Understanding this utterance requires one to create a blended space in which Venice is temporarily moved to the North of England and the interlocutor is forced to draw analogies between Venice and Manchester (in this case, it is largely the presence of canals that is being referred to). Because there is often a lack of surface-level 'logic' to utterances that involve blends, the meanings have to be 'soft-assembled' on-line (see Section 7.2) unless they are conventional. To the best of my knowledge there have been no systematic studies of cross-linguistic variation in terms of blending types and degrees of conventionality. This is surprising given that it is these less 'logical' areas of language where linguistic variation is likely to be found. One thing that has been shown however, and which is relevant to this chapter, is the fact that conceptual blends are often accompanied by an increased use of gesture (Parrill and Sweetser, 2004). These gestures serve two important disambiguation functions. First, they indicate that an extra degree of unpacking is required, and second, they provide help with the unpacking process itself.

The strong communicative functions served by all these types of gesture mean that attention to gesture is a crucial part of language comprehension, a fact which is of vital importance to both language teachers and learners. Attending to, and making use of **iconic gestures** can help learners compensate for gaps in their target-language vocabulary, and learn new vocabulary, a fact that has been widely attested in the learning strategies literature (e.g. Oxford, 1990). The key role that **metaphoric gestures** play in elucidating primary metaphors and blends, suggests that paying attention to them will facilitate access to the conceptual system of the target language and help the learner to develop what Danesi (2008) refers to as 'conceptual fluency'. Attending to **beat gestures** and **cohesiveness-marking gestures**, and then learning to produce such gestures themselves in an L2-appropriate way, is likely to help learners develop spoken discourse competence. Understanding and using appropriate **deictic gestures** and **pragmatic function** gestures should help them develop pragmatic competence in both listening and speaking. Finally, the use of gesture to signal and facilitate the understanding of **conceptual blends** is likely to be particularly important for language learners as it is in the fuzzy, 'illogical' areas that different languages and conceptual systems are most likely to vary. Thus one might expect that paying attention to all these types of gesture is likely to make some sort of contribution to their overall language learning. However, the question here is, to what extent do target-language gestures need to be taught? Is the ability to understand and produce appropriate gestures a skill that can simply be transferred from one's own language to the target language, or do languages vary significantly in the ways in which they employ gestures? If they do, then there is an argument for drawing learners' attention to such differences.

7.4 Cross-linguistic variation in the use of gesture

In terms of cross-cultural variation, gestures fall into two broad types: emblems and spontaneous gestures (Stam and McCafferty, 2008). **Emblems** are culture-specific, codified, conventional gestures that carry designated meanings, such as the 'thumbs up' sign in British and American English. These are susceptible to wide cross-cultural variation, but are relatively limited in number, highly salient, and therefore reasonably easy to learn. **Spontaneous gestures** present more of a challenge. We only use them when we speak, and they convey the same or complementary semantic and/or pragmatic content as the words that we are using. What makes them interesting from a language learning point of view is that they are an external manifestation of a speaker's 'thinking for speaking' (see Chapter 2). Although spontaneous gestures are often highly idiosyncratic, it has been pointed out that 'there seem to be cultural repertoires [of gestures] whose characteristics are motivated both by culture and by language' (Gullberg, 2008: 281). An ability to interpret and produce these 'cultural repertoires' of preferred gestures of the target language community is therefore likely to contribute both to communicative competence and to cultural awareness. It may therefore be important for learners to have some sort of focus on gesture in the language curriculum.

Cross-linguistic variation is highly apparent at the level of metaphoric gesture. In particular, one metaphor that does not appear to be universal is the **conduit** metaphoric gesture for communication, in which the information is seen as being in a container and passed from person to person. For instance, when he studied a series of narratives in Chinese and Turkana (the language spoken by the Turkana people of north-western Kenya), McNeill (1992) found no evidence of gestures in which abstract ideas were presented as bounded and supported containers, although there was plenty of evidence of other metaphoric gestures in both of these languages. Conversely, these container-type gestures had a strong presence in the narratives of the other languages he studied (English, German, Italian, Georgian and Japanese). McNeill (*ibid.*: 152) reports that:

> In a context where an English narrator would typically perform a conduit, the Chinese speaker created a boundless substance that she then patted down... This gesture creates an image of a substance without form. The metaphor is that an abstract idea is a mass of some kind, a concrete substance, but it is not supported in the speaker's hands.

This study shows that by examining the gestures used by speakers of different languages, we can obtain information about the different ways in which they subconsciously conceptualize abstract phenomena.

Languages also vary in terms of the way speech and gesture relate to one another. For example, it has been noted that Italian speakers use gesture to emphasize the referential content of the utterances, whereas Yiddish speakers use gesture more to emphasize logical structure (Efron, 1972). Kendon (2004) suggests that there are at least four ways in which structural, or lexico-grammatical differences between languages cause variation in the way speakers of those languages use gesture, and reports on four studies that provide support for these differences. All the studies employed the same technique: participants were shown a silent film and then asked to explain in their own language what the film was about, and the ways in which speakers of different languages did this were then compared. The differences identified are as follows.

Firstly, in languages where more syntactic work is involved to express a particular concept, gesture may be used as a substitute. For example, Spanish-speakers, who do not have manner-of-movement verbs (such as *slither* or *creep*) in their language, tend use significantly more gesture than English speakers, who can express this movement through the language (McNeill and Duncan, 2000).

Secondly, the semantic features of one's language may influence what gesture is used. For instance, Kita and Ozyurek (2003) found that English-speakers are more likely to use an arc-like gesture to show swinging than Japanese- and Turkish-speakers. The equivalent verbs in Japanese and Turkish do not imply an arc-like path.

Thirdly, speakers of languages that differ in the number of separate constructions may differ in the number of separate gestures they use. For example, when they elicited the expression 'he rolled down the street', in speakers of English and Turkish, Kita and Ozyurek (2003) found that the Turkish speakers employed two gestures whereas the English-speakers employed only one. Interestingly, this expression comprises two clauses in Turkish, but only one in English.

Fourthly, differences in how the topic is structured in discourse may give rise to differences in where the pertinent gesture is placed, For example, in Mandarin, the topic is placed at the beginning of the sentence and the action isn't reported until much later. However, the topic itself limits the number of actions that are to be expected. McNeill and Duncan (2000) found that Mandarin-speakers employ gesture to accompany the topic, well before the action is stated. For example, when they produced the utterance 'ge lao tai tai na le ge hao xiang ba ta da dao de da bang' ('The old lady hold big stick, may or may not cause him hit down', meaning: 'The old lady may or may not have knocked him down with a big stick'), they used a hitting gesture to accompany the words 'big stick'.

Other research has shown that cross-linguistic differences in broad discourse patterns can influence the use of gesture. For example, in Japanese the information that is considered most important and 'news-worthy' relates to locations and settings, whereas in Dutch, Swedish and French, actions are considered to be more newsworthy. Gullberg (in press) found that Japanese-speakers mark locations and settings with a beat gesture, whereas Dutch-, Swedish- and French-speakers are more likely to mark the actions.

Gullberg (in press) found that differences in categorization systems (see Chapter 2) can also give rise to different gestural patterns. For instance, Dutch has different words for 'putting down' (*zetten* and *leggen* etc.) depending on the shape of the object that is being put down. French does not have this distinction. When they talk about putting things down, French-speakers simply use a downward motion gesture, whereas Dutch-speakers vary their hand shape according to what it is they are talking about being put down. This suggests that, in comparison with French speakers, Dutch speakers consider it more important to convey what it is that they are actually putting down.

These accounts of cross-linguistic variation in the use of gesture provide further evidence of the fact that events and phenomena are construed in different ways in different languages, and that cognition is embodied in different ways in different languages. This implies that when people learn a second language, it may be useful for them to recognize and use target-language-style gestures. It also implies that in many cases the use of target-language gestures will parallel target language development. But does it? Findings with respect to this question vary according to the learning setting, in particular whether or not the language is being learned in a natural setting and whether or not there is exposure to native speakers of the language, and whether learners actually want to become like native speakers of the language. In general, research shows that the acquisition of a second language tends to be accompanied by a corresponding ability to use appropriate target-type gestures (Gullberg, 2008). For example, Özyürek (2002) found that Turkish-speakers who could use English-like syntax to express manner and path of motion events started to use English-speaker-like gestures. This implies that there may be a link between the acquisition of L2 syntax and the corresponding gestures that L2 users might use. On the other hand, sometimes learners retain their L1 gesture repertoires, even at advanced levels (Yoshioka, 2008). The tendency to adopt L2-style gestures seems to be linked as much to issues such as acculturation and attitudes to the target language culture as it is to language proficiency *per se* (McCafferty, 2008). As with all areas of second language acquisition, the acquisition of L2-style gestures is not a linear process. A learner's knowledge of first- and second-language gesture systems interacts in a complex manner in the target language, and is influenced by the acquisition of syntax, semantics and pragmatics as well as affinity with the target language culture.

7.5 How do learners benefit from seeing gesture when listening to the target language?

We have seen that the main advantage of using gesture is that it allows learners to open up, and to fully exploit, another channel of communication in terms of both comprehension and production. In order to gain access to the conceptual system of the target language, it may thus be beneficial for language learners to see the gestures employed by expert users of that language. In an L2 context, gestures have the potential so serve as a powerful form of **input enhancement**. Input enhancement is a term used by Sharwood Smith (1991, 1993) to refer to methods that a language teacher uses to make certain features of a second language more salient for learners in such a way as to facilitate acquisition. It includes, but is not limited to, a number of techniques such as not reducing vowels, slowing down the rate of speech, providing more repetition, providing less pre-verbal modification and more post-verbal modification, making greater use of gestures, visual stimuli, and the use of video, as well as employing traditional techniques for drawing the learner's attention more overtly to how the language system works. Of all these techniques, exaggerating one's use of gesture is likely to serve as a particularly powerful form of input enhancement as it provides a direct, fast-track route to the conceptualizer, via embodiment.

There is evidence to suggest that the use of gesture by the speaker plays an important part in L2 listening comprehension, particularly amongst beginners (Sueyoshi and Hardison, 2005) or people who are exposed to language that is completely unknown to them (Tellier, 2006, cited in Gullberg, 2008). Gesture is particularly helpful in the understanding of anaphoric reference, again particularly amongst beginners (Kida, 2008). Research is also beginning to show that learners are significantly more likely to remember L2 vocabulary if the teacher accompanies his or her explanations with appropriate gestures (Allen, 1995). The gestures in Allen's study are interesting as they include a mixture of iconic gestures (for example, a dancing gesture to indicate 'will you dance with me?), highly culturally conventional gestures (e.g rotating a closed fist on the nose to indicate 'drunkenness'), and metaphorical gestures (e.g. a swimming gesture to indicate being completely lost or 'at sea'). Unfortunately, Allen did not focus on the relative benefits of *different types* of gesture in her study. If she had done so, she might have discovered that certain sorts of gestures are more likely to facilitate learning than others. For instance, highly culturally conventional gestures are unlikely to facilitate learning unless they are already known by the language learner. On the other hand, introducing learners to culturally conventional gestures may in itself be a useful activity as it increases the chances of the learners being able to reproduce these gestures in communicative situations where they are interacting with native speakers.

Given that being able to see gesture helps with listening comprehension, is it therefore useful for teachers to make use of gesture in the language classroom? Studies have shown that learners are very aware of the gestures that are used by their teachers, that teachers who are perceived as 'excellent' tend to use significantly more gesture than those who tend not to use so much gesture, and that classroom gestures serve to disambiguate meanings, focus attention on important aspects of the lesson and aid memorization (Sime, 2008). On the other hand, Kida (2008) warns against 'visual over-scaffolding' which may engender an over-reliance on gesture in some language learners. Also, Faraco and Kida (2008) point out that some gestures may be too vague, and lead to misunderstandings in the classroom. Classroom gestures may also differ from those used by the target-language community and may in some cases be an exaggerated caricature of 'real-world' gesture. On balance however, findings appear to show that if due care is taken not to over-use it, or to use it in a misleading way, the deliberate use of gesture by language teachers is to be encouraged.

7.6 How do learners benefit from using gesture when working in the target language?

The use of gesture by language learners themselves has been shown to be useful. It serves two important functions: firstly, it has an interactional function in that it facilitates communication; and secondly, it is likely to serve a cognitive function in that learners use it to help them formulate utterances in the target language. As we will see below, these two functions interact to promote language learning.

Let us begin by looking at the communicative function of gesture. In interactive settings, gesture can be used to build intersubjectivity and common frames of reference in dialogues between native speakers and second language learners (McCafferty, 2002; Mori and Hayashi, 2006). Once these common frames of reference have been built up, the native speaker has an idea of what the language learner wants to say, and can help provide the missing vocabulary and constructions to the learner. The learners themselves may use gesture to create zones of proximal development (Vygotsky, 1986), within which they can safely try out new constructions in the target language without the fear of being misunderstood. Thus the use of gesture works as an effective communication strategy that allows learners to negotiate with their interlocutor in order to obtain feedback on their language ability and to shape their input into something that will help them learn (see Gass, 1997; Gullberg, 1998). The use of gesture also contributes to a learner's 'interactional alacrity and resourcefulness' which should, according to Firth and Wagner (2007: 806) contribute to their interactional and learning success.

The use of gesture in interactions *between learners* also appears to facilitate learning. Platt and Brooks (2008) show how pairs of learners engaged in task-based learning activities use gesture to help each other understand the task, to identify opportunities for learning within the task, to make constructions easier for the other person to notice and internalize, and to regulate their learning. Gesture was found to facilitate learning in interaction in the MacArthur and Littlemore (2008) study that was referred to in Chapter 4. It will be remembered that the aim of the study was to assess how learners of English and Spanish might learn the figurative uses of denominal verbs by making use of language corpora. We were particularly interested in the ways in which the students interacted with one another during the learning process, and in this study we found that collaborative reasoning about the senses of the words explored was often accompanied by gesture. In other words, verbal explanations were often supported and elaborated by physical movement, serving to clarify and illustrate the learners' understanding of the sense of a verb. We found that the use of appropriate gesture by the students enhanced both their comprehension and retention of the vocabulary items. The learners were more likely to remember those words that had provoked the use of gesture when first encountered.

The learners of English in the study made noticeable use of gesture when learning the items *worm, snake* and *elbow*, all of which can express a manner of motion which may then be figuratively extended to refer to another type of activity or process. The following exchange (from MacArthur and Littlemore, 2008) illustrates how gesture supports a learner's understanding of the metaphorical use of *elbow*:

T: So how did you remember **elbow** there, Luis?
S9: I just remembered it. There was **elbow** aside and **elbow** out.

T: Yeah, but you get **shoulder** aside too, don't you?

S9: Yes, and it said **shoulder** your way or **elbow** your way through a crowd

S8: Yes, but it's different. If you use your elbows it's like this [*makes jabbing motions outwards with elbows*] like when you get on the bus, it's rude – and when it says 'judo has been **elbowed** out of the next Commonwealth games' it means dejar de lado, ignorar. Es más que eso – quiere decir dejar de lado cuando alguien se impone [*gesture with elbows again*] y no le importan los demás. ['... it means leave to one side, ignore. It's more than that – it means leave aside when someone imposes on others [...] and doesn't care about others.']

The use of gesture in this exchange allowed the learners to distinguish between similar senses of *shoulder* and *elbow*, and to clarify why *elbow* can extend its meaning metaphorically to denote a negatively evaluated action while *shoulder* does not usually do so. As we argue in our paper, the use of creativity and gesture to achieve an understanding of the senses of these verbs is a far from unimportant strategy, and may improve the learner's overall grasp of figurative usage in general. Metaphors, particularly when realized by phraseological units, are rarely neutral in discourse, but are used by speakers to evaluate the events and situations they describe (Nunberg *et al.*, 1994; Moon, 1998). Failure to grasp the evaluative content of a metaphorical expression may lead non-native speakers to use such expressions inappropriately. The use of gesture appeared to be particularly helpful in guiding the learners' appreciation of this aspect of figurative language.

The learners of Spanish in the study also used gesture to work out affective or physical components of the vocabulary items. The three items that triggered the use of gesture were *agostado* ('Augusted' meaning 'withered'), *aletear* ('to wing', meaning 'to flap'), and *torear* ('to bull', meaning 'to dodge'). Interestingly, *agostado* and *aletear* were among those items that were most likely to be remembered by the learners. *Torear* provided an interesting focus for discussion in the first session. It means 'to dodge' and is taken from the behaviour of the bull fighter getting out of the way of the bull. This interpretation is quite culturally specific, and the learners took a long time to work it out. This is because they were working with those aspects of a bull that are perhaps more prototypical for English speakers (size, ferocity, and so on). A sudden, spontaneous use of gesture by one of the learners in the first session was a significant impetus to correct interpretation of the word by the others.

For both sets of students in the study (English and Spanish) those words that had provoked the use of gesture were more likely to be retained than those that had not.

Now let us turn to the cognitive function of gesture. According to the **information packaging hypothesis** (Kita, in press), we use gesture to help put our thoughts into words. Second language learners have been found to make considerable use of these sorts of gestures, as putting one's thoughts into words in another language involves a great deal of repackaging and filtering of information (Yoshioka, 2008). By looking at the gestures they use, we may gain some insight into the ways in which they are attempting to construe and 'package' events in the target language (see Chapter 2). Gestures are also used in private speech when learners are internalizing new information that they have learned about the target language. It has also been found that the use of gesture during vocabulary learning significantly enhances retention (Allen, 1995).

Under a usage-based account of language learning, the communicative and cognitive functions of gesture cannot be seen as separate entities. Producing and attending to gesture helps to promote interaction, which helps learners to expand their zones of proximal development (Vygotsky, 1986). Within these zones, meanings are co-constructed, new constructions can be identified, internalized and then tried out. Gesture has a crucial role to play at every stage of this cyclical, dialectic process.

The only language teaching methodology which gives gesture a central role is **total physical response (TPR)** (Asher, 1988). TPR involves learners acting out the actions as they say them. It has been developed in recent years into a more elaborate version, **total physical response storytelling** (Werstler, 2002), in which entire stories are acted out by the teacher and by the whole class. Lindstromberg and Boers (2005) put the effectiveness of TPR methodology to the test, carrying out a series of rigorous experiments to measure its effect on students' retention and recall of manner-of-movement verbs. Their results were very positive. They found that recall of manner-of-movement verbs is better promoted by watching someone physically demonstrate the meaning of a manner-of-movement verb than by listening to a verbal definition, and that physically acting out the meaning of a manner-of-movement verb oneself promotes retention even more. Although Lindstromberg and Boers' findings are encouraging, two criticisms have been levelled at TPR that to the best of my knowledge have not yet been empirically addressed. The first is that the technique is not as useful for learning abstract senses of words as it is for learning physical senses (although embodiment theory would suggest that it should be). The second is that it relies so heavily on cognates that it cannot be used for more distant language pairs. On the other hand, the fact that abstract concepts are thought to be grounded in embodied cognition suggests that these too may be taught, to some extent through TPR-type approaches. A number of ways in which this might be done can be found in Holme (2004), but it should be noted that there has to date been no research into their effectiveness. Despite the possible limitations of TPR, Lindstromberg and Boers' findings remain important as they imply a central role for gesture in the process of second language learning and teaching. One problem with TPR is that it is not a particularly 'authentic' or 'communicative' approach to language teaching, as the learners are never really involved in genuine communication with one another. It would therefore be useful if we could find ways of combining it with language learning activities that involve more genuine interaction, or if we could find ways of integrating a focus on gesture into a wider variety of teaching activities.

7.7 Concluding comments

In this chapter we have seen how embodied cognition and the use of gesture might be relevant to second language learning and teaching. The embodied cognition hypothesis and work in the field of gesture have inspired various approaches to language teaching. These approaches generally involve making the links between abstract language and physical experience more apparent to language learners. Or, as in TPR, they involve learners in acting out pre-ordained scripts in the classroom. Although these approaches are potentially very powerful, they remain somewhat de-contextualized. To date, there has not been much research into how such approaches can be integrated into more communicative methodologies, such as task-based learning, that allow learners to learn and create meaning through usage. This would be a useful development and more work in the area would be welcome. As for the role of gesture in second language learning, this is a relatively new area of research whose initial findings are very interesting, particularly those that focus on the use of gesture by language learners to create shared ground and open up new zones of proximal development. Most recent research in the area is beginning to look at the use of gesture by language learners to formulate their ideas and to 'package' them in appropriate L2 constructions; the ways in which speakers of languages with different construals of the same event use gesture to accommodate one another when engaged in conversation; and the ways in which an enhanced awareness of gesture relates to L2 proficiency. This work will provide important insights into the ways in which languages are learned through usage, and should eventually lead to a more central role for the interactive functions of gesture in language teaching methodology.

8
'Loud suits' and 'sharp cheese': Motivated Language and Second Language Learning

8.1 Introductory comments

One of the things that all humans do when faced with new input of any kind, is to search for meaning. Although recent approaches to language teaching, such as the lexical approach (LA), have emphasized the arbitrary nature of language, work in cognitive linguistics has shown that many aspects of language are in fact meaningful or **motivated**. Cognitive linguists use the term 'motivated' in a different way from mainstream applied linguists. In applied linguistics, the term is usually used to refer to keen and enthusiastic learners, whereas in cognitive linguistics, the term is applied to the language itself; it is used to refer to the fact that some aspects of language are not arbitrary and that there are sometimes reasons why we say things the way we do. For instance, as we have already seen in Chapter 7, some form–meaning connections are not as arbitrary as people claim, especially if we are aware of the types of processes (such as metaphor, metonymy and embodied cognition) that link form and meaning in language. Using these findings, teachers can explain, in theory, to their students why it is that certain expressions mean certain things, instead of simply telling them 'that's just the way it is' and expecting them to learn expressions by heart. This engages learners in a search for meaning, which is likely to involve deeper cognitive processing which, according to Craik and Lockhart (1982), leads to deeper learning and longer retention. It is important to say at this point that although a great deal of language is thought to be motivated, the ways in which this happens are not entirely predictable, and different languages are motivated in different ways. Thus, much of the analysis of motivated language is necessarily retrospective rather than predictive. Teaching language as a motivated phenomenon is therefore more relevant to language comprehension than language production.

One of the most persuasive papers on this topic is written by Boers and Lindstromberg (2006), who discuss the role of linguistic motivation in language teaching. Boers and Lindstromberg take as their starting point, Radden and Panther's (2004) proposal that motivated language can take three forms. It can be found in explainable form–form connections (e.g. alliteration), explainable form–meaning connections (iconicity), and explainable meaning–meaning connections (e.g. polysemy). This chapter is organized around these three areas. It takes Boers and Lindstromberg's work as a starting point, and then introduces other relevant work in the area.

8.2 Explainable form–form connections

Boers and Lindstromberg draw attention to the fact that fixed phraseological patterns are often characterized by alliteration, assonance and other phonological patterns, and show how this feature may aid their recall by learners. They argue that it is no coincidence that expressions such as *publish or perish* or *cut and thrust* endure in language, as there is something inherently meaningful and pleasurable about phonetic parallelism and rhyme. They have found that expressions such as these account for a startlingly high proportion of fixed expressions in English, that they are relatively easy to learn (Lindstromberg and Boers, 2008), and that their learnability is improved if their alliterative nature is pointed out to students.

Alliteration and other phonological patterns have been found to be particularly important when students are learning through data-driven learning approaches involving the use of corpora. MacArthur and Littlemore (2008) asked two groups of students to work collaboratively with language corpora to identify the meanings of denominal verbs in English and Spanish (see Section 3.2). We found that when working out the figurative senses of the items used, the presence or absence of fixed phraseological patterns affected learners' ability to perceive their meaning. For example, the students found it much easier to work out the meaning of expressions such as *worm one's way* or *weather a storm*, than expressions such as *to mushroom* or *pencilled in*.

The English-speaking learners of Spanish were also much more likely to notice phrases that had conspicuous alliteration. Two expressions that were particularly salient for them were: *cuadrar las cuentas* ('settle the accounts') and *monear las matas* ('climb trees'). These items provoked a significant amount of discussion in the first session, and were among the best retained in the testing session. These findings provide further support for Boers and Lindstromberg's (2008) finding that alliteration and other phonological patterns help learners to notice and remember fixed phraseological patterns.

8.3   Explainable form–meaning connections

Although the majority of form–meaning combinations are not explainable, there are certain cases where the form of the word does correspond in some ways to its meaning. The most widely cited instance of this in the cognitive linguistics literature is Taylor's (2002) 'more form is more meaning' principle. According to Taylor, longer words tend to express more complex meanings than shorter words. Moreover, words in basic-level categories (such as *cat*) tend to be shorter than words in higher-level categories (such as *animal*) or lower-level categories (such as *Siamese*). This principle also works at the level of the sentence. A long sentence, such as 'Would you mind passing me the book please?' manages to convey much more 'distance', and hence politeness than a short sentence, such as 'Pass me the book'. The 'more form is more meaning' principle has applications in the teaching of English for Academic Purposes, where longer words are sometimes seen as being more 'academic', and longer, more roundabout, sentences often indicate a higher degree of hedging. Also, nominalization leads to longer sentences that can sometimes sound more reified and 'academic' than shorter sentences.

Onomatopoeia constitutes another type of 'sound symbolism' in which form and meaning are related. Words like *tinkle, swoosh*, and *roar* all, to some extent, sound like what they mean, and this can be exploited to good effect in the language classroom. Although onomatopoeia is not particularly common in English, it is very common in languages such as Japanese, where it can be used to describe a range of phenonema. In Japanese, there are three types of onomatopoeia. **Gisei-go** involves imitations of the sounds of nature, **gitai-go** is used to talk about external states, and **gijoo-go** is used to talk about internal mental conditions. Gisei-go includes words such as *pili pili*, which describes a particular type of persistent rainfall. Gitai-go includes words such as *ton-ton*, which refers to someone knocking on a door, and gijoo-go includes words such as *nori nori*, which means to be in a good mood. It has been argued that by drawing attention to form–meaning combinations such as these, teachers of Japanese can make them more learnable and more memorable for students (Ivanova, 2006), but to the best of my knowledge these claims have not yet been empirically tested.

Sound symbolism is also present, albeit to a lesser degree, in English, where it manifests itself in the residual meaning of sounds, or phonological clusters, such as /gl + high front vowel/ in *glisten, glint, gleam, glitter* and *glimmer* (see Bergen, 2004). In this case, the relation is etymological (from *glit*, meaning 'brightness' in Old/Middle English). Words with *'udge'* (implying 'heavy stickiness'; Shore, 1996) such as *fudge, trudge, budge, sludge* and *grudge*, show no such etymological connection. Words with *'inkle'*, which connotes something small and cute, as in *twinkle* (visual), *winkle* (tactile), *tinkle* (auditory), seem to represent a halfway house as they derive partly from an Old/Middle English morpheme (*inkle*) denoting 'habitual action'. Clusters such as /gl-/ are sometimes referred to as **phonesthemes**. They are not infallible indicators of meaning, but they often contribute to the overall meaning of a word. As such, they are involved in the construction of 'soft-assembled meaning' that was mentioned in Chapter 5. Phonesthemes do not transfer neatly from language to language, so teacher-led, or facilitated, activities to raise awareness of them in the target language would seem sensible. One approach that has been found to generate good student participation, is to offer students choices involving polar opposites. Littlemore (2004) reports an instance during a lesson in which five advanced Japanese students of English were introduced to the word *stodgy*. At first, they claimed to have no idea what this word meant. However, when they were asked to listen to the sound of the word, and to decide whether they thought 'stodgy food' was more likely to be 'heavy' or 'light', they all immediately replied that it would be heavy. When asked if the word was more likely to have 'positive' or 'negative' connotations, they all immediately replied 'negative'. Therefore, by focusing on the sound of the word, they had managed to infer that 'stodgy' food is heavy and not very nice, a description which corresponds fairly closely to dictionary definitions of the word (e.g. 'heavy and solid' *OALD* (1995: 1174)). This approach might be adapted to less obvious instances of sound symbolism. For example, if a language learner were shown two shapes, an oval and a rectangle, and asked to guess from the sounds of the words, which was the 'oval', and which was the 'rectangle', many students would probably guess the meaning correctly through the use of sound symbolism, as the word 'oval' sounds more rounded than the word 'rectangle' (Ramachandran, 2003; Ramachandran and Hubbard, 2001). The positive results produced by such an approach might give learners confidence to develop a more intuitive side to their language learning, instead of relying heavily on dictionaries and teacher input. In some ways, the type of thinking here resembles the sort of thinking that I described in the discussion of metaphor in Chapter 4. For instance, the knowledge that /ʌʤ/ represents heavy or boring notions is on a par with knowledge about common conceptual metaphors and metonymies; and it can usefully be applied as part of a figurative thinking procedure (Littlemore and Low, 2006a).

A slightly wider view of onomatopoeia relates to **synaesthesia**, which is a mental process whereby different physical senses are conflated or even substituted. Synaesthesia allows us to talk about things such as a *sharp cheese*, a *loud tie*, or *cheerful music*. It is an everyday phenomenon that can be found in all sorts of words. It is important to note here that I am not talking about the rare cases of synaesthesia that cause people, for example, to relate Tuesday idiosyncratically to the colour blue, or the number six. I am only concerned with its more conventional forms, and its more fixed impact on vocabulary. In many ways, synaesthesic expressions such as a *harsh light* or a *gentle flavour* can be seen as a kind of metaphor, and as such, should be susceptible to elucidation by figurative thinking in the same way as other metaphoric expressions are (see Littlemore and Low, 2006a). The learner's task when trying to understand synaesthesic expressions in the L2 is presumably facilitated by the fact that the same types of mappings tend to be made across languages. However, significant variation has been found across languages in terms of the linguistic expressions that are used to describe synaesthesia and the phenomena that typically lend themselves to synaesthesic description (Takada, 2008).

Another problem for language learners relates to cross-linguistic variation in terms of the direction in which synaesthesia usually works. Williams (1976), in an early study on synaesthesia, proposes a hierarchy according to which synaesthesia works in English. According to this hierarchy, *tastes* are likely to be described synaesthesically in terms of *touch*, but not the other way round, *sounds* are likely to be described synaesthesically in terms of *touch* and *taste*, but not the other way round, and so on. Williams' hierarchy is shown here in Figure 8.1. Synaesthesic expressions in English that follow this hierarchy are significantly easier to interpret than those that do not. Other languages have been found to exhibit slightly different hierarchical patterns. For example, by using informants and corpus data, Werning *et al.* (2006) show that in German, colours are more likely to be used to describe tastes and smells than would be the case in English. These findings suggest that English-speaking learners of German may have difficulty understanding

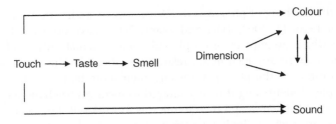

Figure 8.1 Directionalities of synaesthesia, according to Williams (1976: 463)

these expressions, or alternatively, that German-speaking learners of English may transfer them into English. On the other hand, they may, as Kellerman (1987a, b) suggests, be wary of transferring these usages to the target language.

8.4 Explainable meaning–meaning connections

One of the key ways in which language is motivated is through meaning–meaning connections (Radden and Panther, 2004). The theory underlying this view is grammaticalization (Hopper and Traugott, 2003). Under the grammaticalization hypothesis, as we saw in Chapter 1, new words enter the language as lexical (or 'open class' items) and then over time, some of these words acquire a grammatical (or 'closed class') function that is etymologically related to their original lexical meaning. This means that grammatical terms are inherently meaningful, although over time their meanings will become more 'schematic' than those of more clearly lexical items. The most widely cited example of this is the forms *will* and *going to*, which originally referred respectively to 'desire' and 'physical movement' but which, over time, have come to be used as different ways of construing future events. Although their original senses are much less widely used than their temporal senses, there is still a loose link between them which some grammarians use to account for the differences between them in meaning. As words become less lexical and more grammatical, their meaning becomes more schematic and the image schemas that they evoke contribute in part to the overall meaning of an utterance in context. Explaining meaning–meaning connections to language learners involves resurrecting the links with original lexical meanings of grammatical items, and using these links to enhance understanding and memorization.

One of the main ways in which language teachers have tried to apply the cognitive approach to identifiable meaning–meaning connections is in the teaching of phrasal verbs. A number of studies (Kövecses and Szabo, 1996; Li, 2002; Tyler and Evans, 2004) have been conducted, all of which attempt to teach phrasal verbs systematically, exploring the metaphoric and metonymic relationships between the senses of the prepositions in the phrasal verbs and their more basic senses. So for example, students might be encouraged to focus on the basic sense of the preposition *down* and then to use this to work out the meanings of expressions such as: 'look down on someone'; 'get down to work'; and 'go down in someone's estimation'. A full review of this work can be found in Littlemore and Low (2006a; see also Chapter 3). The findings from such studies are mixed, but by and large they show that learners are to some extent able to form these links and that they are then able to use them to infer the meanings of newly introduced phrasal verbs (Kövecses, 2001). However, more work is needed in this area to establish whether or not the approach is equally effective with all types of phrasal verbs and with all types of learners. The fact that, under the cognitive linguistic view, grammar is to some extent meaningful, and not entirely arbitrary, is related to the discussion of embodiment in the previous chapter. For example, Tyler's (2008a, b) approach to teaching modal verbs that was discussed in Section 7.2 relies heavily on explainable meaning–meaning connections.

A useful resource for language teachers who are interested in teaching grammar as a meaningful rather than an arbitrary phenomenon is Radden and Dirven's (2007) *Cognitive English Grammar*. This book provides comprehensive coverage of all the main areas of grammar, explaining them from a cognitive linguistic perspective. Radden and Dirven are able to identify cognitive motivations for a wide range of grammatical phenomena that have traditionally been presented to language learners as arbitrary. Although it is not written for students, the ideas in the book could be used by teachers who are interested in presenting grammar in a meaningful and memorable way. Their book is based, among other things, on Langacker's (1987) system of word classes, and Talmy's (2000) conceptual structuring system. I have referred briefly to elements of both these systems in previous chapters of this book, but it is useful to have an idea of the whole system. In this section, I outline the main ideas in each of these systems, providing examples of how Radden and Dirven use these systems to explain particularly difficult grammar points.

Langacker's system of word classes is different from more conventional systems in which the main 'divisions' are between nouns, verbs, determiners, conjunctions, and so on. Instead, he argues that linguistic expressions can be divided into two main categories: **nominal**

predications (that are conceptually independent entities, e.g. as in English, *car*) and **relational predications** (that rely on other entities to complete their meaning e.g. *before* or *visit*). This division reflects a fundamental conceptual division in terms of the way we divide up our knowledge of the world into things that 'stand alone' and things that need to be defined in terms of their relationship with something else. Nominal predications can in turn be subdivided into those which are **bounded** (i.e. they have some sort of boundary, such as *the sea*) and those which are **unbounded** (i.e. they are limitless, such as *sea-water*). Relational predications can also be subdivided into those which are **temporal** (which are mainly verbs) and those which are **atemporal** (which include adjectives, adverbs and participles). Speakers choose which of these categories to use when talking about particular scenes and events, and their choice of category depends on how they want to package and present, or in cognitive linguistic terms, 'construe', the information. Choices are not fixed, as they reflect different ways of construing phenomena and events, although some ways of construing events are more conventional than others (as we saw in Chapter 2).

Let us now see an example of how this system might be used in second language teaching. Radden and Dirven take the bounded versus unbounded distinction from Langacker's model and use it to explain the difference between *few* and *a few* in sentences such as (45) and (46):

(45) There are few people who believe in fate
(46) There are a few people who believe in fate

They argue that the contribution made by '*a*' to the phrase is to make us see the people as existing within some sort of boundary, as we can see in Figure 8.2. Once they are clearly defined by this boundary, the people can now been seen as real, specific people if necessary and the focus is on the actual existence of these people. The utterance without the article '*a*', as we can see in Figure 8.2, has no boundary, which indicates that it is deliberately vague and implies that we are not talking about

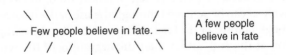

Figure 8.2   A possible illustration of the difference between *few* and *a few*

any specific people who believe in fate, but about a general absence of 'people who believe'.

Teachers may recognize this sort of diagram as resembling the sorts of diagrams that they themselves use in order to try and illustrate this grammatical point. They may however have worried that their diagrams are too idiosyncratic or bizarre for their students to understand. What cognitive linguistics does is provide an underlying rationale for the use of such diagrams, as it shows that they do indeed have a cognitive basis. By providing diagrams such as these, language teachers may help their students gain direct access to the image schemas underlying the 'grammar rules' of the target language. More research however is needed to assess the extent to which students benefit from the use of diagrams representing basic image schemas such as this and, as is noted by Boers (2004), whether some learners are more likely to benefit from them than others.

Talmy's conceptual structuring system also relates to the ways in which phenomena and events are construed. According to Talmy, we can select the way we choose to present information by making choices within four different, yet related systems. The first is the **configurational structure system**, which relates to issues such as boundedness (mentioned above, but also applying to verbs in Talmy's system), dividedness (whether things are countable or countable), and degrees of extension (whether or not events stretch over time). The second system in Talmy's model is the **attentional system**. As its name suggests, this system refers to what aspect of the utterance the speaker wishes to draw attention to. Certain aspects can be foregrounded or backgrounded, depending on the communicative intentions of the speaker. For example, let us compare two utterances, the second of which was uttered by my elder son:

(47) We started fighting and I hit Oscar
(48) There was a fight and Oscar got hurt

Although both of these sentences describe more or less the same scene, my son is much more likely to choose the second option rather than the first. This is because it draws attention away from him as the antagonist. This effect can be achieved through the use of the passive voice (as here), through ellipsis, or (in English) by positioning the backgrounded information at the end, rather than the beginning of the sentence. In cognitive linguistic terminology, the information that is foregrounded is usually referred to as the **figure**, whereas the information that is being backgrounded is referred to as the **ground**. Thinking about 'figure' and 'ground' is thus useful for showing which part of a text is considered prominent by the speaker.

Another advantage of the figure/ground dichotomy is that it provides a useful metalanguage for describing spoken grammar. It has been pointed out that traditional grammars have difficulty in dealing with features of spoken English, which has a flexible clause structure, and is listener-sensitive (Carter, 2007). For example, Carter asks how traditional grammars can deal with spoken utterances that exhibit 'front-loading' and 'tails', such as those appearing in these extracts from the Cambridge and Nottingham Corpus of Discourse English (CANCODE) (http://www.cambridge.org/elt/corpus/corpora_cancode.htm):

(49) She's a very good swimmer Jenny is
(50) It can leave you feeling very weak, it can though apparently, shingles, can't it?

In these utterances, the main idea is placed at the beginning of the utterance and the less important information forms the 'tail' of the utterance. Talmy's notions of figure and ground are useful for describing this phenomenon. In both of Carter's examples, the main information is frontloaded and therefore profiled as the figure, whereas the less important information comes last and is clearly relegated to the ground. These figure/ground construals are also likely to be reinforced through intonation and stress patterns (i.e. the 'figure' is emphasized and the 'ground' is de-emphasized, both phonetically and through use of intonation patterns). Fluent communication involves the ability to engage in constant profiling shifts in order to accommodate one's interlocutor and to co-construct meaning. It also involves the ability to mark these shifts with appropriate changes in word order and intonation. This skill is described by Carter (2007) as **confluence**. This is an extended version of fluency and includes skills such as speaking in a listener-friendly way and co-constructing meaning. Talmy's system of figure/ground contrasts provides a useful way of describing the necessary fluctuations that this entails.

The third and fourth systems in Talmy's model have already been discussed in previous chapters. The third system in the model is the **perspectival system**, which refers to the speaker's own vantage point. Many of the issues related to attention and perspective were discussed in Chapter 2 in the discussion of construal. The fourth system in Talmy's model, the **force dynamics system**, was discussed in Section 7.2 above, so I will not repeat the discussion here.

Let us now see an example of how Radden and Dirven use Talmy's conceptual structuring system to explain a difficult grammatical point. Because I have already focused on the attentional, perspectival and force dynamics systems in earlier chapters, I have chosen an example to illustrate how Talmy's configurational system can be used when presenting grammar. An idea that is present in Talmy's system, but which is not present in Langacker's system is that the boundedness/unboundedness dichotomy can be applied to activities, as well as to nominal predicates. In its most basic sense, the dichotomy applies to temporal events. A typical textbook example (Murphy, 1986: 24) is as follows in examples (51) and (52):

> (51) Yesterday <u>Tom and Jim played tennis</u>. They began at 10 o'clock and finished at 11 o'clock.
> (52) What were they doing at 10.30? <u>They were playing tennis.</u>

> 'They were playing' means that they were in the middle of playing tennis. They had started playing but they hadn't finished.

Although Murphy makes no explicit mention of it, one of the main differences between the two examples is that (51) describes a bounded event (with a clear beginning and end) whereas (52) describes an unbounded event, where the beginning and end are not specified. Radden and Dirven (*ibid.*: 187) argue that boundedness and non-boundedness are radial categories that extend beyond temporal notions, as in the following pairs of contrasts, here numbered (53)–(55):

> (53) a I talked to Mr Green (bounded)
>   b I was talking to Mr Green (unbounded)

> (54) a What did you do before you came to work here? (bounded)
>   b What were you doing before you came to work here? (unbounded)

> (55) a What did you do in my office? (bounded)
>   b What were you doing in my office? (unbounded)

In all three cases, the unbounded option adds vagueness (Channell, 1994). In (53b) it introduces an element of vagueness in terms of the amount of time spent talking to Mr Green, and possibly the topic of the conversation. The unbounded question in (54b) would probably elicit a slightly different, less specific response than its bounded equivalent (54a). The question in (55b) goes well beyond the basic sense of the words it contains, and carries a number of pragmatic implications that are not present in its bounded equivalent (55a). By and large, questions (54a) and (55a) are intended to elicit more precise answers than questions (54b) and (55b), although it is possible to imagine different interpretations, depending on the speaker's tone of voice and body language. Without boundaries, there are thus more opportunities for vagueness and pragmatic extensions. In some ways this can be seen as a metaphorical extension of the concrete function of physical boundaries to the more abstract function of unboundedness in grammar. This corresponds to the radial category approach to grammar which we discussed in Chapter 3. The prototypical senses of a grammatical construction are motivated by embodied cognition (i.e. our experience of real, physical boundaries), and then are extended metaphorically to take on more abstract meanings. This process lies at the very core of cognitive linguistics, and is perhaps one of the areas that has the most to offer language teachers. Grammar rules could perhaps be explained through reference to embodied cognition, and then presented as being flexible enough to accommodate extensions into more abstract domains.

Niemeier and Reif (2008) develop this idea even further and propose some practical teaching ideas designed to help (in their case German) students to understand the difference between the progressive and the non-progressive aspect in English. They note that German speakers of English often have problems with this area of grammar, due in part to the fact that German does not mark these different aspects grammatically. Speakers of German tend to rely on additional particles and adverbial clauses (such as 'at the moment' or 'right now'), as well as contextual information. Niemeier and Reif suggest that, when it is used with actions that are normally bounded (e.g. 'she made me a cup of tea'), the main function of the progressive aspect is to de-emphasize the boundaries (i.e. to remove the focus from the beginning or the end point of the action) and to zoom in on the action itself. They believe that it is important for the students to realize that the progressive and non-progressive aspects represent particular construals of the same action. In order to show how a particular scene is being construed by the use of the progressive aspect they suggest illustrating the scene with a large magnifying glass placed over it, or showing the scene through a keyhole cut-out to show how, in this particular construal, the viewer is intended to focus on one part of the action. They plan to carry out empirical studies in order to test the relative efficacy of these different approaches.

In this chapter, we have seen so far that there are a number of explainable form–form, meaning–form and meaning–meaning connections that are of potential use in the language classroom. We have seen that there are good arguments for raising students' awareness of these motivated aspects of language as they help show why languages behave in the way they do, and reduce the number of arbitrary associations that the learners have to make. However, there are limitations to this approach, as we will now see.

8.5   Limitations to the teaching of motivated language in the classroom

One limitation to the idea of teaching language as a 'motivated' phenomenon is the fact that a great deal of language simply isn't motivated. Many form–meaning connections are simply arbitrary and have to be learned that way. The role of the teacher is thus to help learners notice connections that are motivated, and to help them use those motivations to learn. A second limitation, as Boers and Lindstromberg (2006) point out, is the fact that languages are motivated in different ways, and that it is difficult to predict exactly how the motivation patterns in a given language will work. That is to say, although the explanations such as those outlined above can be observed retrospectively, they are very difficult to predict. This means that although linguistic motivation may help learners to understand language input, it will not necessarily help them to produce appropriate target-language forms. At any one time, there are many potential, motivated relationships that can be formed, but only a few ever come into existence. For example, in English, a teacher can 'run through' the homework, or 'go over' it, and both of these expressions are to some extent explainable in terms of the 'path' metaphor, but he or she cannot literally 'run over' the homework as this expression means something entirely different indeed (Low and Littlemore, 2009). Thus to some extent, we have to accept that there is still a degree of arbitrariness in language in terms of which motivated routes are followed and which are not. On the other hand, if learners are sufficiently confident, they should be able to use the patterns of motivation that they have identified thus far in their target language, to develop and test out new expressions. If they are sufficiently proficient to signal these usages as *novel*, then, through the use of feedback from their interlocutor, they should be able to learn from their experiments.

Another important observation to make is that the methods proposed in this chapter are heavily biased towards the explicit teaching of grammar, albeit with a slightly different focus from the more conventional approaches to grammar teaching in the classroom. We saw in Chapter 2 that the most lasting learning effects are most likely to result when explicit knowledge is brought to bear on implicit knowledge and vice versa. Therefore, as well as being presented with motivated language explicitly, learners need to see evidence of it in authentic discourse, and test out their own hypotheses in as natural a setting as possible.

8.6 Concluding comments

In this chapter we have looked at three forms of linguistic motivation: form–form motivation; form–meaning motivation; and meaning–meaning motivation. We have seen examples of how these different types of motivation might be exploited in second language classrooms and noted the need for more research in the area. I have ended by sounding a note of caution and observing that motivated language is best observed retrospectively, and that the particular direction that a language will take is often unpredictable. Attending to the motivated aspects of language is a strategy that is perhaps more suited to language comprehension than to language production. On the other hand, students might use the principles of cognitive grammar to make predictions about the target language and then test out these predictions when communicating in that language. In the next chapter I look at how linguistic motivation works at a phraseological level.

9
'Brian sent Antarctica a walrus': Construction Grammars and Second Language Learning

9.1 Introductory comments

In this chapter I take the idea of linguistic motivation that was discussed in the previous chapter and extend it to the level of the phrase, by focusing on **construction grammars**. In Chapter 3 we saw that different aspects of language, such as words, morphemes, parts of speech and even intonation patterns, have been found to exist within radial categories. Findings from cognitive linguistics are starting to show that this phenomenon stretches beyond the word, operating at a phraseological level too. In other words, grammar patterns, or **constructions**, also carry their own meanings, independently of the words they contain. These meanings exist within radial categories that have more concrete, prototypical, and more abstract peripheral members. For example, if we look at the following instance of what Goldberg (1995: 152) describes as the 'caused motion' construction, in example (56):

(56) Jake pushed the vase off the table

We can see that it bears some sort of semantic relationship to other sentences that have the same grammatical pattern, for example (57)–(59):

(57) Sue squeezed her head through the neck of the jumper
(58) She ordered Jack out of the meeting
(59) Jamie sneezed the napkin off the table

These sentences are all instances of the 'caused motion' construction. We can see that there is a clear semantic link between them and that their meaning appears to be inherent in the actual grammar pattern, or 'construction', rather than the words it contains. Thus, *sneeze*, which does not normally operate as a transitive verb, begins to do so when it is placed in this construction. *Sneeze* is, in many ways, much less prototypical for a construction such as this than for example the verb *pushed*, so could be said to lie more towards the periphery of the category. The other verbs in the above examples (*squeezed* and *ordered*) are progressively less 'prototypical' within this construction, which shows how constructions operate within radial categories.

Unlike most of the other examples used in this book, the above examples are not corpus-based. This is because the majority of accounts of construction grammar rely on artificial examples which allow for a more succinct explanation of the theory. Although there have been some recent attempts to address the problem (e.g. Stefanowitsch and Gries, 2007), the fact that so many accounts of construction grammar rely on artificial examples is a serious drawback of the theory. Of course the advantage of using artificial examples is that they can be simple, allowing the reader to focus on what can be complicated concepts. For this reason, I have followed suit in this chapter, although I discuss the implications of the theory's lack of authentic data below.

One of the main aims of construction grammars is to provide a single, coherent account of both the 'regular' and 'idiomatic' properties of language. Therefore some constructions, such as the 'simple past' construction, bear a strong resemblance to regular 'grammar rules', whereas others, such as the 'what's X doing Y?' construction (e.g. 'What's that gorilla doing in a bikini?' BofE example), are much more idiomatic. Construction grammar has at least two things in common with views of language that have grown out of corpus linguistic approaches.

Firstly, the construction grammar approach incorporates the 'idiom principle' that was proposed by Sinclair (1991). According to the idiom principle, our choice of which word comes next in a sentence is limited by the phraseology of the sentence. However, construction grammarians part company with Sinclair over the idea that there is also, at times, an 'open choice' principle at work in language, where the choice of words is not restricted by what has gone before. Construction grammarians would argue that the open choice principle operates rarely, if ever, in language. For the construction grammarian, the idiom principle operates all the time, but with varying degrees of strength.

Secondly, construction grammar has a great deal in common with Hunston and Francis's (1999) **pattern grammar**. Both approaches to grammar emphasize the fact that the construction, or pattern, determines the meaning of the verb it contains. However, there are differences between these two approaches which, if anything, should make them complementary. Unlike construction grammar, pattern grammar is data-driven and relies entirely on authentic language. It is also vast, with 85 basic patterns having been identified for verbs, along with numerous extensions to these patterns, and an equivalent number of patterns for nouns and adjectives. Construction grammarians have identified a much smaller number of patterns and these are not based on authentic data. However, they have identified ways in which constructions relate to one another, and have attempted to isolate the meanings of certain constructions. Both approaches reveal that traditional grammatical categories such as 'object', 'complement', and so on, do not adequately account for the behaviour of words, but construction grammarians have gone on to create a meta-language to describe the components of constructions in terms of what they actually do. It would therefore be advantageous if the systematicity of construction grammar could be combined with the real-world approach of pattern grammar to create an authentic, yet usable, description of English grammar.

A number of different versions of construction grammar have been proposed, including: Langacker's (1987) original 'cognitive grammar', which is based on action chains and force dynamics; Goldberg's (1995) construction grammar which was the first to extend the constructional approach from 'irregular' idiomatic constructions to more 'regular' types of constructions; Bergen and Chang's (2005) 'embodied construction grammar', which focuses on language processing and looks at how embodied knowledge is used in the comprehension and production of constructions; and Croft's (2001) radical construction grammar (RCG), which emphasizes the degree to which the meaning of words is dependent on the constructions in which they appear. According to RCG, words themselves cannot be categorized into word classes that have any kind of independent reality. It is the construction in which a word appears that gives a word its class, and it is meaningless to talk of word class outside the construction.

In this chapter, my aim is to focus on those areas of construction grammar that have the most relevance to language teaching and learning. I therefore concentrate on Goldberg's model, as this has been the most widely studied to date. I also refer at times to Bergen and Chang's embodied construction grammar, as this has clear implications for language teaching. Although my focus is mainly on these two approaches, at times I draw on ideas from the other approaches where they have something to offer to second language learning and teaching. I also draw attention to the limitations of construction grammars and their applications to second language learning and teaching. I begin in Section 9.2 by outlining Goldberg's approach to construction grammar, introducing it through a series of examples that are adapted from Goldberg's own work, and assessing its applicability to language teaching. In Section 9.3, I introduce Goldberg's account of how constructions relate to one another. Having examined Goldberg's approach in detail, in Section 9.4, I look at how constructions might be *explicitly* taught and learned in the second language classroom. Then, in Section 9.5, I look at the *implicit* learning of constructions by second language learners. I begin by looking at the role of construction grammar in first language acquisition, and describe Tomasello's (2003) work, which constitutes the first fully usage-based theory of first language acquisition. His book-length treatment of the subject investigates how infants use intention-reading skills and pattern-recognition skills to acquire and use the constructions in their first language. Tomasello's findings are likely to have strong implications for SLA, particularly when it takes place in non-classroom settings. I discuss the contribution that Tomasello's work may make to existing theories of SLA, and to methodologies such as task-based learning. In this section, I look at studies that have attempted to simulate L1-style learning settings, by providing learners with skewed input in order to see whether they can learn from such input.

9.2 Goldberg's (1995) construction grammar

As we have seen, one of the main claims in a construction grammar approach to language is that the patterns, or 'constructions', in which words are organized are as capable of conveying meaning as the words themselves. Words can therefore have different senses depending on what construction they are used in, and from a comprehension point of view, constructions can serve a strong disambiguating function. As we saw with the 'caused motion' construction, constructions are also thought to exist within radial categories. Although all the examples above reflect the same construction, each of them is, in some way, less 'literal' or 'basic' than example (56) 'Jake pushed the vase off the table', implying that these examples all inhabit different spaces within the same radial category. When atypical words, (such as *sneezed* in example (59) above) are pulled into a construction, they acquire slightly new senses that are more in line with the overall meaning of that construction. Arguably, the word *sneeze* would not normally be associated with a transitive construction, but the fact that it sits in one here gives it a particular transitive meaning. This is an important point in cognitive linguistics, and relates back to the discussion of encyclopaedic meaning that we had in Chapter 4. Different aspects of a word's encyclopaedic meaning can be activated by its presence in a particular construction.

The fact that constructions are thought to occupy radial categories has interesting implications for language learning and teaching. For example, students could be taught these 'core' meanings, and then encouraged to extrapolate from them to other more peripheral meanings. Moreover, as we will see below, constructions are thought to be organized in a relatively systematic manner, and have clear, motivated relationships with each other. Focusing on constructions, and the relationships between them, could perhaps help learners to come to terms with the phraseological nature of language, without them being overwhelmed by a sense of apparent arbitrariness and lists of unrelated phrases. These ideas are discussed in more depth in Section 9.4, but as we will see later in the chapter, construction grammars are a relatively new and untested phenomenon, so we should proceed with caution when discussing their potential applications to language teaching.

Another advantage of constructions from the point of view of the language learner is that by and large, they are thought to be motivated by embodied schemas (Bergen and Chang, 2005). One of the main claims of construction grammarians is that there is a close correlation between conceptual structures and syntactic structures. Two of the key cognitive processes that are reflected in different constructions are those of foregrounding and backgrounding, which were briefly introduced in Chapter 8. Reference to these processes gives rise to more transparent, meaningful terminology to describe the components of a construction. Table 9.1 shows how the caused-motion construction would be described in both traditional syntactic terminology and cognitive linguistic terminology.

We can see from Table 9.1 that cognitive linguistic terminology is much more closely related to the semantics of the phrase than conventional syntactic terminology. As it is more closely related to the embodied meaning of the construction, the cognitive linguistic terminology is arguably more likely to be remembered by language learners. It is easier to visualize, and therefore remember words such as *cause, motion, figure, path* and *ground* than words such as *subject, verb, object,* and *adverbial*. The reason for this is that the cognitive linguistic terminology is closer to what is actually happening in the construction, and is much less abstract than the conventional terminology.

Table 9.1 Conceptual and syntactic accounts of the caused-motion construction

Example	*The draught*	*blew*	*the pencil*	*off*	*the table*
Cognitive linguistic terminology	CAUSE	MOTION	FIGURE	PATH	GROUND
Conventional terminology	Subject	Verb	Object	Adverbial	

One of the main advantages of construction grammar is that is allows teachers to give their students meaningful accounts of grammatical phenomena. To illustrate the meaningfulness of constructions, let us look at part of Goldberg's (1995:153) account of the 'caused motion' construction:

(60) We coaxed/asked/invited/allowed him out of the room.

Which can be contrasted with the somewhat fuller construction:

(61) We instructed/told/advised/begged him to go out of the room

Although these two constructions appear to be semantically equivalent, there are a number of words that do not fit well into the caused motion construction:

(62) * We instructed/told/advised/begged him out of the room

Equally, there are other words that do not fit well into the longer construction:

(63) * She lured him to go out of the room

A traditional grammatical account of the above examples might argue that verbs such as *instruct* are 'infinitival', verbs such as *lure* are 'prepositional', which means that they are followed by a preposition, and verbs such as *order* are both 'infinitival' and 'prepositional', which means that they are followed by an infinitive or a preposition. The problem with explanations such as this is that they do not tell us *why* these particular verbs are followed by these particular parts of speech. The learner therefore has nothing to hold onto, and simply needs to learn the lists off by heart. A construction grammar approach arguably offers a better way of presenting the information to learners as it appeals to the semantics of the construction itself. By examining those words which fit the construction well, we can identify a number of conditions that need to be more or less satisfied in order for the construction to make sense. The full set of these conditions constitutes the semantics of the construction.

We will now see how Goldberg (1995: 167–73) illustrates two of the five conditions identified for this particular construction, by looking at two sets of examples. For reasons of space, I will not provide details of all five of Goldberg's conditions for this particular construction. Firstly, let us look at the following two sentences:

(64) Fans booed the striker off the pitch (BofE example)
(65) ? They booed him into the car

The reason why (65) sounds slightly marked is that getting into a car requires some agency on the part of the protagonist. This means that it does not fully meet the first condition of the caused motion construction:

No cognitive decision can mediate between the causing event and the entailed motion.

Now let us look at two more sentences:

(66) Arts West flew me to Barcaldine last Wednesday (BofE example)
(67) ?Mum flew me to London for a holiday

Sentence (67) sounds odd as parents do not conventionally fly people round the world, whereas companies do. Thus it does not meet the second condition of the caused motion construction:

If the activity being referred to reflects 'conventional' behaviour in the language community then the activity can be packaged as a single event even if an intervening cause exists.

The two conditions shown in italics form part of the actual meaning of the caused motion construction. Both of the utterances that are preceded by a question mark describe events that are somewhat unlikely to occur in everyday life (though a convincing meaning scenario could perhaps be put together at a stretch) and they therefore sound slightly marked within this construction. This shows how the behaviour of constructions reflects real-life experience and is not simply arbitrary. This is a good illustration of how semantic and pragmatic information can actually be encoded in the syntax. It is a powerful indicator of the fact that grammar is a process that draws on the full resources of our knowledge frame rather than relying solely on a subcomponent of the mind concerned purely with some sort of narrowly defined 'linguistic knowledge' (Lee, 2001: 89). Moreover, according to *embodied* construction grammar, the central and typical senses will always be experientially grounded, and the less basic senses are arranged around them in radial categories, with the senses that lie towards the periphery of the categories being less typical of everyday behaviour and experience.

Looking at language via construction grammar is potentially useful for second language educators because it provides a sort of middle ground between the categorical yet inadequate traditional 'grammar rules' approach and the more accurate yet potentially overwhelming 'lexical' approach, which relies on rote memory of thousands of unrelated phrases. Construction grammars are able to show the phraseological nature of language whilst providing a system within which these 'phrases' can be learned. In doing so, it downplays the dichotomy between predictability and arbitrariness.

However, there are at least two problems that need to be addressed before we can start to use construction grammar in the language classroom. The first problem relates to the meta-language that is used to explain the various conditions that the constructions must meet. Many language learners would probably be somewhat put off by explanations, such as: *'No cognitive decision can mediate between the causing event and the entailed motion'*. Serious thought needs to be given to the ways in which this sort of language can be paraphrased, and made more student-friendly. For example, the two conditions that were mentioned above for the 'caused-motion' construction could be paraphrased as follows:

The caused motion construction is used to refer to actions that lead directly to some sort of movement

and

You can use your knowledge of what is conventional to infer that movement has taken place

However even these explanations are somewhat long and unwieldy without illustrative examples. The best approach would probably be to give students examples such as those shown above, and have them work out the conditions for themselves. This would arguably lead to a greater degree of metalinguistic awareness, and possibly deeper learning. The problem with this approach is that it is very time-consuming. It would therefore need to be restricted to constructions that are particularly productive in the target language, or markedly different from those in the student's native language. Corpus studies would be useful to identify such constructions. We also need to consider how they might best be presented to learners.

A second, more serious problem with construction grammars, as we saw above, is that they are not based on authentic language data. Although some researchers are starting to investigate the ways in which individual constructions behave in authentic discourse (e.g. Stefanowitsch and Gries, 2007), construction grammar as a whole has not yet been exposed to large-scale systematic validation using corpus linguistic techniques. To illustrate, the sentence 'Jake sneezed the napkin off the table' that we saw above is a widely cited example of the caused motion construction in cognitive linguistics, but a search of the 450 million-word Bank of English reveals no instances of this transitive use of *sneeze*. Although this does not undermine the theory as a whole (it is easy to think of other examples that do fit the pattern) it does raise questions about the frequency of such constructions and of how worthwhile it is to teach them. We therefore need to investigate the frequency and distribution of constructions across large amounts of authentic language data in order to establish which ones to focus on in the language classroom. Cross-linguistic studies would also be useful in order to identify potential areas of difficulty for language learners.

Corpus-based studies that have been carried out in order to investigate construction grammar have revealed that the reality of constructions is much messier than cognitive linguistic theories would predict. For example, Hopper (2001) looked at the cleft construction (e.g. 'What we're going to do is...') in the London-Lund corpus of spoken English and found little evidence of prototypical instances of this construction and many instances of sentence fragments which, under a cognitive linguistic account, would lie more towards the periphery of the category. The findings here are similar to those discussed in Chapter 3, which showed that in authentic discourse, the majority of the utterances tend to lie towards the periphery of radial categories, rather than at the centre. This fact needs to be taken into account in any attempts to implement a construction grammar approach in the language teaching curriculum. With these caveats in mind, let us now turn to a second area of construction grammar that may be useful in language teaching: the relationships between constructions.

9.3 Relationships between constructions

An observation made by Goldberg (1995: 75–81) that has potential applications to second language learning and teaching is that constructions (and the utterances that operate within them) are related to one another in ways that are logical and meaningful. Constructions that look similar to one another will have meanings that are similar to one another, so learners can presumably use their existing knowledge of constructions to infer the meanings of ones that are new to them. We will see below that this mirrors the way in which children learn constructions in their own language. Goldberg identifies four ways in which constructions (and the utterances that they contain) are related. Let us now look in more detail at Goldberg's account of the relationships within and between constructions.

Firstly, within a particular construction, Goldberg argues that the various utterances that are possible are linked through **polysemy**. For instance, the ditransitive construction is associated with a range of senses, all of which share some aspects of the semantics of transfer, as we can see in the following examples:

X causes Y to receive Z (central sense):
(68) 'Rachel gave Kim a CD'

Conditions of satisfaction imply X causes Y to receive Z:
(69) 'Mum promised Joe a new bike'

X intends to cause Y to receive Z:
(70) 'Dan baked Jeannette a cake'

Although these examples all share some element of transfer, they differ according to whether the transfer is actual, as in (68), intended, as in (69) or implied, as in (70). Thus constructions are polysemous in much the same way as individual words are, as we saw in Chapter 3. Indeed, for many cognitive linguists this is not surprising, as individual words are also viewed as constructions; they are merely simple, rather than complex constructions.

Secondly, one of the main ways in which constructions are related *to each other* is through **subpart links**. For example, if we compare the two utterances (71) and (72):

(71) Karen drove Jake to the airport
(72) Karen drove

The first utterance is an instance of the caused motion construction, whereas (72) is an instance of the intransitive motion construction. Whereas (71) 'lexically profiles' (i.e. expresses in words) a CAUSE (*Karen drove*), a THEME (*Jake*) and a GOAL (*to the airport*), the second only 'lexically profiles' a THEME (*Karen drove*). The second construction is therefore a subpart of the first.

The third way in which constructions can be related is through **instance links**. These occur when one construction is a special case of a related construction. The most common type of instance link is that of substantive idioms (where the idiomatic reading is only applicable when one of a restricted set of expressions is present). For instance, let us consider the resultative construction:

(73) Tim drank himself under the table

When this construction has the word *drove* in it, it tends to take on an idiomatic meaning which means to 'make someone crazy', as in:

(74) Jack drove me mad/round the bend/up the wall

The meaning of the construction is restricted to this sense, which means that it sounds odd with other adjectives, such as:

(75) * Jack drove me happy/sad/excited/bored

This idiomatic reading is thus a special instance of the more general resultative construction, which is why it is described as an 'instance link'.

Fourthly, constructions can be linked by **inheritance links**, which usually involve metaphor. For example, the caused motion construction:

(76) Jack kicked Peter out of the room

can be metaphorically extended to form the resultative construction:

(77) Jack kicked Peter senseless

In this example, *senseless*.... is a type of metaphorical goal, which parallels the actual goal in the caused motion construction. Despite the metaphorical inheritance link, Goldberg maintains that it is important to recognize that these are in fact two separate constructions as they each sanction different sets of verbs. For instance, the resultative construction licenses *made*, whereas the caused motion construction does not:

(78) Joe made Oscar happy
(79) * Joe made Oscar into the cupboard

In contrast, the caused motion construction licenses *pushed*, whereas the resultative construction does not:

(80) Joe pushed Oscar into the cupboard
(81) * Joe pushed Oscar happy

An awareness of these types of inheritance links is likely to be useful to language learners as it brings a degree of systematicity to the apparently overwhelming number of constructions that need to be learned. This should in theory go some way towards helping learners to deal with one of the greatest hurdles in phraseological approaches to language learning: that of 'data overload' (Broccias, 2008). However, in the language teaching profession we have a long way to go before we can produce suitable materials to introduce learners to L2 constructions and the relationships between them in a realistic, systematic and learnable manner. Before this can be done, more research is needed using authentic data to establish the exact nature of constructions, and then pedagogical research is needed to investigate the best ways of introducing them, either explicitly through the use of accessible terminology or implicitly through carefully selected L2 input. Bearing in mind the fact that we are at such an early stage of research in this field, the ideas presented in the following two sections, which look at how constructions might be taught and learned explicitly and implicitly, must be seen as provisional.

9.4   Learning constructions explicitly: classroom applications of Goldberg's theory

We have seen in the above section that there are a number of features of constructions that should make them attractive to language learners and teachers: that there is a close correlation between conceptual structures and syntactic structures; that constructions may be stored in the long-term memory; that constructions have meanings of their own; and that these meanings exist in radial categories. Instead of providing lists of arbitrary rules concerning the behaviour of individual words and then asking students to learn these rules by heart, teachers should be able to use construction grammar to explain why it is the case that these words behave in the way they do. In other words, they should be able to present phraseology as being a partially motivated, rather than an entirely arbitrary, phenomenon. Although some of the explanations in the preceding section contained terminology that would be inappropriate for most language classrooms, other constructions that Goldberg has identified could be introduced inductively through the use of examples, without the use of any unnecessary metalanguage. For instance, let us look at Goldberg's (1995: 200–1) *way* construction, as illustrated by the following set of examples (which I have taken from the Bank of English):

(82) he'd *bludgeoned his way through,* right on the stroke of half time
(83) [the players will] *maul their way up* the middle of the field
(84) …glaciers which had repeatedly *nudged their way between* England and Wales

Goldberg points out that without a constructional approach to language we would need to find additional senses for each of the verbs in italics, and we would then have to stipulate the fact that these new verb senses can only occur in this particular syntactic structure. As she very neatly puts it: 'Clearly it is more parsimonious to attribute the motion interpretation directly to the construction itself' (1995: 201). In this case, learners could simply be shown the examples above and asked to infer the meaning of the construction. They could then be asked to work out the subtle nuances provided by the different verbs in the examples. The teacher could also draw on the fact that these expressions are highly metaphorical.

A second way in which teachers might introduce constructions explicitly is to teach the difference between apparently very similar constructions. For example, in English, we have the ditransitive construction (e.g. 'Alex gave him the book') and the prepositional construction (e.g. 'Alex gave the book to him'). In many ways, these two constructions are very similar, but a cognitive linguistic account, such as the one below, that is adapted from Lee (2001:75), could be used to explain the differences. For example, a teacher might begin by showing the students the following pairs of expressions and asking them if either of the expressions sounds odd:

(85)   a   Sheila gave the office a new coat of paint
      b   ?Sheila gave a new coat of paint to the office

(86)   a   Bob taught me all I know
      b   ?Bob taught all I know to me

(87)   a   Brian sent a walrus to Antarctica
      b   ?Brian sent Antarctica a Walrus

(88)   a   Jeannette cleared the floor for Terry
      b   ?Jeannette cleared Terry the floor

The teacher might then go on to explain that to many speakers of English, the 'b' sentences in each pair sound marked. The students could be asked to work out why they think this is so. They could then be given the cognitive explanation, which is as follows: The ditransitive construction focuses on the *result* of the process, whereas the prepositional construction focuses on the *movement*. The object (or 'patient') must be seen in some way as a *recipient*, rather than simply being the place to which the direct object moves. This explains why the sentences (89) and (90) sound unusual:

(89) * I mowed Gill the lawn
(90) *I opened Gill the door

This explanation is better than a traditional 'grammatical' one in which the learner would simply be told that some verbs take the ditransitive construction and some verbs take the prepositional construction, with no explanation being offered as to why this might be. The cognitive linguistic explanation shows *why* it is that some words sit more comfortably in one construction than another. Cognitive linguistic explanations such as this could be supplemented with the use of diagrams and mime, which would then give the students a second and perhaps more powerful and memorable mode of input. As Lee (2001: 90) points out:

> the claim that different constructions express subtle meaning differences provides an explanation for the fact that certain verbs which appear to be closely related semantically nevertheless exhibit distributional differences with respect to the range of constructions in which they occur.

This is very important information for second language learners as it could be used to teach them about the subtle differences between near-synonyms in the target language.

Another area of construction grammar which could be introduced explicitly through the use of examples relates to 'change of state' verbs (Levin and Rappaport Hovav, 1991). For example, although the three sentences (91)–(93) sound unmarked in English:

(91) They cleared the debris from the road
(92) They emptied the chocolate off the shelves
(93) He mopped up the milk from the floor

When they are expressed in a slightly different way, the third sentence sounds somehow odd:

(94) They cleared the road of debris
(95) They emptied the shelves of chocolate
(96) ?He mopped the floor of milk

Levin and Rappaport Hovav argue that the reason for this is that *clear* and *empty* are 'change of state verbs'. That is to say, they refer to processes that result in a particular state of affairs, without specifying how that result was achieved. Their focus is on the resultant state rather than on the process. *Mop* is not a change of state verb as it focuses slightly more attention on the action itself rather than simply describing the end result. This is why *clear* and *empty* fit the second construction, whereas *mop* does not. Examples such as these exemplify the close synchrony between semantics and syntax and show how syntax is semantically motivated. Again, this sort of knowledge is likely to be useful for second language learners.

One of the main proponents of the idea that language teachers should explicitly focus on the subtle meanings or construals of constructions is

Achard (2008). He argues that instead of giving learners sets of grammar rules with corresponding lists of exceptions, or lists of words that can be used in one construction but not in another, it is much more useful to try and explain, perhaps through the use of examples such as those given above, the exact construals implied by the constructions, and use this explanation to show why certain words sit more comfortably within those constructions than others. In order to illustrate his point, he refers to French definite articles, which are often taught in combination with particular words. As an example, he cites the French textbook *Deux Mondes*, in which students are advised:

> To choose the appropriate article, look at the kind of verb used in the sentence. With verbs describing likes or dislikes, such as **aimer, adorer, detester, préférer**, use the definite article because you are talking about things in a general sense... On the other hand, if the verb deals with having, obtaining, or consuming, use **du, de la, de l'** or **des** because you are talking about some amount of thing. Such verbs include **avoir, acheter, manger, boire, prendre**, and many others. Les Francais **boivent du** café après le dîner "the French drink coffee after dinner". Nous **mangeons de la** pizza tous les vendredi soir "We eat pizza every Friday night." (Extract from *Deux Mondes*, cited in Achard [2008: 443] ; emphasis in the original)

In this extract, the *Deux Mondes* textbook presents a couple of very general rules but then presents article selection as being mainly a property of individual verbs. Using corpus data, Achard identifies a number of examples that violate the supposed restrictions cited above and uses this data to argue that the use of the definite article reflects a choice by the speaker to construe the event in a certain way. Often it will serve to evoke cultural rituals, such as the fact that at four o'clock, many French families 'prennent le café' (literally, 'take the coffee') or when a new person arrives in a neighbourhood, they may be invited to 'boire l'apéritif' (literally, 'drink the l'apéritif'). These culturally determined schemas are an important aspect of construal and are reflected in the types of constructions discussed above. Helping learners gain access to these schemas will not only help them to better understand the target-language culture, it will also give more meaning to their learning, and should in theory prove to be much more motivating than simply learning by rote which verbs are used in which constructions.

Also of potential relevance to language learners is the fact that languages vary in terms of the extent to which they exploit the potential of a given construction category. For example, Taylor (2003: 242) points out that if we look at the transitive construction in English and German, we can see that it has undergone considerable extension in English, whereas in German its usage is relatively restricted. Prototypical uses of the transitive construction exist in both languages. For example, a straightforward transitive construction is used in both languages for expressions like 'I'm eating toast'. However, a number of more peripheral uses are permitted in English, which in German have to be rendered through the use of a different type of construction. For instance, the sentence 'I like James' has to be rendered 'Mir gefällt James' (James pleases me) in German. 'Joe brushed his teeth' has to be rendered as 'Joe hat sich die Zähne geputzt' (Joe brushed - to himself - the teeth). Moreover, German does not permit the use of instruments in the subject position of this construction, so it is not possible to say things like 'The key opened the door' or 'The hotel does not allow dogs'. And finally, sentences which sit 'at the very limit of the construction' (*ibid.*: 243) such as 'The tent sleeps six' have no transitive equivalents in German. It would be useful for language learners to be aware of the ways in which constructions such as these differ from those in their own language. It may be useful to employ a contrastive approach to teaching so that learners can be made aware of the differences, rather than having to infer them for themselves. More research is needed to measure the benefits of such an approach.

9.5 Learning constructions implicitly: Tomasello's usage-based account of L1 acquisition and its applications to L2 acquisition

So far, the discussion has focused on the usefulness of explicitly teaching constructions to second language learners. The methods proposed in the preceding section are however very de-contextualized and grammar-focused. It remains to be seen whether teaching grammar in this way carries with it all the problems that are typically associated with traditional, explicit grammar teaching, or whether such an approach offers a better route to learning, as the grammar being presented is a more accurate representation of reality. In other words, we do not know whether the problems associated with the traditional grammatical approaches to language teaching are more to do with the way in which it is taught, or whether they are more related to the artificial nature of the 'grammar' that is actually being presented. Answers to this question will no doubt emerge as cognitive linguistic approaches to the explicit teaching of grammar are tested in language classrooms. So for now, we will leave this debate and consider implicit learning.

An excellent account of the way in which children learn form–meaning pairings of constructions in their first language is offered by Tomasello (2003). He argues that two key cognitive processes that children employ to learn the meanings of constructions are **intention reading** and **pattern formation**. In other words, by predicting what it is that the other person is likely to be telling or asking them in a given context, and then mapping the language that they actually hear onto these predictions, children learn to associate particular expressions with particular meanings. They then use their ability to compare utterances with one another and to detect similarities and differences between them, and they use their implicit knowledge of the sorts of relationships that typically exist between constructions to build their knowledge of language. For example, if, when offering their child something to eat, to drink, or to play with, a carer always uses the words 'Would you like a....?', the child will eventually start to associate this expression with the fact that they are being offered something, and work out that the word on the end indicates what it is that they are being offered. They then use their pattern-finding skills to relate this utterance to other utterances within the same construction, such as 'Would teddy like a cup of tea?', and other related constructions, such as 'would you like to go to the zoo?' or 'Would you like a new doll for Christmas?'

In cognitive linguistic terminology, intention-reading and pattern-finding skills are used to identify the context or the 'ground' within which the language can be learned. The object to which the carer is trying to draw the child's attention (for example, the food on his or her plate) is thus perceived as the 'figure'. Because the figure is perceptually salient, the child will pay more attention to it and will try to relate it to the words their carer is uttering. Within this setting, two facilitative processes can then come into play: lexical contrast, and use of the linguistic context. The phenomenon of **lexical contrast** means that in any language there is strong pressure against synonyms, so if the child hears a new word or a new construction, he or she will automatically assume that it means something different from things that he or she has heard previously in the same context. He or she will then use **the linguistic context** along with knowledge of other constructions and of the typical links that exist between them, to work out what the new construction means. Infants and children also use their ability to work out what particular perspective their interlocutor has on a situation and match this with the construction that their interlocutor habitually uses to reflect this viewpoint. Through repeated performances of this matching activity, they are able to work out how different constructions reflect different construals of the same event. They are thus able to generalize to a set of more abstract, overarching, schematic constructions that correspond to conventional ways of construing events in the language that they are acquiring. In order to do this, they use basic cognitive operations such as analogy, segmentation, and schema formation.

Children get a great deal of help from their carers when learning their first language. This help takes the form of **skewed input**. Goldberg (2006) found that in child-directed speech, and in the speech of the children themselves, the 'lion's share' of the verb slot in three-argument structure constructions is taken by just one verb, and that this is usually its most prototypical verb. This serves to reinforce the relationship between that particular verb and that particular construction in the child's mind. Prototypical verbs are said to have **high cue validity** in that they are more likely than other verbs to occur within a particular construction in child-directed speech. This allows the child to learn the association of a particular verb with a particular construction through a process of **contingency learning** (see Chapter 2). The probability that that particular verb will trigger that particular construction is high, and vice versa; if the child hears that particular construction, there is a strong chance that it will be used with that particular verb.

So how applicable are these ideas to second language acquisition? The ability to extract a set of abstract schematic constructions from the input one hears, and to associate different constructions with different construals is a good example of implicit learning. It involves sensitivity to the meaning, frequency and distribution of constructions, and takes place largely below the level of consciousness, thus reflecting the type of probabilistic processing described by Ellis (2006a, b, c) which was discussed in Chapter 2.

So does this mean that we can simply put second language learners in a situation where they are exposed to plenty of authentic discourse and then expect them to use their intention-reading skills and pattern-finding skills in order to make sense of the input and extract the relevant form–meaning pairings? The short answer to this question is: probably not. Second language learners rarely find themselves in the same situation as small children learning their first language, with a dedicated carer pointing things out to them, deliberately simplifying and repeating constructions, using verbs with high cue validity, exaggerating the intonation patterns of certain constructions, and employing all the other pedagogical features of child-directed speech. Rather, in many ESL situations, learners are more likely to find themselves surrounded by the target language in its unadulterated form and will have far fewer cues as to their interlocutor's intended meaning than are normally available to the average two-year-old learning their first language. For these reasons, it is unlikely that second language learners will be able to pick up L2 constructions in the same way that L1 learners do, via implicit learning, without any assistance or input modification. On the other hand, research has shown that the ability of L2 learners to attend to constructions helps them learn the different senses of 'de-lexicalized' verbs, such as *get* (Waara, 2004). Waara argues that 'the semantic contribution is highly if not solely dependent on the construction, and can be an asset for the L2 speaker' (*ibid.*: 73). In other words, it is the construction, not the word, that conveys the meaning. The key issue here relates to the types of input that second language learners are exposed to; our role as teachers and/or researchers is to assess whether this input provides sufficient opportunities for learners to extract target-language constructions.

Looking at first language acquisition, Casenhiser and Goldberg (2005) attempted to simulate, under laboratory conditions, the task that children face when learning a new construction in their own language. They studied the ability of children to learn constructions through a contingency learning process in a controlled setting, introducing children learning English as an L1 to a 'new' (artificial) construction which was associated with five 'new' (artificial) verbs. They split the children into three groups. Each group was played a video showing two side-by side scenes portraying objects appearing in various ways. One group heard the construction more often with one particular verb (which resembles the way in which new constructions are introduced in child-directed speech), another heard it with different verbs more or less evenly distributed, and a third, control, group heard no sound. Their results showed that of the three groups, the group that had heard the construction with the same verb used more often were significantly better than the other two groups at learning the meaning of the construction, and that both experimental groups significantly outperformed the control group. These findings suggest that when people encounter a new construction they find it easier to learn if it is associated with the same verb every time. In other words, the frequent use of verbs with high cue validity promotes the acquisition of constructions in the L1. Casenhiser and Goldberg's findings provide interesting insights into first language acquisition, but do they hold for second language acquisition?

An attempt to apply Casenhiser and Goldberg's findings to second language acquisition was made by Nakamura (2008), who, in a highly controlled experiment, manipulated the frequency of two constructions in the incoming data for a group of mixed-nationality, adult 'learners' of Samoan. The word 'learners' is in inverted commas here as the participants were only in fact 'learning' Samoan for the purposes of the study. After having pre-taught the learners the necessary vocabulary he exposed them to two constructions in Samoan: the novel appearance construction 'the rabbit, the hat, appeared' (the rabbit came out of the hat) and a Samoan ergative construction 'drove (ergative marker) the boy the car' (the boy drove the car). He exposed four matched groups of students to these constructions. Two of the groups received skewed input and two received balanced input. He hypothesized that those students who had received the skewed input would learn the constructions better than those who had received the more balanced input. In fact Nakamura's findings did not support his hypothesis. The students who received the skewed input were no better at learning the construction than those who had received the balanced input. This finding suggests that second language learners will not necessarily learn from skewed input in the same way that first language learners do.

There are several possible explanations for this finding. Nakamura himself notes that it could be to do with individual differences among his participants in terms of their sensitivity to input manipulation. This is certainly an avenue of research that is worth pursuing. Other explanations might include the fact that second language learners are simply not used to receiving skewed input in the way that first language learners are. People rarely speak to adult second language learners in the same way as they speak to children who are learning their first language. Adult second language learners therefore have no reason to expect that naturally occurring input will be skewed in order to facilitate learning. Therefore they will be unlikely to automatically employ the same sort of contingency learning that children employ in order to attach form–meaning relationships to constructions. Moreover, as we saw above, corpus-based research into the nature of radial categories suggests that in authentic adult native-speaker discourse, peripheral members of the category are just as common, if not more common, than prototypical members. Therefore, in the sort of language that adult learners are used to hearing, prototypical meanings may have less cue validity than they do in child-directed speech. The adult learners in Nakamura's study may have become sensitized to this fact and may therefore have lost the habit of using cue validity to learn new constructions.

On the other hand, Nakamura did find that those students in the study who had *noticed* the construction were significantly more likely to learn it than those who had not. This finding suggests that it may be beneficial to alert adult second learners to the presence of constructions in the target language (see Section 2.7 for a discussion of the role of noticing in SLA). One of the roles for the language teacher might therefore be to help learners to develop ways of noticing new constructions and their corresponding verbs. This could be done either through explicit teaching (as we saw above) or, as we will see below, through some form of input enhancement.

Input enhancement (which was discussed in Chapter 4) refers to any kind of manipulation of the language that learners will be exposed to in order to make a target item more salient to them. The studies by Casenhiser and Goldberg and Nakamura described above both involved a kind of input enhancement in which the learners were exposed to the target constructions more frequently and in a much more systematic way than they would be in uncontrolled input. However this manipulation of input was not found to be sufficient to help the second language learners acquire the constructions. This means that in order to facilitate learning, the input needs to be enhanced more explicitly than this. One way to do this would be to underline key constructions in written text, or better still, to have the students underline new constructions themselves. Such an approach would combine explicit awareness-raising activities with learning activities that otherwise promote implicit learning. In some ways, this is similar to Lewis's (1993) lexical approach where learners are encouraged to identify and learn set 'lexical phrases', but it is a slightly broader approach as it reflects the fact that language is *entirely* made up of constructions that display varying degrees of flexibility.

Another way to incorporate explicit awareness-raising activities into otherwise implicit-learning situations is through a modified form of task-based learning. In presenting their definition of a task, Willis and Willis (2007) outline a series of questions which help to determine the extent to which a task is really a 'task'. They ask: (1) whether there is primary focus on meaning, (2) whether there is an outcome, (3) whether success is judged in terms of the outcome, (4) whether completion is a priority, (5) and whether the activity relates to real world activities. They also argue that a task will only facilitate language learning if it actively engages the learners' interest, and a desire to engage in meaning. This is very similar to some of the joint attentional settings described by Tomasello above. If learners could be put in a situation where they genuinely want to exchange meaningful information with an 'expert language user' (or at least a user from whom they can learn new constructions), they would be learning in the sort of optimal conditions described by Tomasello. With children and beginners, it would be good if the 'expert language user' were to employ some of the features of child-directed speech such as the use of prototypical verbs with high cue validity, and exaggerated intonation, to introduce new constructions. Due care would need to be taken so as not to sound patronizing. With adult or advanced learners it would be more appropriate for them to use the less prototypical verbs that were identified above as being more typical of authentic discourse. Most importantly, learners would need to be told beforehand that their input is going to be modified in this way so that they know to look out for the cues. If on the other hand, the learners are performing the task with their peers whose knowledge of the target language may be the same as or worse than their own, they could be shown short video recordings of expert users performing the task and then, during the language-focus phase, the teacher could draw attention to specific constructions that helped the speakers perform the particular task.

It is important to acknowledge the extent to which language learners themselves are able to produce communicatively effective constructions in the target language, even though they may not always be 'perfect'. Waara (2004), who looked at the actual constructions produced by Dutch learners of English, observed that although the constructions were not always an exact match for the types of things that an English speaker would produce, they were good enough to convey meaning and keep up the interaction that would lead to subsequent learning. She argues (*ibid.*: 53) that:

> a learner construction is a construction i.e. a meaning and syntax correspondence, but which is used in a slightly unconventional manner. Although usage does not result in a communication breakdown between participants, it deviates in some way.

The quality of these learner constructions should not be underestimated as it is testimony to what Firth and Wagner (2007: 801) describe as the learner's ability to 'modify, adapt, and creatively deploy what to them are new forms of language'. This links neatly to Ellis's ideas that were introduced in Chapter 2: Waara's findings show how L2 speakers are able to blend and generalize from the constructions they have learned.

9.6 Concluding comments

In this chapter we have seen that construction grammar is potentially a very useful concept in second language teaching as it provides a meaningful and systematic account of the phraseological aspects of language. However, it has also been noted that research in this area is not yet extensive. Before we draw any firm conclusions, more work is needed to identify the nature and distribution of constructions in authentic discourse, and to assess how they might be presented to second language learners. Initial attempts to replicate studies conducted in first language acquisition have not produced particularly encouraging findings. Second language learners do not appear to engage spontanesously in the sort of contingency learning that would allow them to learn constructions from the types of skewed input that first language learners receive. Therefore, some explicit teaching and/or input enhancement may be beneficial. Learners could be told what to look out for, and then be provided with enhanced input which would make the new constructions easy to identify.

In this chapter I have only really scratched the surface of construction grammar, which is potentially of great significance to second language learning and teaching. In the coming years I expect to see the collection of significantly more data concerning the exact nature of the constructions in different languages, and look forward to seeing a convergence of construction grammar and pattern grammar in the study of language. Work in both of these areas is already forcing us to change our views on how languages develop, how they are understood, and how they are learned.

10
Conclusion

We saw at the beginning of this book that although cognitive linguistics is a relatively new discipline, it has a number of contributions to make to second language learning and teaching. These have been discussed in detail on a chapter by chapter basis so my aim in this chapter is simply to make a few final points.

Construal, categorization, metaphor, metonymy and embodiment are first and foremost *dynamic* cognitive processes that can move in a variety of directions, within the boundaries of human experience. However they each leave their own lasting imprint on language, and the fact that they can work in different ways enables different languages to incorporate different ways of seeing and describing things. Back in 1993, John Taylor argued that one of the main contributions that cognitive linguistics could make to theories of second language teaching and learning was to highlight such differences between languages. This is very much in line with current work in SLA, which is starting to show the benefits of using a modified version of the **contrastive analysis** approach to both grammar (Ammar and Lightbrown, 2005) and vocabulary (Laufer and Girsai, 2008). The research to date shows that linguistic variation in the way events are construed is a good predictor of the sorts of problems that language learners are likely to face, particularly in the early stages of learning, when the L2 still has a parasitical relationship with the L1. Other areas that would lend themselves well to a contrastive analysis approach are metaphor and metonymy, and the role that they play in category extension and polysemy. We saw in Chapter 3 that languages vary considerably in this respect, but that this is rarely discussed explicitly with students. It is an area of knowledge that they are simply expected to acquire implicitly over time, through exposure, and research shows that in many cases this knowledge is simply not acquired.

Another contribution that cognitive linguistics has made to second language learning and teaching is that it shows the extent to which **languages are motivated and therefore explainable**, whilst stressing that different languages are motivated in different ways. We have seen that by drawing students' attention to the motivated, embodied nature of language, teachers can promote deep learning and therefore longer retention. Focusing on motivated language constitutes a radical departure from those approaches to language teaching that play down the role of linguistic analysis in favour of communication and information exchange. Providing learners with opportunities to pause and reflect on the reasons why certain things are expressed in certain ways is beneficial, as it reduces the rote memory load.

One way of introducing learners to differences between languages, and of raising their awareness of the motivated elements of the target language, is through **input enhancement** (Sharwood Smith, 1993). In other words, as we saw in Chapter 2, the input that they receive can be 'doctored' in order to make certain features more salient. In written input, input enhancement can take the form of highlighting, underlining, special fonts and, in the case of poetry, particular layout. In spoken input, it can take the form of exaggerated intonation (so that learners pick up on new constructions and their corresponding intonation patterns), excessive use of gesture (to give learners increased access to the conceptual content that corresponds to the linguistic utterances), slowing down and repetition. In a recent review of research on input enhancement, Han *et al.* (2008) demonstrated that it is more beneficial in some areas than others. For example, it is particularly likely to promote learning when there are strong, transparent form–meaning relationships. One of the things that I hope to have shown in this book is that form–meaning correspondences are often motivated, but in different ways in different languages. When language is viewed through the lens of cognitive linguistics, its motivated elements become much more apparent. Future research could usefully investigate how input enhancement can be used to make form–meaning relationships more transparent to students.

We have seen that by acquiring a second language people develop the ability to see or describe things in different ways from what they have been used to. Learning a second language requires us to **overcome the cognitive habits** that we have developed as a result of speaking our first language. Learning a second language involves the ability to reorganize our encyclopaedic knowledge and corresponding word association networks, thus deepening our knowledge of L2 vocabulary. It also involves overcoming the ways in which conceptual metaphor and metonymy are conventionally exploited in our L1, in order to take on board metaphorical and metonymic extensions of word meaning that are used by the target language. Finally, learning a new language involves **learning how to re-package our ideas** into different types of constructions that may emphasize different things from those that we use in our first language.

We saw in Chapter 2 that bilingual people tend to exhibit particularly high levels of the sort of **cognitive flexibility** that is necessary for them to do the types of things outlined in the previous paragraph. For those of us who are unfortunate not to have been brought up in a multilingual environment successful second language acquisition may require us to develop a degree of cognitive flexibility and openness to new ways of seeing things. This is not to say that monolingual people are always, by definition, 'cognitively inflexible', for cognitive flexibility is equally likely to operate as a trait that varies from person to person, a fact which may account for some of the individual differences that have been observed between language learners in terms of attitude and cognitive style. For example, twenty years ago, findings were being made regarding the relationship between **tolerance of ambiguity** and **language learning strategy preferences** (Ely, 1989). Tolerance of ambiguity is a measure of the extent to which a person feels comfortable in unfamiliar or ambiguous situations. Ely found that tolerance of ambiguity was a significant predictor of strategies such as looking for overall meaning in reading, guessing a word from its context, and using mental images to aid memory. It was found to be a significant *negative* predictor of strategies such as looking for exact correspondences between new words and L1 words, and of various strategies which involve focusing on individual language elements. It was also found to be related to risk-taking ability, which means that learners who can tolerate ambiguity are more likely to take risks in language learning. Tolerance of ambiguity thus appears to be an important learner trait if learners are to accept the idea that the new language has different ways of construing and presenting information from their own.

More recently, researchers have talked of another learner trait that may also be important in the learning of new construals and constructions. This is what Grigorenko *et al.* (2000) refer to as 'cognitive ability for novelty in acquisition of a foreign language' (CANAL-F) Basically, this involves the ability to spot new patterns in the language input and to use one's existing knowledge selectively, along with analogical reasoning, to work out new form–meaning pairings. This sort of ability is needed to identify and learn new constructions, and is a crucial prerequisite of **learning language through language use**. 'Cognitive ability for novelty' may also be important to overcome the effects of L1 transfer which were discussed at length in the earlier chapters of this book. As well as requiring flexibility on the part of the learner, we have also seen that according to the cognitive linguistic view, **language itself is a flexible phenomenon** which is not constrained by sets of rigid rules and their accompanying lists of 'exceptions'. Cognitive linguists view grammar and pronunciation 'rules' as operating within flexible, interconnecting radial categories. They have identified forces within these categories, such as metaphor and metonymy, which allow systematicity and flexibility to co-exist. The prototypical members of the categories are more likely to be experientially grounded and related to embodied cognition, whereas the more peripheral members are often more abstract, and less transparent. If both lexico-grammatical and phonological features of the target language could be presented to learners in these radial categories, this would provide them with a more accurate representation of how the language really works. It would also help them to perceive a degree of systematicity underlying authentic language that they are likely to encounter, and give them a better understanding of how 'real' language works. Research is now needed into how a radial category approach might best be incorporated into language teaching materials.

Over the years, in the SLA literature there has been much discussion of 'focus on form' versus 'focus on meaning'. The general consensus appears to be that the best approach is to provide a mixture of meaningful input alongside some explicit focus on form (de Bot *et al.*, 2005). What both cognitive and corpus linguistics bring to this debate is an awareness of the fact that, to a large extent, **form *is* meaning, and meaning *is* form**. Construal is simply the flipside of phraseology. This is an important insight as it downplays the arbitrary nature of language and emphasizes the extent to which it is motivated, and thus easier to grasp. What is now needed is more research into how far motivated language can be exploited in the language classroom. A number of studies into the effectiveness of this approach were outlined in Chapter 8, but we need to know whether learners are able to transfer the declarative knowledge that they have learned in this way into procedural knowledge, and whether all areas of language can be taught through this approach, or whether we are restricted to the areas of tense, modality and phrasal verbs.

Finally, it needs to be borne in mind that **representations in the multilingual lexicon are not stable entities** on which operations can be carried out. The data imply that they are far more fluid than many models suggest (de Bot *et al.*, 2007). This means that the acquisition of L2 'thinking-for-speaking' patterns, construals and constructions will not follow a predictable linear sequence. Future research into the effectiveness of cognitive linguistic-inspired approaches to language teaching will need to be characterized by a degree of sophistication that takes them beyond the study of experimental and control groups and short-term measurable gains. If the long-term, cyclical, dynamic nature of second language learning is to be properly taken into account, then we need to combine qualitative and quantitative approaches to research, and to take a longitudinal perspective. Future cognitive linguistics-inspired language teaching research, over the next ten years, could usefully address the following questions:

- To what extent do L1 construal and categorization patterns influence the learning of L2 construal and categorization patterns?
- How can learners best be helped to learn how metaphor and metonymy operate in the L2?
- What kinds of explicit instruction and/or input enhancement are most effective in helping students to notice and learn construal, categorization, metaphor, metonymy and constructions in the L2?
- How can activities involving 'language play' be most effectively integrated into communicative teaching methodologies in order to promote language learning?
- What can the study of gesture reveal about the acquisition of L2 thinking-for-speaking patterns?
- To what extent and in what ways can cognitive flexibility be developed in the language learner?
- How can L2 constructions be systematically introduced to the language learner?

By finding answers to these questions, we will learn more about the cognitive processes underlying second language learning. This will help us to gain a more complete and accurate understanding of how second language learners comprehend, produce and learn language in the classroom as well as in everyday communicative contexts.

References

Achard, M. (2008). 'Teaching construal: cognitive pedagogical grammar'. In P. Robinson and N. Ellis (eds.) *Handbook of Cognitive Linguistics and Second Language Acquisition* (London: Routledge), pp. 432–55.

Aitchison, J. (1994). *Words in the Mind. An Introduction to the Mental Lexicon*, 2nd edn (Oxford: Blackwell).

Alejo, R. (2008). 'The acquisition of English phrasal verbs by L2 learners: a cognitive linguistic account'. Paper presented at the LAUD Symposium on Cognitive Approaches to Second/Foreign Language Processing: Theory and Pedagogy. Landau, Germany, March 2008.

Allen, L.Q. (1995). 'The effect of emblematic gestures on the development and access of mental representations of French expressions', *Modern Language Journal 79* (4): 521–9.

Ameel, E., Storms, G., Malt, B. and Sloman, S. (2005). 'How bilinguals solve the naming problem', *Journal of Memory and Language 3*: 60–80.

Ammar, A. and Lightbrown, P. (2005). 'Teaching marked linguistics structures – more about the acquisition of relative clauses by Arab learners of English'. In A. Haussard and M. Pierrard (eds.) *Investigations in Instructed Second Language Acquisition* (Berlin: Mouton de Gruyter), pp. 167–98.

Aoyama, K. Flege, J.E., Guion, S.G. and Akahane-Yamada, T. (2004). 'Perceived phonetic dissimilarity and L2 speech learning: the case of Japanese /r/ and English /l/ and /r/', *Journal of Phonetics 32*: 233–50.

Asher, J. (1988). *Learning Another Language Through Actions: A Teacher's Guide* (Los Gatos, CA: Sky Oaks).

Athanasopoulos, P. (2006). 'Effects of the grammatical representation of number on cognition in bilinguals', *Bilingualism, Language and Cognition 9*: 89–96.

Barcelona, A. (2004). 'Metonymy behind grammar: The motivation of the seemingly 'irregular' grammatical behavior of English paragon names'. In G. Radden and K.U. Panther (eds.) *Studies in Linguistic Motivation* (Berlin: Mouton de Gruyter), pp. 357–74.

Barcelona, A. (2006). 'The role of metonymy in discourse-pragmatic inferencing'. In J.-L. Otal Campo, I. Navarro, I. Ferrando and B. Belles Fortuno (eds.) *Cognitive and Discourse Approaches to Metaphor and Metonymy* (Castello de la Plana: Publicationes de la Universitat Jaume I), pp. 29–44.

Banta, P. (1981). 'Teaching German vocabulary: The use of English cognates and common loanwords', *Modern Language Journal 65* (2): 129–36.

Bergen, B. (2004). 'The psychological reality of phonaesthemes', *Language 80* (2): 290–311.

Bergen, B. and Chang, N. (2005). 'Embodied construction grammar in simulation-based language understanding'. In J.-O. Ostman and M. Fried (eds.) *Construction Grammars: Cognitive Grounding and Theoretical Extensions* (Amsterdam: John Benjamins), pp. 147–90.

Bergen, B, Narayan, S. and Feldman, J. (2003). 'Embodied verbal semantics: Evidence from an image–verb matching task'. In R. Alterman and D. Hirsh (eds.) *Proceedings from the Twenty-Fifth Annual Conference of the Cognitive Science Society* (Hove and New York: Psychology Press), pp. 493–504.

Berman, R. and D. Slobin (1994). *Relating Events in a Narrative. A Crosslinguistic Developmental Study* (Hillsdale, NJ: Lawrence Erlbaum).

Bialystok, E. (1999). 'Cognitive complexity and attentional control in the bilingual mind', *Child Development 70*: 636–44.

Bialystok, E. (2002). 'Cognitive processes of L2 users'. In V. J. Cook (ed.) *Second Language Acquisition; Portraits of the L2 User* (Clevedon: Multilingual Matters), pp. 163–72.

Block, D. (2003). *The Social Turn in Second Language Acquisition* (Edinburgh: Edinburgh University Press).

Boers, F. (2001). 'Remembering figurative idioms by hypothesizing about their origin', *Prospect, 16* (3): 35–43.

Boers, F. (2004) 'Expanding learners' vocabulary through metaphor awareness: what expansion, what learners, what vocabulary?' In M. Achard and S. Niemeier (eds.) *Cognitive Linguistics and Foreign Language Teaching* (Berlin/New York: Mouton de Gruyter), pp. 211–32.

Boers, F. and Lindstromberg, S. (2005). 'Finding ways to make phrase-learning feasible: The mnemonic effect of alliteration', *System 33* (2): 225–38.

Boers, F. and Lindstromberg, S. (2006). 'Cognitive linguistic applications in second or foreign language instruction: rationale, proposals and evaluation'. In G. Kristiansen, M. Achard, R. Dirven, F-J Ruiz de Mendoza (eds.) *Cognitive Linguistics: Current Applications and Future Perspectives* (Berlin: Mouton de Gruyter), pp. 305–55.

Bohn, O.-S. (2000). 'Linguistic relativity in speech perception. An overview of the influence of language experience on the perception of speech sounds from infancy to adulthood'. In S. Niemeier and R. Dirven (eds.) *Evidence for Linguistic Relativity* (Amsterdam: John Benjamins), pp. 1–28.

Bouton, L.F. (1988). 'A cross-cultural study of ability to interpret implicatures in English', *World Englishes 7* (2): 183–96.

Bouton, L. F. (1994a). 'Conversational implicature in the second language: Learned slowly when not deliberately taught', *Journal of Pragmatics, 22*: 157–67.

Bouton, L.F. (1994b). 'Can NNS skill in interpreting implicature in American English be improved through explicit instruction? A pilot study'. In L. Bouton and Y. Kachru (eds.) *Pragmatics and Language Learning, Monograph Series 5* (Illinois: University of Illinois), pp. 2–23.

Bouton, L.F. (1999). 'Developing nonnative speaker skills in interpreting conversational implicatures in English: explicit teaching can ease the process'. In E. Hinkel (ed.) *Culture in Second Language Teaching and Learning* (Cambridge: Cambridge University Press), pp. 47–70.

Bowerman, M. (2008). 'Language acquisition and semantic typology'. Paper presented at the LAUD Symposium on Cognitive Approaches to Second/Foreign Language Processing: Theory and Pedagogy, Landau, Germany, March 2008.

Bowerman, M. and Choi, S. (2001). 'Shaping meanings for language: universal and language-specific in the acquisition of spatial semantic categories'. In M. Bowerman and S. Levinson (eds.) *Language Acquisition and Conceptual Development* (Cambridge: Cambridge University Press), pp. 475–511.

Bowerman, M. and Choi, S. (2003). 'Space under construction: language-specific spatial categorization in first language acquisition'. In D. Gentner and

S. Goldin-Meadow (eds.) *Language in Mind. Advances in the Study of Language and Thought* (Cambridge,MA: MIT Press), pp. 387–428.

Bowerman, M. and Pederson, E. (1992). 'Cross-linguistic studies of spatial-semantic organization', *Annual Report of the Max Planck Institute for Psycholinguistics* (Nijmegen: Max Planck Institute), pp. 53–6.

Brazil, D. (1985). *The Communicative Value of Intonation in English: Discourse Analysis, Monograph No. 8* (University of Birmingham: English Language Research).

Broccias, C. (2008). 'Cognitive linguistic theories of grammar and grammar teaching'. In S. De Knop and T. De Rycker (eds.) *Cognitive Approaches to Pedagogical Grammar* (Berlin/New York: Mouton de Gruyter), pp. 67–90.

Brown, A. and Gullberg, M. (2008). 'Bidirectional crosslinguistic influence in L1–L2 encoding of manner in speech and gesture', *Studies in Second Language Acquisition 30* (2): 225–51.

Butcher, A. (1976). *The Influence of the Native Language on the Perception of Vowel Quality* (London: University of London Press).

Cadierno, T. (2004). 'Expressing motion events in a second language: a cognitive typological perspective'. In M. Achard and S. Niemeier (eds.) *Cognitive Linguistics and Foreign Language Teaching* (Berlin/New York: Mouton de Gruyter), pp. 13–50.

Cadierno, T. and Lund, K. (2004). 'Cognitive linguistics and second language acquisition: Motion events in a typological framework'. In B. VanPatten, J. Williams and S. Rott (eds.) *Form–meaning Connections in Second Language Acquisition* (Hillsdale, NJ: Lawrence Erlbaum), pp. 139–54.

Cadierno, T. and Ruiz, L. (2006). 'Motion events in Spanish L2 acquisition', *Annual Review of Cognitive Linguistics 4*: 183–236.

Cameron, L. and Deignan, A. (2006). 'The emergence of metaphor in discourse', *Applied Linguistics 27* (4): 671–90.

Carter, R. (2007). 'Spoken English/written English: Challenging assumptions'. Plenary paper, presented at the annual conference of the Japanese Association for Language Teaching, Tokyo, Japan.

Casenhiser, D. and Goldberg, A. (2005). 'Fast mapping between a phrasal form and meaning', *Developmental Science 8* (6): 500–8.

Channell, J. (1994). *Vague Language* (Oxford: Oxford University Press).

Chantrill, P.A. and Mio, J.S. (1996). 'Metonymy in political discourse'. In J.S. Mio and A.N. Katz (eds.) *Metaphor: Implications and Applications* (Mahwah NJ: Lawrence Erlbaum), pp. 171–211.

Choi, S. (1997). 'Language-specific input and early semantic development: Evidence from children learning Korean'. In D. I. Slobin (ed.) *The Crosslinguistic Study of Language Acquisition*, Vol. 5: *Expanding the Contexts* (Hillsdale NJ: Lawrence Erlbaum), pp. 414–34.

Choi, S. and Bowerman, M. (1991). 'Learning to express motion events in English and Korean: the influence of language-specific lexicalisation patterns', *Cognition 41*: 83–121.

Choi, S. and Lantolf, J.P. (2008). 'Representation and embodiment of meaning in L2 communication', *Studies in Second Language Acquisition 30* (2): 191–224.

Chomsky, N. (1965). *Aspects of the Theory of Syntax* (Cambridge, MA: MIT Press).

Cisneros, I. (1992). *Spanish in Three Months* (Woodbridge, Suffolk: Hugo's Language Books Ltd).

Coates, J. (2003). *Women, Men and Language* (London: Longman).

Cook, G. (1997). 'Schema', *English Language Teaching Journal 51* (1): 86.

Cook, V. (2002). 'Background to the L2 user perspective'. In V.J. Cook (ed.) *Portraits of the L2 User* (Clevedon: Multilingual Matters), pp. 1–32.

Cook, V., Bassetti, B., Kasai, C., Sasaki, M. and Takahashi, J. (2006). 'Do bilinguals have different concepts? The case of shape and material in Japanese L2 users of English', *International Journal of Bilingualism 10* (2): 137–52.

Corballis, M. (1994). 'Neuropsychology of perceptual functions'. In D. Zaidel (ed.) *Neuropsychology Handbook of Perception and Cognition*, 2nd edn (San Diego, CA: Academic Press), pp. 83–104.

Craik, F.I.M. and Lockhart, R.S. (1982) 'Levels of processing: a framework for memory research', *Journal of Verbal Learning and Verbal Behaviour 11*: 671–84.

Croft, W. (2001). *Radical Construction Grammar: Syntactic Theory in Typological Perspective* (Oxford: Oxford University Press).

Croft, W. and Cruse, D.A. (2004). *Cognitive Linguistics* (Cambridge: Cambridge University Press).

Cruttenden, A. (1981). 'Falls and rises: meanings and universals', *Journal of Linguistics 17*: 77–91.

Cuyckens, H., Berg, T., Dirven, R. and Panter, K.-U. (eds.) (2003). *Motivation in Language* (Amsterdam: John Benjamins).

Danesi, M. (1992). 'Metaphorical competence in second language acquisition and second language teaching: the neglected dimension'. In J.E. Alatis (ed.) *Language Communication and Social Meaning* (Washington, DC: Georgetown University Round Table on Languages and Linguistics), pp. 489–500.

Danesi, M. (2008). 'Conceptual errors in second language learning'. In S. De Knop and T. De Rycker (eds.) *Cognitive Approaches to Pedagogical Grammar* (Berlin/New York: Mouton de Gruyter), pp. 231–57.

Davey, J. (2004). *English Correspondence* (London: Vintage Books).

de Bot, K., Lowie, W. and Verspoor, M. (2005). *Second Language Acquisition. An Advanced Resource Book* (London: Routledge).

de Bot, K., Verspoor, M and Lowie. (2007). 'A dynamic systems theory approach to second language acquisition', *Bilingualism, Language and Cognition 10* (1): 7–21.

Deignan, A. (2005) *Metaphor and Corpus Linguistics* (Amsterdam: John Benjamins).

Deignan, A., Gabrys, D., and Solska, A. (1997). 'Teaching English metaphors using cross-linguistic awareness-raising activities', *English Language Teaching Journal 51* (4): 352–60.

DePaulo, B.M. and Friedman, H.S. (1997). 'Nonverbal communication'. In D. Gilbert, S. Fiske, and G. Lindzey (eds.) *Handbook of Social Psychology*, 4th edn (Oxford: Blackwell), pp. 44–59.

Dornyei, Z. and Thurrell, S. (1994). 'Teaching conversational skills intensively: course content and rationale', *English Language Teaching Journal 48*: 40–9.

Doughty, C. (2003). 'Instructed SLA: constraints, compensation and enhancement'. In C.J. Doughty and M. Long (eds.) *The Handbook of Second Language Acquisition* (Malden, MA: Blackwell), pp. 256–310.

Downing, A. and Locke, P. (2002). *A University Course in English Grammar* (London: Routledge).

Efron, D. (1972). *Gesture, Race and Culture* (The Hague: Mouton and Co).

Ellis, N. (2002). 'Frequency effects in language processing. A review with implications for theories of implicit and explicit language learning', *Studies in Second Language Acquisition 24*: 143–88.

Ellis, N. (2006a). 'Language acquisition as rational contingency learning', *Applied Linguistics 27* (1): 1–24.

Ellis, N. (2006b). 'Selective attention and transfer phenomena in L2 acquisition: contingency, cue competition, salience, interference, overshadowing, blocking, and perceptual learning', *Applied Linguistics 27* (2): 164–94.

Ellis, N. (2006c). 'Cognitive perspectives on SLA', *AILA Review 19*: 100–21.

Ellis, N. (2008). 'Usage-based and form-focused language acquisition: the associative learning of constructions, learned attention, and the limited L2 endstate'. In P. Robinson and N. Ellis (eds.) *Handbook of Cognitive Linguistics and Second Language Acquisition* (London: Routledge), pp. 372–405.

Ellis, N. and Larsen-Freeman, D. (2006). 'Language emergence: implications for applied linguistics', *Applied Linguistics 27* (4): 558–89.

Elston,-Guttler, K.E. and Williams, J.N. (2008). 'First language polysemy affects second language meaning interpretation: evidence for activation of first language concepts during second language reading', *Second Language Research 24* (2): 167–87.

Ely C. (1989) 'Tolerance of ambiguity and use of second language strategies', *Foreign Language Annals 22* (5): 437–45.

Ervin, S.M. (1961). 'Semantic shift in bilingualism', *American Journal of Psychology 24*: 233–41.

Evans, V. (2007). *A Glossary of Cognitive Linguistics* (Edinburgh: Edinburgh University Press).

Evans, V. and Green, M. (2006). *Cognitive Linguistics: An Introduction* (Edinburgh: Edinburgh University Press).

Faraco, M. and Kida, T. (2008). 'Gesture and the negotiation of meaning in a second language classroom'. In S. McCafferty and G. Stam (eds.) *Gesture: Second Language Acquisition and Classroom Research* (New York: Routledge), pp. 280–97.

Fauconnier, G. and Turner, M. (1998). 'Conceptual integration networks', *Cognitive Science 22* (2): 137–88.

Fauconnier, G. and Turner, M. (2002). *The Way We Think: Conceptual Blending and the Mind's Hidden Complexities* (New York: Basic Books).

Fillmore, C. (1975). 'An alternative to checklist theories of meaning'. In *Proceedings from the First Annual Meeting of the Berkeley Linguistics Society* (Amsterdam: North Holland), pp. 123–31.

Firth, A. and Wagner, J. (2007). 'Second/foreign language learning as a social accomplishments: elaborations on a reconceptualized SLA', *The Modern Language Journal 91*: 800–19.

Flege, J. (1995). 'Second-language speech learning: theory, findings, and problems'. In W. Strange (ed.) *Speech Perception and Linguistic Experience: Theoretical and Methodological Issues* (Timonium, MD: York Press), pp. 565–77.

Flege, J., Bohn, J., and Jang, S. (1997). 'The production and perception of English vowels by native speakers of German, Korean, Mandarin and Spanish', *Journal of Phonetics 25*: 437–70.

Fodor, J. (1983). *The Modularity of Mind* (Cambridge, MA: MIT Press).

Gallese, V. and Goldman, A. (1998). 'Mirror neurons and the simulation theory of intelligence', *Trends in Cognitive Science 2*: 439–50.

Gallese, V., Fadiga, L. and Fogassi, L. (1996). 'Action recognition in the premotor cortex', *Brain 119*: 593–609.

Gallese, V., Ferari, P. and Umilta, M. (2002). 'The mirror matching system: a shared manifold for intersubjectivity', *Behavioural and Brain Sciences 25*: 35–6.

Gallop, J. (1987). *Reading Lacan* (London: Cornell University Press).

Gass, S. (1997). *Input, Interaction, and the Second Language Learner* (Mahwah NJ: Lawrence Erlbaum Associates).

Gass, S. (2008). 'Interaction: from description to explanation'. Paper presented at the LAUD Symposium on Cognitive Approaches to Second/Foreign Language Processing: Theory and Pedagogy. Landau, Germany, March 2008.

Gentner, D. and Goldin-Meadow, S. (2003). 'Whither Whorf'. In D. Gentner and S. Goldin-Meadow (eds.) *Language in Mind. Advances in the Study of Language and Thought* (Cambridge, MA: MIT Press), pp. 3–14.

Gibbs, R. (1994). *The Poetics of Mind* (Cambridge: Cambridge University Press).

Gibbs, R. (2003). 'Understanding metaphor as cognitive simulation'. Paper presented at the fifth conference of Researching and Applying Metaphor, Paris, France.

Gibbs, R. (2006). *Embodiment and Cognitive Science* (Cambridge: Cambridge University Press).

Goatly, A. (1997). *The Language of Metaphors* (London: Routledge).

Goddard, C. (2004). ' "Cultural scripts": a new medium for ethnographic instruction'. In M. Achard and S. Niemeier (eds.) *Cognitive Linguistics and Foreign Language Teaching* (Berlin/New York: Mouton de Gruyter), pp. 143–63.

Goldberg, A. (1995). *A Construction Grammar Approach to Argument Structure* (Chicago: University of Chicago Press).

Goldberg, A. (2006). *Constructions at Work: The Nature of Generalization in Language* (Oxford: Oxford University Press).

Goossens, L. (1990). 'Metaphtonomy: the interaction of metaphor and metonymy in expressions of linguistic action', *Cognitive Linguistics 1*: 323–40.

Grady, J. (1997). 'Theories are buildings revisited', *Cognitive Linguistics 8*: 267–90.

Grady, J. and Johnson, C. (2002). 'Converging evidence for the notions of *subscene* and *primary scene*. In R. Dirven and R. Pörings (eds.) *Metaphor and Metonymy in Comparison and Contrast* (Berlin: Mouton de Gruyter), pp. 533–54.

Grafton, S., Fadiga, L., Arbib, M. and Rizzolatti, G. (1997). 'Premotor cortex activation during observation and naming of familiar tools', *Neuroimage 6*: 231–6.

Gries, S. T. (2006). 'Corpus-based methods and cognitive semantics: The many senses of to run'. In Gries, S. T. and A. Stefanowitsch (eds.). (2006). *Corpora in Cognitive Linguistics: The Syntax-Lexis Interface* (Berlin/New York: Mouton de Gruyter), pp. 57–99.

Gries, S. T. and A. Stefanowitsch (eds.). (2006). *Corpora in Cognitive Linguistics: The Syntax-Lexis Interface* (Berlin/New York: Mouton de Gruyter).

Grigorenko, E., Sternberg, R. and Ehrman, M. (2000). 'A theory-based approach to the measurement of foreign language learning ability: the canal-f theory and test', *The Modern Language Journal 84* (3): 390–405.

Gullberg, M. (1998). *Gesture as a Communication Strategy in Second Language Discourse : A Study of Learners of French and Swedish* (Lund: Lund University Press).

Gullberg, M. (2008). 'Gestures and second language acquisition'. In P. Robinson and N. Ellis (eds.) *Handbook of Cognitive Lingistics and Second Language Acquisition* (London: Routledge), pp. 276–305.

Gullberg, M. (in press). 'Language-specific encoding of placement events in gesture'. In E. Pederson and J. Bohnemeyer (eds.) *Event Representations in Language and Cognition* (Cambridge: Cambridge University Press).

Guy, G. and Vonwiller, J. (1989). 'The high rising tone in Australian English'. In P. Collins and D. Blair (eds.) *Australian English: The Language of a New Society* (Queensland: University of Queensland Press), pp. 21–34.

Haastrup, K. and Henriksen, B. (2000). 'Vocabulary acquisition: acquiring depth of knowledge through network building', *International Journal of Applied Linguistics 10* (2): 221–39.

Han, Z., Park, E.S. and Combs, C. (2008). 'Textual enhancement of input: issues and possibilities', *Applied Linguistics 29* (3): 597–618.

Heine, B., Claudi, U. and Hunnemeyer, F. (1991). *Grammaticalization: A Conceptual Framework* (Chicago: Chicago University Press).

Holme, R. (2004). *Mind, Metaphor and Language Teaching* (Basingstoke/New York: Palgrave Macmillan).

Hopper, P. (2001). 'Grammatical constructions and their discourse origins: prototype or family resemblance?' In M. Pütz , S. Niemeier and R. Dirven (eds.) *Applied Cognitive Linguistics II: Language Pedagogy* (Berlin: Mouton de Gruyter), pp. 109–29.

Hopper, P. and Traugott, E. (2003). *Grammaticalization* (Cambridge: Cambridge University Press).

Hunston, S. and Francis, G. (1999). *Pattern Grammar. A Corpus-Driven Approach to the Lexical Grammar of English* (Amsterdam: John Benjamins).

Hunt, E. and Agnoli, F. (1991). 'The Whorfian hypothesis: a cognitive psychology perspective', *Psychological Review 98*: 377–89.

Ijaz, I.H. (1986). 'Linguistic and cognitive determinants of lexical acquisition in a second language', *Language Learning 36*: 401–51.

Ikegami, Y. (2000). *Nihongo-ron e shoutai* (An invitation to theories of Japanese language). Tokyo: Kodansha.

Imai, M. (2000). 'Universal ontological knowledge and a bias toward language-specific categories in the construal of individuation'. In S. Niemeier and R. Dirven (eds.) *Evidence for Linguistic Relativity* (Amsterdam: John Benjamins), pp. 139–60.

Ivanova, G. (2006). 'Sound-symbolic approach to Japanese mimetic verbs', *Toronto Working Papers in Linguistics 26*: 103–14.

Jakobson, R. (1971). 'The metaphoric and metonymic poles'. In R. Jakobson and M. Halle (eds.) *Fundamentals of Language 2* (The Hague/Paris: Mouton de Gruyter), pp. 90–6.

Jiang, N. (2004). 'Semantic transfer and its implications for vocabulary teaching in a second language', *The Modern Language Journal 88* (3): 416–30.

Johns, T.F. (1991). 'Should you be persuaded: two examples of data-driven learning'. In T.F. Johns and P. King (eds.) *Classroom Concordancing* (Birmingham: English Language Research), pp. 1–13.

Johns, T.F. (1994). 'From printout to handout: grammar and vocabulary teaching in the context of data-driven learning'. In T. Odlin (ed.) *Perspectives on Pedagogical Grammar.* (New York: Cambridge University Press), pp. 293–313.

198   *References*

Kasper, G. and Roever, C. (2005). 'Pragmatics in second language learning'. In
E. Hinkel (ed.) *Handbook of Research in Second Language Teaching and Learning*
(Mahwah, NJ: Lawrence Erlbaum), pp. 317–34.

Kasper, G. and Rose, K.R. (2002). *Pragmatic Development in a Second Language*
(Oxford: Blackwell).

Kaufman, D. (2004). 'Constructivist issues in language learning and teaching',
Annual Review of Applied Linguistics 24: 303–19.

Kay, G. 1995). 'English loanwords in Japanese', *World Englishes 14* (1): 67–76.

Kecskes, I. (2006). 'On my mind: thoughts about salience, context and figurative
language from a second language perspective', *Second Language Research 22* (2):
219–37.

Kellerman, E. (1987a) 'An eye for an 'eye'. In E. Kellerman *Aspects of Transferability in Second Language Acquisition. A Selection of Related Papers.* (Nijmegen:
University of Nijmegen Press), pp. 154–77.

Kellerman, E. (1987b) 'Towards a characterisation of the strategy of transfer in
second language learning'. In E. Kellerman *Aspects of Transferability in Second Language Acquisition. A Selection of Related Papers.* (Nijmegen: University
of Nijmegen Press), pp. 89–124.

Kellerman, E. (1995). 'Cross linguistic influence: transfer to nowhere?', *Annual
Review of Applied Linguistics 41* (3): 251–69.

Kendon, A. (2004). *Gesture: Visible Action as Utterance* (Cambridge: Cambridge
University Press).

Kida, T. (2008). 'Does gesture aid discourse comprehension in the L2?' In
S. McCafferty and G. Stam (eds.) *Gesture: Second Language Acquisition and
Classroom Research* (New York: Routledge), pp 131–56.

Kita, S. (in press). 'How representational gestures help speaking'. In D. McNeill
(ed.) *Language and Gesture: Window into Thought and Action* (Cambridge:
Cambridge University Press), pp. 165–82.

Kita, S. and Özürek, A. (2003). 'What does cross-linguistic variation in semantic
coordination of speech and gesture reveal? Evidence for and interface representation of spatial thinking and speaking', *Journal of Memory and Language 48*:
16–32.

Koltun, D. (2006). 'A cross-linguistic corpus-based study of metaphor use by intermediate Polish learners of English', Unpublished MA dissertation, University of
Birmingham.

Kövecses, Z. (2001). 'A cognitive linguistic view of learning idioms in an FLT context'. In M. Pütz , S. Niemeier and R. Dirven (eds.) *Applied Cognitive Linguistics
II: Language Pedagogy* (Berlin: Mouton de Gruyter), pp. 87–115.

Kövecses, Z. (2002) *Metaphor: A Practical Introduction* (Oxford: Oxford University
Press).

Kövecses, Z. and Szabo, P. (1996). 'Idioms: A view from cognitive semantics',
Applied Linguistics 17 (3): 334–55.

Kuhl, P., Williams, K., Lacerda, F., Stevens, K. and Lindblom, B. (1992). 'Linguistic
experience alters phonetic perception in infants by 6 months of age', *Science
255*: 606–8.

Kuno, S. (1987). *Functional Syntax: Anaphora, Discourse and Empathy* (Chicago:
University of Chicago Press).

Kusuyama, Y. (2005). 'The acquisition of deictic verbs by Japanese ESL learners',
NUCB Journal of Language, Culture and Communication 7 (2): 31–43.

Laccoboni, M. (in press). 'Understanding others: imitation, language, empathy'. In S. Hurley and N. Chater (eds.) *Perspectives on Imitation: From Cognitive Neuroscience to Social Science* (Cambridge, MA: MIT Press), Vol. 1, ch. 2 ; see http://www.sscnet.ucla.edu/CBD/downloads.

Lakoff, G. (1970). *Irregularity in Syntax* (New York: Rinehart and Winston).

Lakoff, G. (1987). *Women, Fire and Dangerous Things: What Categories Reveal About the Mind* (Chicago/London: University of Chicago Press).

Lakoff, G. (1993). 'The contemporary theory of metaphor'. In A. Ortony (ed.) *Metaphor and Thought*, 2nd edn (Cambridge: Cambridge University Press), pp. 202–51.

Lakoff, G. (2007). 'Cognitive models and prototype theory'. In V. Evans, B. Bergen and J. Zinken (eds.) *The Cognitive Linguistics Reader* (London: Equinox), pp. 130–67.

Lakoff, G. and Johnson, M. (1980). *Metaphors We Live By* (Chicago: University of Chicago Press).

Lakoff, G. and Johnson, M. (1999). *Philosophy in the Flesh: The Embodied Mind and its Challenge to Western Thought* (New York: Basic Books).

Langacker, R.W. (1987). *Foundations of Grammar* , Vol. 1: *Cognitive Prerequisites* (Stanford, CA: Stanford University Press).

Langacker, R. (1991). *Foundations of Cognitive Grammar*, Vol. 2: *Descriptive Application* (Stanford, CA: Stanford University Press).

Langacker, R.W. (2008). 'Cognitive grammar and language instruction'. In P. Robinson and N. Ellis (eds.) *Handbook of Cognitive Linguistics and Second Language Acquisition* (New York: Routledge), pp. 66–88.

Lantolf, J.P. (1999). 'Second culture acquisition: cognitive considerations'. In E. Hinkel (ed.) *Culture in Second Language Teaching and Learning* (Cambridge: Cambridge University Press), pp. 202–51.

Lantolf, J.P. and Appel, G. (eds.) (1998). *Vygotskyian Approaches to Second Language Research* (Norwood, NJ: Ablex).

Larsen-Freeman, D. (2006). 'The emergence of complexity, fluency, and accuracy in the oral and written production of five Chinese learners of English', *Applied Linguistics 27* (4); 590–619.

Larsen-Freeman, D. and Cameron, L. (2007). *Dynamic Systems Theory and Applied Linguistics* (Oxford: Oxford University Press).

Laufer, B. and Girsai, N. (2008). 'Form-focused instruction in second language vocabulary learning: a case for contrastive analysis and translation', *Applied Linguistics 29* (4): 694–716.

Lee, D. (2001). *Cognitive Linguistics. An Introduction* (Oxford: Oxford University Press).

Levin, B. and Rappaport Hovav, M. (1991). 'Wiping the slate clean: a lexical-semantic exploration', *Cognition 41*: 123–51.

Levinson, S.C. (1996). 'Relativity in spatial conception and description'. In J.J. Gumperz and S.C. Levinson (eds.) *Rethinking Linguistic Relativity* (Cambridge: Cambridge University Press), pp. 177–202.

Lewis, M. (1993). *The Lexical Approach. The State of ELT and a Way Forward* (Hove: LTP Teacher Training).

Li, F.T. (2002). 'The acquisition of metaphorical expressions, idioms and proverbs by Chinese learners of English: a conceptual metaphor and image schema-based approach'. Unpublished PhD thesis, Chinese University of Hong Kong.

Li, Wei (2003). 'Activation of lemmas in the multilingual mental lexicon and transfer in third language learning'. In J. Cenoz, B. Hufeisen and U. Jessner (eds.) *The Multilingual Lexicon* (The Netherlands: Springer Verlag), pp. 57–70.

Lindstromberg, S. and Boers, F. (2005). 'From movement to metaphor with manner-of-movement verbs', *Applied Linguistics 26* (2): 241–61.

Lindstromberg, S. and Boers, F. (2008). 'The mnemonic effect of noticing alliteration in lexical chunks', *Applied Linguistics 29* (2): 200–22.

Littlemore, J. (2001). 'Metaphor as a source of misunderstanding for overseas students in academic lectures', *Teaching in Higher Education 6* (3): 333–51.

Littlemore, J. (2004). 'Interpreting metaphors in the language classroom', *Les Cahiers de l'APLIUT 23* (2): 57–70.

Littlemore, J. (forthcoming). 'The role of figurative language in creating and maintaining a discourse community's identity: the university nursery'. In A. Deignan, J. Littlemore and E. Semino (eds.) *Figurative Communication in Discourse Communities* (Cambridge: Cambridge University Press).

Littlemore, J. and Azuma, M. (forthcoming). 'Promoting creativity in English language classrooms in Japan: An investigation into how Japanese learners of English can be helped to exploit the figurative potential of English'. Article submitted to the *JACET Journal*.

Littlemore, J. and Low, G. (2006a). *Figurative Thinking and Foreign Language Learning* (Basingstoke/New York: Palgrave Macmillan).

Littlemore, J. and Low, G. (2006b). 'Metaphoric competence and communicative language ability', *Applied Linguistics 27* (2): 268–94.

Littlemore, J. and MacArthur, F. (2007a). 'What do learners need to know about the figurative extensions of target language words? A contrastive corpus-based analysis of *thread, hilar, wing* and *aletear*'. In I. Navarro i Fernando, J.L. Otal Campo and A.J. Silvestre López (eds.) *Metaphor and Discourse, a Special Edition of Culture, Language and Representation: Cultural Studies Journal of Universitat Jaume I (5)*: 131–50.

Littlemore, J. and MacArthur, F. (2007b). 'Researching metaphor and language learning'. Workshop presented at conference on Researching and Applying Metaphor, Ciudad Real, Spain.

Littlemore, J. and MacArthur, F. (forthcoming). 'Figurative extensions of word meaning: how do corpus data and intuition match up?' Paper presented at the Corpus Linguistics Conference, Liverpool, UK, July 2009.

Low, G. (1999a). 'Validating metaphor research projects'. In L. Cameron and G. Low (eds.) *Researching and Applying Metaphor* (Cambridge: Cambridge University Press), pp. 48–65.

Low, G. D. (1999b) ' "This paper thinks...". Investigating the acceptability of the metaphor AN ESSAY IS A PERSON'. In L. Cameron and G. Low (eds.) *Researching and Applying Metaphor* (Cambridge: Cambridge University Press), pp. 221–48.

Low, G. (2003). 'Validating models in applied linguistics', *Metaphor and Symbol 18* (4): 239–54.

Low, G. and Littlemore, J. (2009). 'The relationship between conceptual metaphors and classroom management language: reactions by native and non-native speakers of English', *Iberica 17*: 25–44.

Lucy, J. (1992). *Grammatical Categories and Cognition: A Case Study of the Linguistic Relativity Hypothesis* (Cambridge: Cambridge University Press).

Lucy, J. and Gaskins, S. (2003). 'Interaction of language type and referent type in the development of nonverbal classification preferences'. In D. Gentner and S. Goldin-Meadow (eds.) *Language in Mind* (Cambridge, MA: MIT Press), pp. 465–92.

MacArthur, F. and Littlemore, J. (2008). 'A discovery approach to figurative language learning with the use of corpora'. In F. Boers and S. Lindstromberg (eds.) *Cognitive Linguistic Approaches to Teaching Vocabulary and Phraseology* (Amsterdam: Mouton de Gruyter), pp. 159–88.

MacWhinney, B. (1997). 'Second language acquisition and the competition model'. In A.M.B. De Groot and J.F. Froll (eds.) *Tutorials in Bilingualism: Psycholinguistic Perspectives* (Mahwah, NJ: Lawrence Erlbaum), pp. 113–42.

Mahpeykar, N, (2008). 'An analysis of native and non-native speakers' use of the word *out* in MICASE'. Unpublished MA dissertation, University of Birmingham.

Majid, A., Bowerman, B., Van Staden, M. and Boster, J.S. (2007). 'The semantic categories of cutting and breaking events: a crosslinguistic perspective', *Cognitive Linguistics 18* (2): 133–52.

Maldonado, R. (2008). 'Spanish middle syntax: a usage-based proposal for grammar teaching'. In S. De Knop and T. De Rycker (eds.) *Cognitive Approaches to Pedagogical Grammar* (Berlin: Mouton de Gruyter), pp. 155–96.

Massaro, D. (1987). *Speech Perception by Ear and by Eye: A Paradigm for Psychological Inquiry* (Hillsdale, NJ: Lawrence Erlbaum).

McCafferty, S.G. (2002). 'Gestures and creating zones of proximal development for second language learning', *Modern Language Journal 86*: 192–203.

McCafferty, S.G. (2008). 'Material foundations for second language acquisition: gesture, metaphor and internalization'. In S. McCafferty and G. Stam (eds.) *Gesture. Second Language Acquisition and Classroom Research* (New York: Routledge), pp 47–65.

McClelland, J., Fiez, J. and McCandliss, B. (2002). 'Teaching the /r/~/l/ discrimination to Japanese adults: behavioural and neural aspects', *Psychology and Behavior 77*: 657–62.

McDonough, L., Choi, S., and Mandler, J.M. (in press). 'Understanding spatial relations: flexible infants, lexical adults', *Cognitive Psychology*.

McGlone, F., Howard, M. and Roberts, N. (2002). 'Brain activation to passive observation of grasping actions'. In M. Stamenov and V. Gallese (eds.) *Mirror Neurons and the Evolution of Brain and Language* (Amsterdam: John Benjamins), pp. 125–34.

McNeill, D. (1992). *Hand and Mind* (Chicago: University of Chicago Press).

McNeill, D. and Duncan, S. (2000). 'Growth points in thinking for speaking'. In D. McNeill (ed.) *Language and Gesture* (Cambridge: Cambridge University Press), pp. 141–61.

Meara, P. (2007). 'Simulating word associations in an L2: the effects of structural complexity', *Language Forum 33* (2): 13–31.

Meara, P. M. and Wolter, B. (2004). 'Beyond vocabulary depth', *Angles on the English Speaking World 4*: 85–97.

Moon, R. (1998) *Fixed Expressions and Idioms in English: A Corpus-Based Approach* (Oxford: Clarendon Press).

Mori, J. and Hayashi, M. (2006). 'The achievement of intersubjectivity through embodied completions: a study of interactions between first and second language speakers', *Applied Linguistics 27* (2): 195–219.

Murphy, R. (1986). *English Grammar in Use* (Cambridge: Cambridge University Press).

Nakamura, D. (2008). 'Awareness, input frequency, and construction learning: a replication and extension of Casenhiser and Goldberg (2005) to adult second language acquisition'. In *Cognitive Approaches to Second/Foreign Language Processing: Theory and Pedagogy. Papers from the 33rd International LAUD Symposium*, Landau, Germany, March 2008 (Landau, Phalz: LAUD Linguistic Agency), pp. 464–81.

Nakao, K. (1998). 'The state of bilingual lexicography in Japan: learners' English-Japanese/Japanese-English dictionaries', *International Journal of Lexicography 11*: 35–50.

Nation, P. (2001). *Learning Vocabulary in Another Language* (Cambridge: Cambridge University Press).

Negueruela, E. and Lantolf, J. (2008). 'The dialectics of gesture in the construction of meaning in second language oral narratives'. In S. McCafferty and G. Stam (eds.) *Gesture. Second Language Acquisition and Classroom Research* (New York: Routledge), pp. 88–106.

Nerlich, B., Todd, Z. and Clarke, D. (1999). '"Mummy I like being a sandwich". Metonymy in language acquisition'. In G. Radden and K. Panther (eds.) *Metonymy and Cognition* (Amsterdam: John Benjamins), pp. 88–101.

Niemeier, S. (2004). 'Linguistic and cultural relativity – reconsidered for the foreign language classroom'. In M. Achard and S. Niemeier (eds.) *Cognitive Linguistics and Foreign Language Teaching* (Berlin/New York: Mouton de Gruyter), pp. 95–118.

Niemeier, S. and Reif, M. (2008). 'Making progress simpler? Applying cognitive grammar to tense-aspect teaching in the German EFL classroom'. In S. De Knop and T. De Rycker (eds.) *Cognitive Approaches to Pedagogical Grammar* (Berlin: Mouton de Gruyter), pp. 325–56.

Nunberg, G., Wasow, T. and Sag, I.A. (1994). 'Idioms', *Language 70* (3): 491–538.

Oxford Advanced Learners Dictionary /OALD (1995). (Oxford: Oxford University Press).

Odlin, T. (2005). 'Crosslinguistic influence and conceptual transfer: what are the concepts?', *Annual Review of Applied Linguistics 25*: 3–25.

Oe, S. (1975). *Nichi Eigo no Hikaku Kenkyu: Syunkansei o Megutte* (A Contrastive Study of Japanese and English: With a Focus on Subjectivity) (Tokyo: Nanundo Press).

Oxford, R.L. (1990). *Language Learning Strategies: What Every Teacher Should Know.* (Boston: Heinle & Heinle).

Ozcaliskan, S. (2007). 'Metaphors we *move* by: children's developing understanding of metaphorical motion in typologically distinct languages', *Metaphor and Symbol 22* (2): 147–68.

Özyürek, A. (2002). 'Speech-gesture synchrony in typologically differnt languages and second language acquisition'. In B. Skarabela, S. Fish and A. H. Do (eds.) *Proceedings from the 26th Annual Boston University Conference on Language Development* (Somerville, MA: Cascadilla Press), pp. 500–9.

Paganus, A., Mikkonen, V. P., Mäntylä, T., Nuuttila, S., Isoaho, J., Aaltonen, O. and Salakoski. T. (2006). 'The vowel game: continuous real-time visualization for pronunciation learning with vowel charts'. In *Lecture Notes in*

Computer Science: Advances in Natural Language Processing (no editor), vol. 4139 (Berlin/Heidelberg: Springer).

Panther, K.-U. and Thornburg, L.L. (1998) 'A cognitive approach to inferencing in conversation', *Journal of Pragmatics 30*: 755–69.

Panther, K-U and Thornburg, L.L. (2003). 'Introduction: Metonymy across languages'. In K-U. Panther and L.L. Thornburg (eds.) *How Universal are Conceptual Metonymies? Special Edition of Jezikoslovje 4* (1): 5–9.

Parrill, F. and Sweetser, E. (2004). 'What we mean by meaning. Conceptual integration in gesture analysis and transcription', *Gesture 4* (2): 197–219.

Partington, A. (1998). *Patterns and Meanings. Using Corpora for English Language Research and Teaching* (Amsterdam: John Benjamins).

Pederson, E., Danziger, E., Wilkins, D., Kevinson, S., Kita, S. and Senft, G. (1998). 'Semantic typology and spatial conceptualization', *Language 74*: 557–89.

Perez-Hernandez, L. and Ruiz de Mendoza, F.J. (2002). 'Grounding, semantic motivation, and conceptual interaction in indirect directive speech acts', *Journal of Pragmatics 34*: 259–84.

Peters, A. (1977). 'Language learning strategies. Does the whole equal the sum of the parts?', *Language 53*: 560–73.

Picken, J. (2007). *Literature, Metaphor and the Foreign Language Learner* (Basingstoke/New York: Palgrave Macmillan).

Pisoni, D. and Lively, S. (1995). 'Variability and invariance in speech perception: a new look at some old problems in perceptual learning'. In W. Strange (ed.) *Speech Perception and Linguistic Experience: Theoretical and Methodological Issues* (Timonium MD: York Press), pp. 433–59.

Platt, E. and Brooks, F. (2008). 'Embodiment as self-regulation in L2 task performance'. In S. McCafferty and G. Stam (eds.) *Gesture. Second Language Acquisition and Classroom Research* (New York: Routledge), pp. 66–87.

Quek, F., McNeill, D., Bryll, R., Duncan, S. Kirbas, C., Mccullough, K.E. and Ansari, R. (2002). 'Multimodal human discourse: gesture and speech'. *ACM Transactions on Computer-Human Interaction, 9* (3): 171–93.

Radden, G. (2005). 'The ubiquity of metonymy'. In J.-L. Otal Campo, I. Navarro, I. Ferrando and B. Belles Fortuno (eds.) *Cognitive and Discourse Approaches to Metaphor and Metonymy* (Castello de la Plana: Publicationes de la Universitat Jaume I), pp. 29–44.

Radden, G. and Dirven, R. (2007). *Cognitive English Grammar* (Amsterdam: John Benjamins).

Radden, G. and Kövecses, Z. (2007). 'Towards a theory of metonymy'. In V. Evans, B. Bergen and J. Zinken (eds.) *The Cognitive Linguistics Reader* (London: Equinox), pp. 335–359.

Radden, G. and Panther, K. U. (2004). 'Introduction: reflections on motivation'. In G. Radden and K. U. Panther (eds.) *Studies in Linguistic Motivation (Cognitive Linguistics Research)* (Berlin/New York: Mouton de Gruyter), pp. 1–46.

Ramachandran, V. S. (2003). 'The emerging mind'. Lecture presented as part of the *Reith Lecture Series* (London: BBC Radio Four).

Ramachandran, V. S. and Hubbard, E. M. (2001). 'Synaesthesia – a window into perception, thought and language', *Journal of Consciousness Studies 8* (12): 3–34.

Ramirez, L. (2006). 'Manner of movement verbs'. Unpublished MA dissertation, University of Birmingham.

Read, J. (1993). 'The development of a new measure of L2 vocabulary knowledge', *Language Testing 10* (3): 355–71.

Read, J. (2004). 'Plumbing the depths: how should the construct of vocabulary knowledge be defined?' In P. Bongaards (ed.) *Vocabulary in a Second Language. Selection, Acquisition and Testing* (Philadelphia, PA: John Benjamins), pp. 77–98.

Richardson D. C. and Matlock T. (2007). 'The integration of figurative language and static depictions: an eye movement study of fictive motion', *Cognition 102* (1): 129–38.

Rizzolatti, G. and Arbib, M. (1998). 'Language within our grasp', *Trends in Neurosciences 21* (5): 188–94.

Roehr, K. (2008). 'Linguistic and metalinguistic categories in second language learning', *Cognitive Linguistics 19* (1): 67–106.

Rosch, E. (1975). 'Universals and cultural specifics in human categorization'. In R.W. Brislin, S. Bochner and W.J. Lonner (eds.) *Cross-cultural Perspectives on Learning* (New York: John Wiley), pp. 177–206.

Rost, M. (2002). *Teaching and Researching Listening* (Harlow: Longman).

Rudzka-Ostyn, B. (2003). *Word Power. Phrasal Verbs and Compounds. A Cognitive Approach* (Berlin: Mouton de Gruyter).

Ruiz de Mendoza, F. J. (2008). 'The case of Spanish diminutives and reflexive constructions'. In S. De Knop and T. De Rycker (eds.) *Cognitive Approaches to Pedagogical Grammar* (Berlin: Mouton de Gruyter), pp. 121–54.

Ruiz de Mendoza, J. and Mairal Uson, R. (2007). 'High level metaphor and metonymy in meaning construction'. In G. Radden, K.M. Kopcke, T. Berg and P. Siemund (eds.) *Aspects of Meaning Construction* (Amsterdam/Philadelphia: John Benjamins), pp. 45–73.

Schmidt, R. (1990) 'The role of consciousness in second language learning', *Applied Linguistics 11*: 17–46.

Schmidt, R. (1993). 'Consciousness, learning, and interlanguage pragmatics'. In G. Kasper and S. Blum-Kulka (eds.) *Interlanguage Pragmatics* (Oxford: Oxford University Press), pp. 21–43.

Schmitt, N. (1998). 'Tracking the incremental acquisition of second language vocabulary: a longitudinal study', *Language Learning 48* (2): 281–317.

Schmitt, N. (2000). *Vocabulary in Language Teaching* (Cambridge: Cambridge University Press).

Seidlhofer, B. (2004). 'Research perspectives on teaching English as a lingua franca', *Annual Review of Applied Linguistics 24*: 209–39.

Seidlhofer, B. (2005). 'English as a lingua franca', *English Language Teaching Journal 59* (4): 339–41.

Sharwood Smith, M. (1991). 'Speaking to many minds: on the relevance of different types of language information for the L2 learner', *Second Language Research 7* (2): 118–32.

Sharwood Smith, M. (1993). 'Input enhancement in instructed SLA: theoretical bases', *Studies in Second Language Acquisition 15*: 165–79.

Shore, B. (1996). *Culture in Mind* (New York: Oxford University Press).

Shortall, T. (2002). 'Teaching Grammar'. *Developing Language Professionals in Higher Education Institutions (DELPHI) project.* Available online at http://www.delphi.bham.ac.uk/modules.htm.

Sime, D. (2008). ' "Because of her gesture, it's very easy to understand." Learners' perceptions of teachers' gestures in the foreign language class'. In S. McCafferty and G. Stam (eds.) *Gesture. Second Language Acquisition and Classroom Research* (New York: Routledge), pp. 259–79.

Sinclair, J. (1991). *Corpus, Concordance, Collocation* (Oxford: Oxford University Press).

Singleton, D. (1995). 'Introduction: a critical look at the critical period hypothesis in second language acquisition'. In D. Singleton and Z. Lengyel (eds.) *The Age Factor in Second Language Acquisition* (Clevedon: Multilingual Matters), pp. 1–29.

Singleton, D. (1999). *Exploring the Second Language Mental Lexicon* (Cambridge: Cambridge University Press).

Slobin, D. (1996). 'From "thought and language" to "thinking for speaking"'. In S. Gumperz and S. Levinson (eds.) *Rethinking Linguistic Relativity* (New York: Cambridge University Press), pp. 70–96.

Slobin, D. I. (2000). 'Verbalized events. A dynamic approach to linguistic relativity and determinism'. In S. Niemeier and R. Dirven (eds.) *Evidence for Linguistic Relativity* (Amsterdam: John Benjamins), pp. 108–38.

Slobin, D. (2003). 'Language and thought online: cognitive consequences of linguistic relativity'. In D. Gentner and S. Goldin-Meadow (eds.) *Language in Mind: Advances in the Study of Language and Thought* (Cambridge, MA: MIT Press), pp. 157–92.

Soderman, T. (1993). 'Word associations of foreign language learners and native speakers: the phenomenon of a shift bin response type and its relevance for lexical development'. In H. Ringbom (ed.) *Near-native Proficiency in English* (Abo, Finland: Abo Akademi), pp. 91–182.

Stam, G. and McCafferty, S. (2008). 'Gesture studies and second language acquisition'. In S. McCafferty and G. Stam (eds.) *Gesture. Second Language Acquisition and Classroom Research* (New York: Routledge), pp. 3–24.

Stamenov, M. (2002). 'Some features that make mirror neurons and the human language faculty unique'. In M. Stamenov and V. Gallese (eds.) *Mirror Neurons and the Evolution of Brain and Language* (Amsterdam: John Benjamins), pp. 249–72.

Stefanowitsch, A. and Gries, S. (eds.) (2006). *Corpus-based Approaches to Metaphor and Metonymy* (Berlin: Mouton de Gruyter).

Stefanowitsch, A. and Gries, S. (2007). 'Collostructions: investigating the interaction of words and constructions'. In V. Evans, B. Bergen and J. Zinken (eds.) *The Cognitive Linguistics Reader* (London: Equinox), pp. 75–105.

Strange, W. (ed.) (1995). *Speech Perception and Linguistic Experience: Issues in Cross-language Research* (Timonium, MD: York Press).

Sueyoshi, A. and Hardison, D.M. (2005). 'The role of gestures and facial cues in second language listening comprehension', *Language Learning* 55 (4): 661–99.

Svalberg, A. (2007). 'Language awareness and language learning', *Language Teaching* 40: 287–308.

Swales, J. (1990). *Genre Analysis* (Cambridge: Cambridge University Press).

Sweetser, E. (1990). *From Etymology to Pragmatics: Metaphorical and Cultural Aspects of Semantic Structure* (Cambridge: Cambridge University Press).

Sweetser, E. (1998). 'Regular metaphoricity in gesture: bodily-based models of speech interaction', In B. Caron (ed.) *Actes du 16e Congres International des Linguists.* (New York: Elsevier).

Takada, M. (2008). *Synesthetic Metaphor - Perception, Cognition, and Language* (Amsterdam: VDM Verlag).

Talmy, L. (1985). 'Lexicalisation patterns semantic structure in lexical forms'. In T. Shopen (ed.) *Language Typology and Syntactic Description*, Vol. III: *Grammatical Categories and the Lexicon* (Cambridge; Cambridge University Press), pp. 93–121.

Talmy, L. (1988) 'Force dynamics in language and cognition', *Cognitive Science 2*: 49–100.

Talmy, L. (2000). *Toward a Cognitive Semantics*. Vol. II: *Typology and Process in Concept Structuring* (Cambridge, MA: MIT Press).

Tang, P. (2007). 'Figurative language in a nursery setting and a non-native speaker's perspective on this discourse community'. Unpublished MA dissertation, University of Birmingham.

Taylor, J. (1993). 'Some pedagogical implications of cognitive linguistics'. In R.A. Geiger and B. Rudzka-Ostyn (eds.) *Conceptualizations and Mental Processing in Language* (Berlin: Mouton de Gruyter), pp. 201–23.

Taylor, J. (2002). *Cognitive Grammar* (Oxford: Oxford University Press).

Taylor, J. (2003). *Linguistic Categorization* (Oxford: Oxford University Press).

Taylor, J. (2008). 'Prototypes in cognitive linguistics'. In P. Robinson and N. Ellis (eds.) *Handbook of Cognitive Linguistics and Second Language Acquisition* (New York: Routledge), pp. 39–65.

Tellier, M. (2006). 'L'impact du geste pedagogique sue l'enseignement/ apprentissage des languages etrangeres: Etude sur des enfants de 5 ans' (University Paris VII- Denis Diderot) (cited in Gullberg, 2008).

Tomasello, M. (2003). *Constructing a Language. A Usage-based Theory of Language Acquisition*. (Cambridge, MA: Harvard University Press).

Tyler, A. (2008a). 'Cognitive linguistics and second language instruction'. In P. Robinson and N.C. Ellis (eds.) *Handbook of Cognitive Linguistics and Second Language Acquisition* (New York/London: Routledge), pp. 456–88.

Tyler, A. (2008b). 'Applied cognitive linguistics: putting linguistics back into second language learning'. Paper presented at The LAUD symposium on Cognitive Linguistic Approaches to Second Language Learning and Teaching, Landau, Germany, March 2008.

Tyler, A. and Evans, V. (2001). 'The relation between experience, conceptual structure and meaning: non-temporal uses of tense and language teaching'. In M. Pütz , S. Niemeier and R. Dirven (eds.) *Applied Cognitive Linguistics II: Language Pedagogy* (Berlin: Mouton de Gruyter), pp. 63–105.

Tyler, A. and Evans, V. (2004) 'Applying cognitive linguistics to pedagogical grammar: the case of over'. In M. Achard and S. Niemeier (eds.) *Cognitive Linguistics and Foreign Language Teaching* (Berlin/New York: Mouton de Gruyter), pp. 257–80.

Verspoor, M. H. (2008). 'Cognitive linguistics and its applications to second language teaching'. In J. Cenoz and N.H. Hornberger (eds.) *Encyclopaedia of Language and Education,* 2nd edn. Vol. 6: *Knowledge about Language* (New York: Springer Verlag), pp. 79–91.

Verspoor, M. and Lowie, W. (2003). 'Making sense of polysemous words', *Language Learning 53* (3): 547–86.

Verspoor, M., Lowie, W. and Seton, B. (2008). 'Conceptual representations in the multilingual mind'. In *Cognitive Approaches to Second/Foreign Language*

Processing: Theory and Pedagogy. Papers from the 33rd International LAUD symposium, Landau, Germany. (Landau, Phalz: LAUD Linguistic Agency), pp. 928–45.

Vygotsky, L. (1986). *Thought and Language* (Cambridge, MA: MIT Press).

Waara, R. (2004). 'Construal, convention and constructions in L2 speech'. In M. Achard and S. Niemeier (eds.) *Cognitive Linguistics and Foreign Language Teaching* (Berlin/New York: Mouton de Gruyter), pp. 51–76.

Walker, C. (2008a). 'A corpus-based study of the linguistic features and processes which influence the way collocations are formed'. Unpublished PhD dissertation, University of Birmingham.

Walker, C. (2008b). 'Factors which influence the process of collocation'. In F. Boers and S. Lindstromberg (eds.) (2008). *Cognitive Linguistic Approaches to Teaching Vocabulary and Phraseology* (Berlin: Mouton de Gruyter), pp. 291–308.

Wardhaugh, R. (1970). 'The Contrastive Analysis Hypothesis'. Paper presented at the fourth annual TESOL Convention, San Francisco, California, March 18–21.

Weedon, C. (1999). *Feminism, Theory and the Politics of Difference* (Oxford: Blackwell).

Werker, J. and Tees, R. (1984). 'Phonemic and phonetic factors in adult cross-language speech perception', *Journal of the Acoustical Society of America 75*: 1866–78.

Werker, J.F. and Tees, R.C. (1999). 'Experiential influences on infant speech processing: toward a new synthesis', *Annual Review of Psychology 50*: 509–35.

Werning, M., Fleischhauer, J. and Beseoglu, H. (2006). 'The cognitive accessibility of synaesthetic metaphors'. In *Proceedings of the 25th Annual Conference of the Cognitive Sciences Society*, pp. 2365–70.

Werstler, J. M. (2002) 'Total Physical Response Storytelling: a study in actively engaging students across the modalities.' Unpublished Master's thesis, Department of Modern Languages, Central Connecticut State University.

Wierzbicka, A. (1997). *Understanding Cultures through their Keywords* (Oxford: Oxford University Press).

Wierzbicka, A. (2006). *English: Meaning and Culture* (Oxford: Oxford University Press).

Wilks, C. and Meara, P. (2002). 'Untangling word webs: graph theory and the notion of density in second language word association networks', *Second Language Research 18* (4): 303–24.

Williams, J. M. (1976). 'Synaesthetic adjectives: a possible law of semantic change', *Language 52* (2): 461–78.

Williams, J. N. (2005). 'Learning without awareness', *Studies in Second Language Acquisition 27* (2): 269–304.

Willis, J. (1996). *A Framework for Task-Based Learning* (Harlow: Longman).

Willis, D. and Willis, J. (1996). 'Consciousness-raising activities in the language classroom'. In J. Willis and D. Willis (eds.) *Challenge and Change in Language Teaching.* (Oxford: Heinemann), pp. 63–76.

Willis, J. and Willis, D. (2007). *Doing Task-Based Teaching* (Oxford: Oxford University Press).

Wilson, D. and Sperber, D. (2004). 'Relevance theory'. In L. Horn and G. Ward (eds.) *Handbook of Pragmatics* (Oxford: Blackwell), pp. 250–71.

Wolter, B. (2001). 'Comparing the L1 and L2 mental lexicon. A depth of individual word knowledge model', *Studies in Second Language Acquisition 23*: 41–69.

Wolter, B. (2006). 'Lexical network structures and L2 vocabulary acquisition: the role of L1 lexical/conceptual knowledge', *Applied Linguistics 27* (4): 741–7.

Wray, A. (2002). *Formulaic Language and the Lexicon* (Cambridge: Cambridge University Press).

Wu, H.J. (2008). 'Understanding metaphor: Taiwanese students and English language metaphor'. Unpublished MA dissertation, University of Birmingham.

Yoshioka, K. (2008). 'Linguistic and gestural introduction of ground references in L1 and L2 narrative'. In S. McCafferty and G. Stam (eds.) *Gesture. Second Language Acquisition and Classroom Research* (New York: Routledge), pp. 211–30.

Zelazo, P. D. and Jacques, S. (1996). 'Children's rule use: representation, reflection and cognitive control'. In R. Vasta (ed.) *Annals of Child Development, vol. 12* (London: Jessica Kingsley Press), pp. 119–76.

Index